FUTURE CITIES

*42 Insights and Interviews with
Influencers, Startups and Investors*

STEFANO L. TRESCA

SEAHORSE PRESS

FUTURE CITIES: 42 INSIGHTS AND INTERVIEWS
WITH INFLUENCERS, STARTUPS AND INVESTORS

Second Edition

Copyright © 2015, 2017 Stefano L. Tresca
Published by Seahorse Press
ISBN: 978-0-9931095-8-4
E-Book ISBN: 978-0-993109-55-3
Original edition published in 2015

*To all the other book addicts out there -
welcome!*

About the Author

Stefano L. Tresca was employee No. 8 at Wind, a telecom startup company sold for $12.1 billion. He's founding member of Level39 (Europe's largest technology accelerator for fintech and future cities tech), and founder of StartupHome (the co-living for young entrepreneurs). He serves as non-executive director for a university and different companies. Many years ago, he fell in love with the city of London, and that's where he lives today when he's not travelling.

Connect with Stefano

WEB: http://stefanotresca.com
LINKEDIN: http://linkedin.com/in/stefanotresca
TWITTER: https://twitter.com/startupagora
FACEBOOK: http://stefanotresca.com/facebook

Public Speaking and Corporate Training

To invite the author, feel free to use his website:
http://stefanotresca.com/contact
Or Twitter: @startupagora

Table of Contents

Your Neighbourhood Will Never Be the Same

Welcome

Which road do I take? She asked.
Where do you want to go? Responded the Cheshire Cat.
I don't know. Alice answered.
Then, said the Cat, it doesn't matter.

– Lewis Carroll (Alice in Wonderland)

By 2030 nearly 70% of the world's population will be residents of a city. That means 3 billion more urban residents in just 30 years.

Our generation is destined to witness an incredible number of new cities and buildings being built to host our new neighbours. Once these cities are built, they won't be built again. And they won't be easily changed either.

For good or ill, we'll be forced to live in our creations for a very long time. Do it right, and we will provide great quality of life to ourselves and to our neighbours. Do it wrong, and we will condemn ourselves to a miserable existence: endless hours of commuting, loneliness, pollution, disease, crime, stagnation.

Technology is already playing a major role in this scenario. In the last four years I've met more than 120 companies developing new technologies for our cities, and I've shared some of their stories in this book.

Where Is the Money Going?

Cities already provide 80% of the global GDP, and this share is destined to expand in the near future.

Consider just one market – the Internet of Things (IoT). The financial opportunities around smart buildings and cities are estimated to be worth €234 billion ($260 billion), 40% of the entire IoT budget.

As a comparison, the manufacturing industry, with all its robots and technology, will be worth just €17 billion, less than 3% of the IoT budget.

In my job I have the opportunity to meet investors and public officers. I've asked each of them where they think the money will be going, and shared their answers. Some of the responses may surprise you.

The Best Way to Predict the Future

Driverless cars, 3D printers, artificial intelligence and digital medicine are going to change the status quo. The rise of the sharing economy is speeding up the process. These changes are already happening without the help of governments - sometimes despite the government.

Search for "Exponential Growth" on Google and you'll notice a dramatic increase in the number of documents and videos uploaded. The interest in exponential growth is – well – exponential. Because we live exponential growth on a daily basis.

I regularly meet and mentor tech startups. Five years ago there were just one or two companies per year in this area. Now I get at least one pitch every other week. What's going to happen in the next five years?

Wrong Answers Right Questions

As in the tale of Alice in Wonderland, to get the right answers, you first have to find the right questions.

I've travelled to 23 countries in person, and more than that digitally through my email and Skype contacts. I don't have all the answers—nobody does—but I've collected many tools along the road.

These tools may help you and me to understand current and future trends in tech and culture. It's a small competitive advantage, but in the coming days it may be essential.

Enjoy the interviews. I'll be here waiting for your feedback. If you don't agree, I welcome your challenge. This isn't a one-way conversation, after all. This is a global game.

STEFANO L. TRESCA
London, United Kingdom

The Secret Life of an Uber Driver

Interlude

A man's mind, once stretched by a new idea, never regains its original dimension.
— Oliver Wendell Holmes

When I step into the car, I'm greeted by a string of pumpkin-shaped lights circling the inside roof. The driver — Jeff — has a shaved head, and tattoos visible in the orange glow. Not exactly a ride everyone would accept. Well, not before Uber anyway.

Jeff is a five star driver, and his licence is stored somewhere in a server. The company knows who he is and where he lives, and his car is tracked every second of every ride.

When the media talks about Uber, it's all about their status as a "unicorn" — a company worth more than $1 billion — the easy app and the cheap rides. They tend to forget that the sharing economy is more than price and product.

You can take a ride from a tattooed dude in the middle of the night with more confidence than any time in history. (His Halloween décor is just a bonus.)

As with everything, there is — of course — a dark side. Privacy, tracking, and surveillance are giving senators a headache. Even so, the market will never go back to the old ways.

The reason is not Uber. In fact, this is not a post in favour of Uber. It's not against Uber. It's not about Uber at all. This is a post about a person — Jeff — and his receipt to live in our digital age. Jeff's world is our world, he's just adapting in a different way.

Taxi drivers have always been a great source of knowledge and fascinating stories to me. I have been travelling long before the advent of Uber—40 plus countries and counting—and cabs are second only to street food vendors to understand the local environment.

If it's interesting to talk to taxi drivers everywhere, there's no better place to chat with an Uber driver than in Silicon Valley. Here you can find countless programmers and high-paid salaries driving a cab for a few dollars per hour.

Quoting an old movie—Every time a startup fails a driver gets his wings. They don't want to get a "normal" job. They want to live free until the next Big Thing.

Jeff—in a way—is no exception. He's a photographer, and can make $300 in one session. But getting customers can be irregular. So Jeff drives for Uber with his entire photography kit in the back trunk, waiting for a call.

"Uber is great to pay the bills"—he admits.

Today he'd been on the road for less than three hours. While we're chatting, he gets a message on his second iPhone (the first is exclusively for Uber).

"Looks like you're my last ride for the day"—Jeff says. A customer just booked a photo shoot in one hour.

In 10 minutes, we'll reach my destination in Palo Alto. With one tap of his iPhone, Jeff will switch his career from driver to photographer. He'll switch back to driver in the evening—if he doesn't have a date with his girlfriend—or tomorrow morning. One tap is all it takes.

Welcome to Life in the Time of Uber.

Guo Bai

Smart Cities China

The more you know, the more you dare.

— HEC University Paris (Motto)

Guo Bai is the author of "China's Development: Capitalism and Empire", an intriguing book on China's past, present and future. She's a researcher in Paris and an entrepreneur in China, working to develop the Chinese Kickstarter for equity. I'm not going to write a long introduction because you can find all the information in the interview.

With 70% of the world's megacities being located in Asia by 2025, and with the majority being in China, this could be one of the most interesting interviews in the entire book.

The Interview

Good morning Guo, and welcome. Or I should say good evening, since you are probably in China, right?

Yes, I'm in China right now.

Would you like to introduce yourself to the readers?

Okay. My name is Guo Bai. I'm Chinese, and I'm a researcher at HEC Paris (A/N one of the most prestigious business schools in Europe). I'm a firm believer that, in the future, the boundary of organizations and industries is going to blur. That means that with digital technology and the importance of big data rising, the way people work together will be changed.

So right now I'm working on understanding the organizational form and structure, and how people coordinate their work and actions for complex projects such as smart cities, and that's what I'm doing right now. Before that, I have mainly been a macro-economist and I've been working on the book: China's Development: Capitalism and Empire, which tries to explain the real logic of China's reforms.

And what are you doing in China, besides your research?

Actually I'm working on two things at the same time. On one hand, there's my research, so I'm checking massive projects in China, trying to visit their sites and talk with their managers to try to understand how they were managed.

Secondly I'm also working as an entrepreneur. I'm working on a platform to do equity crowdfunding for projects that are more related to creative design and art and promote a more innovative, creative and beautiful lifestyle.

It's kind of like Kickstarter but not completely, because Kickstarter focuses more on the product side of things. And us, we'll be more focused on the startups themselves so it's more on the equity instead of the product.

May I say "the Chinese Seedrs for lifestyle startups?

Right. We have a very specific focus. Like, instead of rushing to show everyone early technologies and digital stuff, we want to really focus on how we use these things to change our lives. And also, we want to spread this idea of crowdfunding to help people who are interested in other aspects of life such as art, design, food, and drink. And also, we do not only focus on Beijing and Shanghai and those very large metropolitan cities, but we spread this idea to local cities such as the second, third, or fourth tier cities in China.

Equity crowdfunding based on communities could work very well. I've done quite a few crowdfunding projects myself—both reward and equity based—and having a community is probably the most powerful tool for a campaign.

So I guess, if you only accept projects that are going to improve their local communities, on one hand they can launch faster, because they are local, and on the other hand the entrepreneur may be already well known and trusted. This definitely helps.

That's exactly what I'm trying to do because nowadays equity crowdfunding is a very hot topic in China. Very hot business, but mostly people are still doing what traditional VC funds were doing. They were focused on very specific industries and they're looking for really high-return projects in the short term. But I think it's a very powerful tool, as you just mentioned, to really mobilize communities. And that's the beauty of the Internet and that's the beauty of crowdfunding, and we want to realize that aspect of it.

Indeed targeting a single community is probably under estimated by entrepreneurs. When I work with someone on a crowdfunding project, they all want to be published in the Financial Times or TechCrunch, and sometimes they don't realize that an article on the home page of TechCrunch stays there probably only for a couple of minutes because there are so many other articles. While an article on an average sized blog in their product's niche could generate many more sales and loyal supporters.

Yeah, bingo. Great minds think alike then. I totally share your view. Eventually if this platform really attracts a lot of attention it could make the front page of the Financial Times, but that's not our purpose. Our purpose is really to mobilize the local communities and to really, not only attract people's attention, but to do things that really can help people's lives. Directly. That's exactly why our platform is very different from other platforms.

This focus on people is the reason why I call our area "future cities" and not "smart cities". I'm interested in anything that can improve our lives in the future, not just buildings and infrastructure. In other words, if we focus on the cities, we may end up with buildings full of gadgets and still have a poor quality of life.

On the contrary, if we focus on people, quality of life comes first.

Sometimes we don't need expensive technology to improve those lives, maybe we just need to use existing technology in another way.

In China, we have a similar trend. We have already hundreds of programs actively applied to the Ministry of Housing. I guess there are around 300 of them already. And there are, I guess, thousands of unofficial ones but also carrying the name "smart cities".

But most projects are mainly related to infrastructure and not enough of them are paying attention to the human side of things.

Also many of these projects want to achieve ground-breaking changes, and it requires a long period of time. But really, sometimes integrating what we already have under the same umbrella is already very helpful and it may provide faster results.

I would like to talk about your book and what's happening in China. Together with Michael Aglietta you wrote a book called "China's Development: Capitalism and Empire".

Besides the questionable high price chosen by publisher, this book is a must read. Cities and megacities are moving East, in particular to China and India. So understanding what works and what doesn't work in China, is a key to understanding our future even in the West. The book is not just about cities, but about every aspect of your country.

What is the hottest topic right now in China?

Okay. Well, the book actually has three parts and only the third part deals with the future. But I think the three parts are closely related to each other. You can see that the first part of the book really deals with China's history. The reason we go so far back into the past is because we believe that China has a very specific state formation process.

We are a country that has been united for thousands of years, relatively without foreign invasion. So the whole country, both its political logic and people's mentalities, is quite inward-looking. We have long realized the importance of administration and we really want to keep the country united, and offer access to the basics to the whole population.

And that leads to the real logic of Chinese reform, which is really not a result of any kind of doctrine, such as a planning economy or

Marxism or the Soviet model. But a process of adjustments to keep this country united and keep providing the people with some basic welfare - that also is the basis actually for the political legitimacy of the regime.

With this kind of very specific state formation process and history, we have a country that is very rich in community culture. I should say, the country has been, for thousands of years, self-organized at a local level. So all these communities, actually they carry a lot of the functions that used to be carried outside China by other institutions such as the state or companies.

That, nowadays, is very interesting because if we talk about smart cities and smart neighborhoods, they are based on a new form of community that encourages a lot of civic participation from everyone. Such kind of participation actually has a very long history in China, and it's very popular and strong.

So this book is not particularly a book about cities, but about China's reform logic and what is going to happen in China in a macroeconomic and a politico-economic sense. But it is related to cities in this way. Chinese people are very used to self-organization, are very used to a community way of thinking, and are very used to, and are good at, a community lifestyle.

So our Chines culture is not only very beneficial and interesting for developing local communities, but also for developing a new form of political regime that is a new type of democracy which is more participative, more based on a civic society, instead of a representative way of choosing who is going to have the final political power.

So this, I think, is something that directly relates my book to the idea of cities, especially smart cities.

So your idea is that, if you add technology to Chinese culture, that is already open to self-organization, then this technology may be way more effective there than outside China. In other words, the impact of tech could grow exponentially if implanted in the right culture.

If your idea is proven correct I see an important consequence. China will become the global beta tester for smart cities. Tech will be tested in China and then exported to the world, inverting the actual trend where tech is developed in Silicon Valley and in the West and then exported to Asia.

Right. I totally agree with you and that's exactly what I've been observing. In fact, I just spent last several months in Boston and in other cities in the United States, and we can already observe China's role.

Of course, nowadays, you (A/N the West) still have a lot of good ideas, good concepts, good technology. But if you're talking about the application of these technologies, we can see that execution in China is nothing less remarkable than anywhere else in this world. For instance apps like WeChat or WeBlog are remarkable.

They have already, I won't say replaced, but really have significantly challenged the traditional way of doing media, advertising, how people self-organize; all these aspects. So I totally agree with you. This cultural heritage and modern technology, the combination of these two will transform this country completely and will make China a leader in future centuries. I'm not saying in a general sense, but more in the application of these products, and also in the way of organization.

I see a glimpse of the Chinese optimist here. I've been working with China since 1996, and you have always been incredible optimistic about your future even when China was not yet recognized as an important player by the West. I remember backpacking China for a couple of months in 2000, and many of my colleagues were asking "If you are interested in business, why you don't go the United States or Germany?"

So at the time, many in the West didn't think of China as a major player in the international community, but all my friends in Hong Kong, Shanghai, Beijing had no doubt about the upcoming importance of their country.

And this trend is so clear nowadays. I'm not going to use the term "superpower" because this has too many geopolitical connotations, but I'm really seeing this country jump forward, that's for sure. We are not just going to be followers or learners anymore. There are going to be aspects in all areas in which we are going to be the innovators, or the pioneers instead of just the followers trying to catch up.

So Guo, you are a researcher but also an entrepreneur. If you had 10 million to invest in a startup, and it cannot be your startup, what area of future cities tech would you pick?

I would still pick business concerning smart neighborhoods. By smart neighborhood, I mean how to change the relationship among people. For example, ideas related to a shared economy would be interesting.

Nowadays in China, you have very interesting apps for hiring a cook; whether a professional or not, who will come to your family and help you cook, either for yourself or for a group of friends. I feel these kinds of applications really change the relationship among people, really change the scope of the people you have contact with.

And they also change the way you socialize, network and the way you live. So I think these kinds of things, related directly with the management of the neighborhood directly with human relationships, would be the project that would be interested in the most.

I like this answer for a specific reason. Smart cities tech can be very slow. Dealing with bureaucracy can be a very long sales process. So if you develop a new transport system or a new energy system that is revolutionary, it can take years before it's implemented and you change the life of the citizens.

On the contrary, if you start providing a service at a neighborhood level, at the bottom, the execution could be very fast. There is no bureaucracy at the bottom.

Exactly. And also, providing services at the bottom is not only economically viable but also I feel it can put pressure directly on the top, for instance on the mayor, to change other systems.

Because when peoples' way of life is already changing, then they demand different means of transportation, buildings, and energy. And that's actually a very good place to dig into the issue and force the government, force the officials, to re-think about what they are doing. And then help them and force them to also change the way they manage energy, transportation and other aspects of urban life.

Also these apps, because they focus on a Chinese neighborhood, they can be tailored to a specific lifestyle. I'll give you an example. There is a sort of Uber in China that empowers the customer to call a taxi.

Nothing special about that but what I found amusing with this app, was that when someone else has booked a taxi, you can offer a tip and "steal" the driver from another customer. Basically if you are in a rush or it's raining, you could outbid another customer.

Such a feature is never going to work well with customers in the United States, I think, but it could work very well in Mumbai or in Rome.

I have another anecdote about Uber in China, which is very funny. Also somewhat of a Chinese characteristic is that they think Uber is a direct competitor of social media platforms like Facebook or WeChat, because it's actually an excellent way for people to meet each other.

So a lot of the Uber drivers I have met in China spend only a few hours driving, because it's not their real job. Their primary goal is to meet new people and make more friends, or even potentially girlfriends or boyfriends. I found this idea very, very funny and very Chinese. It also shows how people are very used to this idea of socializing, meeting people: community.

You definitely know this; you've been to China so many times and have known China for such a long time. If you go to China's parks you can see all these old people. They have self-organized these singing groups, dancing groups, whatever. All these are signs of that demonstrate how this country loves self-organization. And with technology, it just brings it to another level.

I found this story about Uber as a dating app so fascinating that I want to know more. So what you mean is that, some people in China who already have a job and make the same amount of money of a Uber driver, or a bit more, at some point in the day, they stop their full time job, to go out and be a Uber driver so they can meet new people and maybe the love of their life.

Indeed. For example, there is one Uber driver I met. He's the client relationship manager of a big company, and he needs to get out of the office often to meet their clients. Between these meetings he has some free time. So instead of sitting in the office, he prefers to use this time to drive around, and meet more people. And that's why he became an Uber driver.

I'm not sure if other people are sacrificing their time, but are more like using the gaps of the time they have to get out and to be more human-oriented instead of sitting in the office and handling the paperwork. And that's what I observed.

So we have to tell Uber that they can become a dating app in China.

It already is. [Laughs]

Do you know how many Uber drivers found their girlfriend or wife driving people around?

I don't know the statistics on that, but there are many rumors and people are talking about how huge a threat Uber actually is to dating websites.

When I interview someone about Future Cities I often ask if they think that technology will improve or reduce the gap between poorer and richer countries. You have already replied to this question. China is not a poor country but because the size of its territory and population, it's hard to provide a high quality of life to everybody. Based on your information, tech is reducing the gap between China and the West.

Well, I guess it's very difficult to give a general answer saying that the gap is for sure going to enlarge or to shrink. Because it really depends on whether the country, for instance a developing country such as China, has the proper infrastructure and institutional background that allows this catching up. But that's just a general comment.

I do believe that tech can be expensive, but what tech really does nowadays is to bring expensive things down to a more affordable price. So there's definitely a chance. I can't guarantee that it will, for sure, shrink the gap between the developed and developing countries, but there is a chance. There is also the chance it will achieve that. And that's exactly what we have learned in China - we are catching up. Inequalities among different localities are also shrinking, thanks to these technologies.

What I see is that, with those technologies, information spreads much faster than ever. I'll give a very concrete example. Let's take education, for example. It's not just about whether you have a good teacher or not. It's not just about educational resources. Sometimes it's about information. We all know that good universities have scholarships to help poor families, poor kids. But so many poor families and poor kids do not even know that those scholarships exist. And with technology, they can capture this information much easier.

Also they can go on free courses online and have a better chance of self-education. So all these are really, I think, are very positive improvements and I can see that they are going to be tools to help close the gap between the poor and the rich. And that's my comment.

And one of those tools is going to be your crowdfunding platform.

I hope so.

What suggestions would you give to someone that wants to do something with China, not necessarily business? Especially someone who is not a top manager.

Well, in my mind, I think they don't need to do anything special. What I mean is, it's that China is not this purist country anymore. So basically they just need to be really good at what they are doing and bring this expertise to China.

Buy a plane ticket, do not hesitate, do not heed all the stories they have heard about in China in their own country. Buy a plane ticket to come, learn the language, and then just deal with this world and their business as normal, in the same way they would, or should, do in their own country. And that's how you should do business with China nowadays.

In the '80s or '90s it was different. If you came at that time, you would see a country that was completely lagging behind. You brought to China whatever advanced product or service you had in your country, you traded, and then you were successful.

That age has already passed. So really they have to understand this and really try to build up their own expertise. Try to think about what they can really offer to this market, and then learn the language, be friends with the locals, with the Chinese. And that's the way they should do it.

Would you suggest a specific place to start? Because your options are not limited anymore to a few cities like Shanghai or Hong Kong.

There are many cities that come to mind. I would suggest cities in the center of China such as Wuhan, or in Sichuan province like Chengdu, or anywhere actually. It depends on their Chinese level of course, but if they really want to learn the language and learn the culture then they should consider those cities that are more towards the interior of China instead of Beijing and Shanghai where they tend to hang out with their friends from the same country.

Really they should take a backpack, like you did several years ago, and travel the country. They should just look and listen and experience and feel by themselves, and then they would decide because China is so broad and so diverse. I guess everyone has different tastes. So taste it and then decide.

Indeed something that foreigners don't realize until they go to China is that the north of China is more northerly than Denmark, and the south of China is more southerly to Dubai.

So they tend to think of China as a country like others, but it's almost a subcontinent in a way. And the cuisine so different, and the people can be very different, although they all have a something important in common. So I agree with you, for someone that wants to do something in China it would be extremely helpful, and enjoyable, to spend a few months traveling around and then eventually picking a place that they like, or a place where they meet people that they like.

In my case, I was extremely, extremely well-treated in Nanjing (A/N the old capital and a university city). Although I didn't plan to stay there for a long time because there are probably cities that are more suitable in which to do business.

But there is more in Nanjing than business. It's funny because I have a friend who has just opened a very good French restaurant in Nanjing. The business has been hugely successful, and I just visited Nanjing last week and it was fantastic to see. People there are still very nice. And the city, as you said, maybe does not have too many special features but altogether is very agreeable; a very lovely city to live in.

Actually my train reached Nanjing late in the evening, I had no hotel booked, there were no smartphones at the time, but I was invited to sleep in an apartment belonging to the military college by students I met in the street.

And also what you have just mentioned, to be invited by strangers you met on the street to their home, it actually could happen everywhere in China. Because Chinese people are quite curious and they are very natural with close human relationships.

That's for example, the reason for the dating feature of Uber in China, and also why we think community, and especially smart communities apps, have very good potential in China. It's because of this natural closeness with human relationships, I believe.

And what you have just described, I also have experienced with my foreign friends in China in different areas actually. There was one in Beijing, one in Sichuan; they all had very interesting experiences.

People who have just met you and are so happy to meet you and invite you to their family, remain friends, keeping contact for years after. This is just another piece of evidence that shows that China is a country with very long traditions of community and *Guanxi* in a general sense.

It's probably easier in a university city like Nanjing and in big cities because so many of the students speak an okay level of English, with some being very fluent. While when you backpack the interior of China, people can still be very friendly but it's difficult to communicate because at least at the time, it was very hard to find English speakers.

Do you want to add something to close this little chat, or we call it a day?

Well, maybe a general message. I'm really a firm believer that all this technology, Internet, big data, these things are not just for business. And these things are not just technology. They are going to change profoundly the way we organize our activities, the way people relate to each other, and they are going to significantly change what we can do as a group, as a race altogether. We're in this work for this work. So, well, fasten your seatbelt.

Links

1. Get "China's Development: Capitalism and Empire"
by Michel Aglietta and Guo Bai
http://futurecitiesbook.com/101

2. HEC Paris – Business School
http://www.hec.edu

Simon Menashy

MCC Ventures

You can make a good product through hard work, but you can make an amazing product only through the feedback of your customers.

—Simon Menashy

Simon Menashy is not just a venture capitalist but a figure extremely present in the startup scene at every level. I had the opportunity to have Simon as a speaker on my panel at Fintech Week, and I like his practical suggestions for startups. When he talks to the founders, it's never academic or self promotional, but very practical and useful. In a world where marketing and hustling have become the main goal of so many investors and startups, listening to Simon is always refreshing.

The Interview

Hi Simon. Let's go straight to the business. What are the hottest areas in future cities tech?

There are two areas: one that is hot because everybody talks about it, and one that is hot for real. The area that everybody talks about is tech at the highest level: Corporations and government agencies organizing conferences and hackatons about the future of future cities. There is a lot of marketing going on, but eventually it doesn't mean that many things are going to happen.

The second area where things are really happening is at the bottom. Things for example that are happening to City Mappers or

Google Maps; tech that is in the smartphone of every person. And these are the hot technologies that are really going to change the life of the citizens.

On top of that, there are many technologies developed by startups and other companies that are not necessarily small, that are completely unsexy and nobody talks about them. But this is where you can find the hottest opportunities for investments.

So the first tip for an entrepreneur is that you don't need to be famous to be successful. Everybody knows the name of Mark Zuckerberg and other founders of consumer companies. Not many people know the name of Marc Benioff, the founder of Salesforce, and yet this is a very successful company.

Absolutely. An example is the Daily Mail. Everybody talks about this online newspaper and how they are successful and innovative, because an online newspaper is sexy. But the Daily Mail Group spent the last ten years developing and acquiring business-to-business services that are of real value and of real use but just not enough sexy to be talked about.

What do you think these corporations and government agencies could do to help these areas to grow?

For instance they can open their data to the public. London transport made their data free and accessible to everybody a couple of years ago, and in a few months there were more than one hundred startups born thanks to this access, and of them, at least ten were good.

Clearly this has to be balanced with concerns about security and privacy. Not everything can be accessible. But when access to public data has been released in a smart way, it has always proved to be valuable.

Transport for London shut this experiment down unfortunately, and this was probably not a good idea.

Another example. Tom Steinberg—founder of MySociety—at the beginning took the impossible-to-use website belonging to the city of Birmingham and reshaped it to provide a great user experience. He achieved this result with a new design, but by also scraping data from the internet or by using data that was already there but very difficult to access for the users. After his intervention the website became extremely popular.

He did the same with the Odeon website, the movie theatre chain, that at the time was very hard to use. Eventually it was so successful that—if I recall correctly—the Odeon asked to stop the project [laughs].

You are the director of investment at MMC Venture, a venture capital. What's your one piece of advice to the founder of a startup for pitching to an investor?

My first advice is to not approach the investor to sell something, but to be open to discussing it with us. The pitches that work the best are two way discussions.

On one hand the startup founder should have a very strong vision, and negative comments should not be capable of changing his mind and his commitment. On the other hand, he should be open to discussion and to be open to changing the execution of his vision on the basis of the feedback and the experience of the investor.

The second piece of advice is to be personal. To find out in advance what we like and our peculiarities. Even checking our website is sometimes enough. Then contact us and interact with us on a personal level and in a targeted way.

I receive many pitches, because that's my job, and I see that many of them have been prepared by consultants who are proposing the same pitch to fifty different investors. And I don't necessarily want to work with a person who is not interested in working with me specifically; he's just looking to find some funds no matter the source.

We the venture capital, plan to work with people who receive our investments for the next five to ten years. We don't want to work with people that we just like, but with people that we are excited to work with.

I'd like to add a third point. I'm not a venture capital, although I don't exclude entering this arena at some point, but I receive many requests from startups for investment or to be introduced to investors. When I ask "how many investors have you met already and how many of them have agreed to invest in you?" they often reply that they have met twenty or fifty investors but nobody has agreed to invest in them. Than the issue is maybe not that they have a bad approach, but that they have a bad business model.

True. Many startups spend a lot of time and energy on two important activities, developing the product and contacting investors, but not enough time on the third pillar of success — that is spending time with their customers.

You can make a good product through hard work, but you can make an amazing product only through the feedback of your customers.

What other actionable suggestions can you give to a startup that wants to raise funds?

When you are at seed stage the vision and the team can be extremely important, but when you access a series A investment or a following series, you need to show something more. So if you want to access multiple investors for an important funding round, you need to prove that there is at least some customer interest .

Maybe you don't have many customers yet, but you have to be able to prove that when you contact the customers they are open to paying. It's not enough if the potential customers show an interest in your product, they should open their wallet too.

As they say, "Go out and sell"

True. And I'd like to add another suggestion. A startup founder should be able to create its own serendipity. Go out and meet people that can not necessarily be useful now, but might be useful in the near now and in the future.

I totally support this suggestion but how do you suggest balancing this networking activity with good time management? In another interview, Goncalo Agra Amorin who is also a venture capital and runs an acceleration program, talks about "startup tourism". How many founders lose time going to every conceivable event?

The risk of losing time exists and it is usually connected to a passive concept of networking. A new startup founder tends to go to every event that he's invited too. On the contrary, part of the job of a CEO is to actively plan who he wants to meet and what invitations he should refuse.

I really believe in serendipity, and up to a certain point you can create your own serendipity.

Can you give an actionable example?

For instance, follow ups. When you meet someone who seems like an interesting person, many startups are so busy that they never follow up. A good actionable tip is to contact the interesting person you met at an event, as soon as you are back home or in the office.

No matter how busy you are, when you come back home from an evening event, you pick your business and shoot a one line email with a link to your project. If you can't do it, you take some time first thing the following morning.

You have to create your own serendipity, surrounding yourself with the right people, even if you don't need them that very exact moment.

Links

1. MMC Ventures
http://www.mmcventures.com

2. My Society
https://www.mysociety.org

The Future Is a Megacity

Interlude

In a globalized world, the problems of the poor today can, tomorrow — through migration, terrorism, and disease epidemics — become the problems of those at the pyramid's top.

—Richard Heeks

East West East

In 1950 there were only two megacities, metropolises with a population of over 10 million; London and New York. That world is gone. In our brave new world, the megacities are growing in number and at the same time they are moving East. It is estimated that by 2025, there will be about 40 megacities, out of which 28 will be in Asia, and only 5 in the West (London and Paris in Europe; New York, Chicago and Los Angeles in North America).

It's not just a matter of the number of megacities, the population is also slowing down in the West. European and North American megacities are estimated to grow less than 3% per year, versus twice this rate in Africa (Lagos and Kinshasa).

This is not something that will take place in the distant future; in fact it's already happening. Of the top ten cities in the world, just one — New York — is in the West, and it ranks only in 9th position.

London is further down the list in 32nd position. However, with the massive growth in the financial and technological sector, the city is expected to increase its population by more than 25% by 2030.

China will soon be the leader in this game, with the relatively unknown Pearl River Delta to become the biggest megacity in the world. With a gigantic urban area of 16,000 square miles, the Pearl River Delta will be twice the size of Wales and 26 times larger than London.

Back to the Future

For most Westerners it is difficult to fathom that their cities are losing the spotlight, in fact this is nothing new. From an historical perspective, the West has been the land of big cities for only a small parenthesis of time.

Beijing had reached a population of one million by 1775, which London reached only in 1825. Baghdad was acknowledged to have reached a population of one million in 925, and Rome by the end of the 1st century B.C. You could argue that Rome is indeed in the West, but this is not strictly true. Western culture was born in Europe with the industrial revolution, and the culture of ancient Rome does not exist anymore.

It's (Not) the Technology, Stupid

There is a common question in the startup ecosystem: why are people moving to the cities when they have technology and gadgets that allow them to work from a beach?

The first wave of urbanization that took place during the industrial revolution is easy to understand. Factories need people and people appreciate the stable source of income provided by a salary. In the rural areas farmers were subject to famine and instability.

This is not true anymore. Today we can work online while sitting in a farmhouse where the cost of living is just a fraction of what we would pay in a city. Still, cities are growing. Technology writer George Gilder wrote in 1995 that "Cities are leftover baggage from the industrial era". He predicted that in 10 years, we would have the technology to abandon the cities. Gilder was right about the technology, but wrong about everything else. Instead of shrinking, London is growing bigger and richer because of technology.

The reality is that technology has become so sophisticated that it can be easily used by anyone , but it is unlikely to be built by a single individual. Think about the video game. Back in the '80s it was possible to build a successful company in your garage. Today you'd need a staff of programmers, designers and story tellers to have any chance at competing in the market. If Leonardo Da Vinci was born today, he would probably be the CEO or CTO of a startup.

Everything Is a Social Game

This level of sophistication requires an appropriate ecosystem to exchange ideas, find skilled human resources and meet investors.

The progress of a city is not just a technological competition, but a social one. Of the 100+ startups that I interviewed, those who are based in London, or who want to be in London, mentioned the vibrant international community as one of the top 3 reasons why they have relocated or would want to relocate here. A great community is the reason behind the success of Berlin, New York and of course Silicon City, the latter of which is further helped by a beautiful beach and fantastic weather. We can do business in front of a computer, but we start that business in front of a glass of wine, pitching to a partner or an investor.

There Is One More Thing

The megacities in the developing world presents the same catalysts, plus a few others. An example is the leather industry that flourishes under the tinned roofs of one of the biggest slums in the world: Dharavi in Mumbai, India. The concentration of the work force in the same area reduces costs and provides a massive resource for training on the job. A farmer moving from a rural area to the slum can find someone who can teach him to work with leather in a matter of hours.

In an ideal world there would be no space for these slums, but in our world they are a reality. This is where technology could (and should) have a direct and large impact to improve the quality of life.

There Should Be a Better Way

Steve Jobs was famous for approaching any problem with the phrase "There should be a better way". This approach built one of the most successful companies in history. The same approach could be even more effective in the poorer areas of a megacity. An iPod can improve your life with music; smart city technology can save your life by providing clean water or health assistance.

ACCESS health built a system of smart ambulances that have reduced infant mortality by a factor of 5x. Guo Bai — one of the interviewees in this book — talks about developing smart neighborhoods and pushing the changes from the bottom to the top. Cities and megacities are the hottest thing to follow in the next five years. It's not just a matter of cold, hard numbers. The most fascinating thing will not be about the number or the location of megacities, but watching how technology can improve the quality of life for such a large mass of humanity concentrated in the same place. After thousands of years, we finally have the technology to make something truly useful. Hopefully we will not mess everything up as humans so often do.

Links

1. Interactive map by McKinsey&Company
http://futurecitiesbook.com/102

2. Interactive map by The Guardian
http://futurecitiesbook.com/103

Minerva Tantoco

New York City CTO

Access to the internet is the electricity and water supply of the Digital Age.
— Minerva Tantoco

Programmer, patent holder, and mum are three words that don't often come together in the same description. Minerva Tantoco is the exception. Raised in Queens, then attending the Bronx High School of Science, described as 'badass' (Forbes), former CTO of UBS in Hong Kong, and first CTO ever of New York City.

In my job, I meet many successful men and women around the planet, and they rarely impress me anymore. Again Minerva is the exception. She got me talking about William Gibson as her preferred sci-fi author. I mean, how many interviews with government officers end up talking about Gibson and his book Neuromancer? In my career? Zero. Besides, he's my preferred sci-fi writer too.

Much has been written about Minerva as a 'woman in tech' or a 'Queen Geek'. She said in another interview "For years, I dreamed of being a mom and becoming a CTO, but I certainly didn't expect both to happen at the same time." But I feel that focusing on gender in this article is rather reductive. This is the interview with a very interesting human being in a very interesting city. I am sure you will enjoy reading it as much as I did writing it!

The Interview

So Minerva, you have been appointed CTO (Chief Technology Officer) of New York City, a role that is usually reserved for companies. It clearly shows they have an interest in tech and in smart cities. Would you talk about what's going on in your city and in general in the US from this point of view?

Well, here in the U.S., the dialogue around smart cities was not as strong as I find it is in Europe, and in particular in Barcelona and in the UK. I think New York City has a very unique opportunity in its position as a global city to add to the dialogue around smart cities.

In New York we're leading the charge in the concept of "Smart city as an equitable city." It's really about technology at the service of the citizen to build an equitable city.

One of my favorite science fiction writers is William Gibson, I guess you know him?

Absolutely! I will add the link to the trilogy Neuromancer, Count Zero, and Mona Lisa Overdrive for the readers at the end of the interview. We definitely have similar tastes.

I love his quote, "The future is here. It's just not evenly distributed." More and more, we see that this distribution of technology access is divided, not just across cities, but across gender, income, and racial lines. This tech divide is both a cause and a symptom of economic equality. So in New York City, we recognize that you cannot have a smart city without it being an equitable city, as well.

That is our organizing principle. And I am finding in my conversations with other cities like Medellín (Colombia), Barcelona, (Spain), and elsewhere in Asia, that this theme is coming on strong.

Since you are familiar with the space you know that a lot of the smart city dialogue to date has been about very important things like energy efficiency, growth, and sustainability. Transportation is a huge component too. They are all very much a part of New York City's smart city strategy.

Our addition to the global dialogue on the subject of smart cities wants to be around equity. We look at the people-centric view of technology. It's almost the difference between designing a city from the air and designing a city from the ground.

Could you tell us a bit more about the specific activity that is going on in New York?

For New York, our tech strategy is based on three pillars: talent, access, and innovation. And the innovation part is where our smart cities strategy sits. Jeff here (A/N Jeff Merritt also from the Major Office of NYC joined our meeting) is our Director of Innovation and is responsible for preparing New York for the Internet of Everything.

And so our focus is people-driven tech, using technology in creative ways to close the tech divide. I can tell you more specifically about a few things we're doing so you'll have a better idea of what we mean by that, if that helps, Stefano.

I would love that. Both me and the readers are always interested in looking at a few practical examples. Also, the majority who usually follow my interviews aren't based in New York but in Europe and Asia with a growing number in Africa and South America; so practical updates that may look obvious to a New Yorker, are very interesting to us.

I'll cover the top three. I'll start from .NYC, the internet domain of the city of New York. NYC is the fastest growing city-owned top-level domain. And the idea behind that is, as top-level domain, we can provide New Yorkers with availability to domain names that they might not have access to in the .COM, because most of those are long gone.

You have to be a New Yorker to have a .NYC domain name, or you have to run a New York business. We verify the address, of course, because it is a branding tool as well. It was an experiment we started last year. We launched it in October, and there has been tremendous response to it.

The second is the website Digital.NYC, which is the one-stop online shop for all things tech in New York City.

Again, the idea is to democratize access to the tech scene. So when you arrive in New York City or are thinking about setting up shop here, you need access to all kinds of information.

Through a public-private partnership, we created this one-stop online site that is a mash up of all of the different tech scenes in New York. It lists jobs. It has a database of every startup and their locations. It has articles and blogs. It lists like 800 events and 5,000 different startups, where can you take a class, so there are educational opportunities included. It's all listed there. And it's all for free.

Giving access is truly going to become one of the main goals of governments all over the world. I am lucky enough to have a privileged view of the sector thanks to my job and these interviews, and it's fascinating to see the similar reaction in places far away from each other.

For instance, in my last interview in China, Guo Bai pointed out exactly the same point that you just made. In her case, the focus was more on all the grants and scholarships and online courses that the government is launching. They may not work properly if nobody knows they exist. So part of the effort now in China is to increase the access to this information, especially among lower income families.

Precisely. And that is the power of the internet. As long as you have access to the internet, you can have that. And that is another area that we're working on. I'm sure China is as well.

Now we see other cities replicating the idea of Digital.NYC and launching similar websites for their cities. And we are very flattered. They say imitation is the greatest flattery, right?

True. It could be frustrating in business, but in government, the more entities learn and copy the good practices of others, the better.

We're very pleased that all these other cities are following us. Of course, to benefit from Digital.NYC at the higher level, you need broadband access. So part of our citywide tech strategy is to provide city-wide internet access. This is the third example, and probably the best-known—and one of my favorites. We are turning all of the payphones on the city's streets into free high-speed Wi-Fi hotspots.

This sounds like one of my favorites, too. Would you like to go a bit more into details on this third example?

Sure. In our view the payphone of the future isn't a payphone at all. You don't pay for it and it's not a phone. Really it's the un-payphone.

The pay telephones here are paid for through a very innovative franchise granted through the city of New York. In exchange, whichever company has that franchise may sell advertising that wraps around the payphones.

When we were reinventing the payphone, we put out a proposal to companies to say, "Give us your best idea for turning these payphones into Wi-Fi hotspots."

The winner was chosen last December, and we hope to see the first of these payphones appearing in New York City by the end of the year. These are going to be beautiful and sleek; basically kiosks that will have Wi-Fi available up to 170 feet around them.

And the speeds, depending on where the payphones are, will be at least 100 Megabits speed over Wi-Fi, and some of them will have the new radios for 1 Gigabit speed Wi-Fi. When it's completed over the next few years, it will be the largest free municipal Wi-Fi in the world.

This also sounds like the base for a grid for the Internet of Everything.

Yes, exactly. The free Wi-Fi is just the tip of the iceberg, I'm sure. Because once these things are in place, the possibilities are endless. In the wearable conversation, there is much talk about the connected self. When everyone is connected, a smart city can provide benefits to all the citizens, and make the city a better place to live.

And then finally, the connected citizen can guide and influence public policies, government services, and also have a voice in the direction of the city. And we want that for everyone, truly everyone, not just the people with the money for an Apple Watch, right?

It really has this huge potential to truly democratize society. So that's the tip of the iceberg and sort of the ultimate vision of connected self, connected city, and connected citizens.

In short, you make the effort to provide the access to everybody, therefore you inject human talent in the society that would have not have access because their low income. Then you leave the people and the companies free to develop their own solutions.

Exactly. And I would say that certainly the federal government and the President of the United States have a very similar view, which is that internet access is really a core infrastructure, similar to electricity and fresh water, right?

Access to the internet is the electricity and water supply of the Digital Age. In the past, private companies might not have brought electricity to all of the farmlands out in the middle of nowhere, right?

And in those cases, the government came in paid for electricity access to be made available in those rural areas. And there is now a trend I see with people thinking of internet access in exactly the same way, where the private companies, for purely commercial reasons, have not blanketed the city in broadband access.

And so what is government's role in that? I'm sure they were thinking the same question about water and electricity 100 years ago or 150 years ago.

Are you seeing that in Europe as well?

I probably see this even more in Europe. The European Union is made up of many countries and historically they have developed their own specific culture. With such a diversity, at least some Member States will debate strongly about this subject.

Some companies would probably prefer to avoid any involvement from the State in providing free internet access. It's probably a situation similar to what happened in Europe over 100 years ago with electricity. At the beginning, in some countries, access to electricity was not considered a right for everyone, but reserved for the higher social classes.

It's interesting. I used to live in Hong Kong. The minute you went over to the border into China, the internet access would just drop down slower. And I know China's grappling with this as well. I think they view it as essential to their economic future to improve it. So Hong Kong enjoys super-fast and inexpensive internet access.

Indeed in Hong Kong everything is concentrated in the city, and they have always been very innovative. I remember in the '90s they already had a prepaid card — the Octopus — with touch payments. When in Hong Kong, I was able to purchase not only the transport ticket, but pay in small shops. We have a similar card, the Oyster, in London, twenty years later.

And it's not just Hong Kong anymore.

Indeed. We are used to thinking that Asia and India copy Europe and the US, but many services now are coming to us from what they call "Developing Countries". M-Pesa comes from Africa and so do the prepaid meters. China is not a follower anymore and India is famous for their tech hubs.

I was thinking that exact thought when I was traveling through Asia. Innovation, in some ways, as you said, will come from countries that have to improve the life of many low income people.

Much of it will come from Asia because they've had to figure out how to do mobile payments with a non-smart phone, for example, right? That's why I also feel that we can have innovation come from our lower income areas here in the US as well.

Innovation doesn't come from only wealthy places; in fact, it often comes from poorer places, as you said. So in New York City we can provide access and education to many talented individuals who will, in turn, create innovation. I think a big part of a smart city has to include a strategy to educate all people.

Asia is investing a great deal in universities and degrees and training people for the next generation of jobs, and that's an essential component. Education has to be a big piece of a smart city plan.

So a fourth example that I can add to the point above, is that New York City has the first tech talent pipeline where we're directly training adults for jobs.

We made a unique public-private partnership. We find what jobs need to be filled, and then we connect them with the educational institutions and schools that do the training.

We literally build the pipeline of people to go into those jobs. And this is something that New York is leading the way in, also.

In many cases, of course it's educating our young in the public school system. But also we need to train people who don't have a job right now so they can be more fully employed.

What's the secret to do that balancing public encouragement and private activity?

A great example is New York City's Tech Talent Pipeline, which is actually funded by several grants. So we actually act as the coordinator and convener and matchmaker. But we have the partnership directly with the tech companies in New York City, whether it's a Facebook or a Google or Etsy. And then we also have those partnerships with the schools that teach web development, iOS, etc.

Really we function as the place where the matchmaking takes place. We find the students. We can, in some cases, use the grant money that we received to pay for the course. Because if your class is too expensive and you don't have a job, how could you afford it?

What kind of budget is already assigned on this project, if you can say?

We're starting this off as a relatively small $10 million initiative and we're seeing what works. So far, it's been very successful. And hopefully, it will expand not only here in New York, but to other cities and countries.

Can we say that part of your mission is to be copied?

Yes, being copied is a marker of success. It shows we got something right with that.

Links

1. Digital.NYC
http://www.digital.nyc

2. Download "Neuromancer"
by William Gibson
http://futurecitiesbook.com/104

3. Download "Count Zero"
by William Gibson
http://futurecitiesbook.com/105

4. Download "Mona Lisa Overdrive"
by William Gibson
http://futurecitiesbook.com/106

Milos Milisavljevic

Strawberry Energy

In order to succeed with limited resources you need to focus. I know it's not a sexy answer but it's true.

—Milos Milisavljevic

What do they have in common?

One of the best tennis players of all time.

One of the greatest inventors in history.

One startup in London.

Well, they all come from Serbia, and they refuse to passively accept the common knowledge.

The inventor is Nikola Tesla and the tennis player is Novak Djokovic. The mantra made famous by Steve Jobs — *There should be a better way* — seems to be a common characteristic in Serbia.

It's easy to see this attitude in Nikola Tesla. He was an inventor after all.

Novak Djokovic is just a click away. Go to Amazon and order his book *Serve to Win*. At first glance, it looks like a book about food and diet. However it's much more than that. This book is a quest to deconstruct whatever is accepted as common knowledge. It's a manual of self-improvement lean and funny. I always recommend Djokovic's book to my students, especially to managers, entrepreneurs and consultants.

The third character of our story is Milos Milisavljevic and his startup is Strawberry Energy. We meet during the Cognicity acceleration program where I mentor.

Milos is not famous like the other two (yet) but they have the same commitment: finding new solutions to old problems.

Strawberry Energy's main product is an artificial tree that recharges your smartphone and can provide free WiFi in the surrounding area. The sleeves are solar panels so the tree became autonomous once it's planted.

Let's repeat that again. A tree with solar panels as sleeves that recharges smartphones and provides free WiFi. Don't you love the idea? Anywhere else in the world this would be considered at least bizarre. In Serbia is business as usual.

The Interview

Hi Milos. Let's start introducing yourself to the reader.

I developed a strong interest in renewable energy sources while I was still in secondary school. After graduating, I went on to study Electrical Engineering at the University in Belgrade and started Strawberry Energy when I was 22 as a hobby. Today Strawberry Energy is a business with real employers presents in ten locations.

How has Strawberry Energy evolved since then?

Our goal was to bring solar energy into people's everyday lives; that's how it all started. Back then we were just producing solar powered charging stations to help people power their devices outdoors using solar energy.

We installed the first Strawberry Tree in the city of Obrenovac, in Serbia and we got an order for the next four stations immediately after so we decided to create the company, Strawberry Energy.

The next thing we did was adding Wi-Fi internet to our trees so people could sit, recharge their devices and have an internet connection. Soon after we realized that energy and connectivity in these standalone devices across cities is all you need in order to bring IoT (Internet of Things) into the public spaces so we thought: Let's make public spaces smart!

This is your product now. What's your grand vision for the future?

When you look at today's startups and smart city industry you see huge amounts of innovation happening around smart homes, smart transport, smart waste management, and so on, but when it comes to smart outdoor public spaces, there's very little being done.

Our goal is to bring smart technology to the outdoors, to our bus shelters, benches and phone booths and to have smart hubs in universities, parks, shopping malls and schools. Ultimately, we want to have these smart connected devices communicate between themselves, which will bring the power of the IoT to outdoor spaces in every city.

It sounds an ambitious plan. There are less investments available for outdoor spaces. Also, these spaces are often communal areas, without a specific private owner to turn into a customer. How are you going to do that?

There are four directions we are following: power and connectivity, improved security, disaster preparedness and smart city sensors and data. For example, Strawberry Trees have LED lights and it's incredible but just by providing light in a dark part of the road we can increase security for passersby.

We're also building emergency buttons, so if something happens to you, you can go to any Strawberry smart station and push the button to call for help. In terms of disaster preparedness, if there's a big storm or a fire and you have a blackout, our standalone systems will be the only place which will provide you energy and connectivity.

Finally, we want to have sensors in our devices so public authorities can use the data gathered to understand their environment in real time: pollution levels, air quality, traffic, pedestrian flow.

Imagine having sensors which detect particles in the air that cause asthma. If you deploy them across the city, people can have a real time map of the city with the parts of town they should avoid in a mobile app. That's our vision. Bringing smartness and the IoT to public spaces.

What's your secret sauce? What makes you different from every other IoT startup?

We're seeing a lot of competition arising, but most companies are focused on building solar powered street infrastructure with one or two features. We think that's a real shame. It's like building a phone with just calls and SMS. We want our Strawberry devices to be platforms where you can install any app you want, from CCTV to public announcement systems, screens with local info, coupons for nearby stores.

All you need is energy, connectivity and smartness, the computing power inside. Everything else is just modular; you can add it physically or use the software. So, the core value of our mission is not to build these simple, isolated devices. We want to build a smart connected infrastructure.

Where are you now in terms of growth?

So far we have installed 13 systems in ten cities in three countries. All of them have smart connected apps and they gather real data so we know how much energy they saved, how much carbon dioxide they saved, what is the average amount of time people spent recharging and how many people have used it.

By mid-2015, we'll have 20 systems and almost half a million users. We are also seeing huge possibilities to grow not only in existing cities but in new ones.

On top of that, I see that you are turning your weakness — serving public spaces — into a point of strength. Your company is taking part in every public competition and event out there.

You won an investment from the Bulgarian Accelerator Venture Fund Eleven and expand to their country. You were selected by Cognicity — the London acceleration program where we meet. In short, you can leverage the public benefits of your product where a typical startup usually leverage the economics.

Yes and the public interest is destined to growth. You have huge smart cities being developed from scratch in China, Malaysia and India and we have started working with a couple of companies who are designing these whole smart cities and are looking for solutions for outdoor IoT tech.

We have talked about you and the company. Can you introduce us to your team?

We are eight people at the moment. Half of us are dedicated to engineering and solving technical problems and the other half deal with business development and marketing.

I must say that we develop not just the software but the hardware too. We control the whole process of the production because that's the best way to ensure you get a quality product, by understanding not only the outside but the inside too.

You're based in London at the moment participating in the Cognicity challenge. What do you think of the ecosystem here?

London is one of the most entrepreneurial cities in Europe and also, as far as we're concerned, where more is being done to support small businesses who want to develop smart city technologies.

In the entrepreneurial world there's a lot more buzz about apps, software as a service or consumer electronics but when it comes to smart city services and infrastructure, the market is small at the moment. I think London is being quite visionary by taking the lead and investing in these types of entrepreneurial projects. It's great to be able to take part in it.

What piece of advice can you give other startups?

Focus. In order to build something and succeed in a reasonable amount of time with limited resources you need to focus. I know it's not a sexy answer but it's true.

Moving to something more personal. Can you name a person—dead or alive—who inspires you or your company?

Tesla, but the scientist, not the car maker! Nikola Tesla was born in Serbia and was one of those people who used technology to push the human race forward. He envisioned clean technology, a goal we share with him at Strawberry Tree.

Allow me to finish with a trivial question. What gadget would you love to own?

I want to buy a Tesla car actually. Imagine having solar panels in your roof which provide energy that can power your car. It's an insanely intelligent way to move without spending energy and I just want to own one.

Basically you don't want a Tesla just to drive it, but to experiment. If you get the car, you would try to fix solar panels on the roof. An electric car with solar panels doesn't need to stop at the power station. Elon Musk, you have been warned!

Links

1. Company website
http://senergy.rs/?lang=en

2. Download "Serve To Win"
by Novak Djokovic
http://futurecitiesbook.com/107

3. Eleven - Accelerator Venture Fund
http://11.me

4. Cognicity - Acceleration Program
http://cognicity.london

One Drone in Every Home

Interlude

Progress is impossible without change, and those who cannot change their minds cannot change anything.

—George Bernard Shaw

One day a drone with Artificial Intelligence will look back and thanks Jeff Bezos for promoting the civil role of its drone peer. Every other news bulletin is about war.

Claire Danes is the (War) Drone Queen in the TV series *Homeland*, Ethan Hawke is a war drone pilot in the movie *Good Kill*, and the news is all about drones and the war on terrorism.

Bezos and his idea of delivering Amazon goods by civil drones put them in a different spotlight. A startup could be involved in drone market even if they don't want to compete with the big military providers, no matter whether it is for moral reasons or just business.

The US Consumer Electronics Association estimates a $1 billion market in drones by 2018, an exponential growth from the $130 million this year, with the prevision of 425,000 units sold in 2015.

These numbers are still nothing compared to the estimates made by the Association for Unmanned Vehicle Systems International (between you and me, that means Association for Drones. Toqueville would be so proud.) AUVSI projects an international market of $82.1 billion between direct sales (i.e. drones) and indirect revenue (patents, jobs, etc.) with the creation of more than 100,000 high-paying new jobs.

These are 'just' estimates at the moment. The consumer drone market is growing fast, so fast that the US Federal Aviation Administration is working to reduce their limits, and US Congress has ordered a regulatory framework for the testing and licensing of commercial drones (the 2012 FAA Reauthorization Act).

Where Is the Money Going?

This is the question that we ask every time a new market booms: "Where is the money going?" Before you launch a startup or a new line of products in your company, you want to be sure that the market is big enough, and not just afflicted by momentary hype.

In the drone market there is definitively space for the private and leisure industry.

At the time of writing you can buy a flying drone for just $78 dollars on Amazon; the Parrot Minidrone Rolling Spider. It's a toy, but it can fly for real and take aerial shots and video from the sky with the embedded vertical mini-camera. Just make sure you have a look at criminal law if you want to use it in a—well—'particular way'.

Timothy Reuter, CEO of a startup called AirDroids, pledged $35,000 on Kickstarter to build a drone equipped with a GoPro camera. He ended up raising almost $1 million in 60 days (2,655% of his initial target).

Drones are used to shoot porn too. I know that many of you would love to see a link for 'educational purposes'. I can't do that if I want to distribute this book in every country and to customers of every age. You can, however, Google "Drone Boning Movie" and see what's going on (It's nothing X rated, I swear).

Another booming use of the consumer drone will be in the police forces. The Grand Forks sheriff's department in North Dakota was the first to publish videos of their use of Qube, a drone built specifically for the police forces by AeroVironment, a company that has developed a their expertise with the military.

Deputy sheriff Alan Frazier of Grand Forks stresses how drones are not an extravagant expense; on the contrary they help save money. According to Frazier's statement a human-manned helicopter costs around $12 million a year while a drone costs his department just around $10,000.

Despite all these activities, private customers, police, and city councils (i.e. firefighters) combined can't top the amount spent by agriculture, the biggest market of the civil drone industry.

It may sound surprising that we are talking about agricultural application in a book about cities, but it's not. In fact, the agricultural use of drones is going to push the growth of the cities even further.

On one hand, more programmers and engineers who want to develop drones will move to the cities to access the networking opportunities with investors and the pool of human talent.

On the other hand, more 'farmers' if we can still call them that, will move to the cities to access the lifestyle and networking opportunities, and run their farm comfortably from their apartment.

With the rise of the drone economy, farmers and soldiers don't need to be on a farm or in a war zone to conduct their business anymore. It's not yet clear if this is a good or bad thing, but it seems to be an unstoppable phenomenon.

The Real Deal

The real issue will not be if the use of drones is growing or not (it's growing already), but one of privacy and security. During the Urban Shield Conference, HaloDrop—a company in the drone business—reported to be developing software capable of filming a face from 300 meters away, and passing the images to the police's face recognition databases.

For good or for ill, the drone technology is already out there. "One computer in every home" was Bill Gates' dream and the reality has greatly improved people's lives. "One 3D printer in every home" is also going to revolutionize our cities for the better. "One drone in every home" could be somewhat alarming, especially if the drone is not yours.

Links

1. US Consumer Electronics Association
http://www.ce.org

2. AUVSI - Association for Unmanned Vehicle Systems International
http://www.auvsi.org

3. FAA - Federal Aviation Administration
http://www.faa.gov

4. US Congress 2012 FAA Reauthorization Act
http://thomas.loc.gov/cgi-bin/query/z?c112:H.R.658:

5. Check the Parrot Mini-drone Rolling Spider on Amazon
http://futurecitiesbook.com/108

6. The Pocket Drone on Kickstarter
http://kck.st/1hPUDOG

7. Urban Shield conference
https://www.urbanshield.org

Thomas Davies

Seedrs

Tech, sales, and marketing are a bit like a three legged chair, if you haven't got one of those legs it will fall over, and each is just as important as the other.

—Thomas Davies

Love it or hate it, Kickstarter and Indiegogo have created an entire generation of companies that would have not be possible without them. They have made the word "crowdfunding" popular and hot. However, they represent only a part of the market, the reward based crowdfunding,. "Reward based" means that you typically raise money pre-selling a product. Your supporters are customers, in fact they buy a product in pre-order before it's built.

Sometimes there are nasty consequences, with companies that, after years, still haven't shipped their product, but in general reward based crowdfunding has been an extremely good thing.

The interviewee today—Thomas Davies—is the Chief Investment Officer in Seedrs, a new generation of crowdfunding, where the company doesn't pre-sell products but offers equity (company shares).

The supporters are not customers but investors. To give you an idea, one of the most successful campaigns on Kickstarter last year was Oculus Rift, the company behind virtual reality goggles and technology. They were so successful, that they were acquired by Facebook for $2 billion just after the campaign. If Oculus would have raised money on a crowdfunding for equity platform, their supporters would have been incredibly wealthy today.

The Interview

Hey Thomas, I am so happy to have you here. Because your company — Seedrs — is one of the top crowdfunding platforms for equity in the world, why don't we skip the talk about smart cities in general, and make a list of actionable advice that a company could use to raise money. Is this okay with you?

Sure. I would say that when thinking about the initial stages of raising money, bootstrapping is perfectly fine for a while, but there comes a time where it's more efficient to raise money externally, rather than trying to do it yourself.

If the founders are considering crowdfunding, the really important thing to remember is that there are a number of benefits, in addition to just the money.

So the money is one part of the reason why people use crowdfunding, but the other reasons are PR. Companies get a lot of publicity when they successfully crowdfund. For example, a newspaper is much more likely to write about a company that's just raised money through crowdfunding, rather than just raised money from one angel investor.

This is a controversial point and I want to make some clarification. An easy access to the media was true in the past when only a few companies were using reward crowdfunding. It's much harder today. However, Seedrs is not reward crowdfunding but equity crowdfunding (you don't pre-sell products but offer shares in your company).

Only a few startups are solid and interesting enough to access crowdfunding for equity, many of them just get rejected or don't even bother to try. Therefore it's easier to catch the attention of the media if you have a crowdfunding for equity campaign. Don't get me wrong, I am not saying it's easy. But it's definitely easier.

Public relations are the first benefit. And then the second benefit is having lots and lots and lots of investors who are now behind you and are there to provide you with support and mentorship and advice.

By having several hundred people who are accountants, lawyers, marketing executives, exiting entrepreneurs themselves, there's a whole wealth of knowledge that you can tap into, often in areas which are all very useful when you're just starting a business.

And then of course you get the money, so there are a number of benefits, one of which is money but it's not the only reason, and I think that's a very important vote for very early stage businesses in particular.

There is also another aspect peculiar to Seedrs but not to every crowdfunding platform. You represent the small investors/ shareholders and you help and coordinate them. There is a direct benefit for the startup. If my grandmother invests $100 in a startup, the founders don't have to deal with her and the other thousand investors, but just with one professional investor: you, and maybe a few other big investors that are not represented by you.

These small investors, on the other hand, became evangelists and customers because they want your company to succeed since they have shares.

That's very true and I think that you've hit the nail on the head in that the crowds can be very, very valuable, and mentorship and support doesn't just have to be in the form of one rich person who can provide you with business advice.

It can also come in the form of 100 people who put £50 in each, talking about the product or the service with their friends, talking about it on Facebook, talking about it at dinner parties, buying the product, all of that stuff which is actually often, they tend to be more active in supporting and talking about the product than the big mentors.

And actually the smaller the investment, the louder they talk, which I think is interesting. However, the downside to that is, as you said, if you don't have someone representing them all, you can have a lot of noise and a lot of administration hassle.

So while we know there's lots of benefits, there are downsides to having lots of individual investors. So what Seedrs does is try to give you, and help you maintain, the good stuff, which is access to them through your own investment portal, and they can ask you questions but in one centralized place. But any voting rights, any consents, any agreements you need signing, is all done by Seedrs.

For example, we do all the tax paperwork and all that stuff. And what means is that you get to enjoy all the benefits, while Seedrs absorbs all the administration hassle that comes with having shareholders, just by its very nature.

And that's another benefit—and this is something that we didn't really probably realize at the beginning. It's a bit like what Just Giving has done. Just Giving has essentially provided people a technological solution to raising money from people they already know.

Now with crowdfunding, we are very, very good at raising money for you through our platform, but also we are as much a source of capital as we are a tool to raise money from people you do know, which is your friends, your family, your network. And just like Just Giving, it's a lot easier to get people to donate money for your marathon run by sending them to a link, rather than going around with a clipboard and asking them for cash. It's a lot easier to raise money from all of your network by sending them a link to Seedrs.

And also when you're talking about investments, if things go wrong or there's admin and there's paperwork and there's legal shareholder rights, it actually makes your relationship much healthier if you have a third party in the middle managing it, because it's not like the founder chasing his best friend for payment, it's Seedrs chasing for payment.

And that's a very, very powerful tool, because it puts a slight buffer and makes it much more professional and serious, as opposed to just asking your mates for £50 down the pub.

Another feature of crowdfunding for equity that I've found extremely helpful, but was probably not so clear at the beginning of the venture, is how the escrow account can solve so many problems with angels. A quick example.

When you manage to raise money through a typical angel round, let's say $250,000, you have to convince all the angels to sign the term sheet, in order to have a valid agreement. So when the last angel has signed, sometimes 30-60 days after the first one, you go back to all the angels asking them to wire their money.

And maybe the first angel can't do it because during those 30-60 days he bought a new luxury car, or his business is not doing as well anymore, or any other reason. And you have to start everything from scratch.

On the contrary, if you are on Seedrs or a similar serious platform, you can ask the first angel to wire the money immediately into Seedrs' escrow account. If the fund raising fails, the startup can't steal the money, or use it anyway, because it is in a third party escrow account. The angel get his money back immediately.

Yes exactly. Actually, we're starting to have a number of private angel syndicates using Seedrs for that very reason. We've got one that's just closing now which you'll never see, because it's private. The founders already know the angels, and the Seedrs campaign is used as a way of gathering the money.

Seedrs takes care of all the legal documentation in a very cheap way, and as a third party negotiator, so we haven't got 10 different opinions.

Plus the escrow account mechanism that you just described, and obviously we do a very reduced fee, and provide basically an execution service, as opposed to just a front end raising service as well, and that's proving very popular among angel syndicates at the moment.

What do you think is the biggest mistake that founders make when they join Seedrs or another crowdfunding for equity platform?

I think one of the biggest mistakes is thinking that crowdfunding is a magic solution where money falls from the sky. I think that crowdfunding is a very important tool, it's yet another avenue of funding which is proving very popular and is very useful for certain types of businesses. But the common theme between all successful campaigns is that the entrepreneur was a good hustler and worked very hard at his campaign.

You have to go out and get your network in the first instance to invest, because the platform investors, who are browsing around building up a portfolio, are not going to be interested if your campaign hasn't got any momentum. You have to go and get that momentum yourself, by tapping into your friends, your family, your social media contacts.

And then once you start to get momentum, the platform investors will follow. But if you go up there at 0% and wait for investment, it's not going to work. And I think that people who look at crowdfunding as a passive thing, where you just put it up and wait, will be disappointed. It's an active thing, you have to put it up and then go and tell everyone about it.

We can say that a crowdfunding platform is sometimes more of a marketing channel than an investment channel.

It's a marketing channel, it's a tool. And there is capital there, but we could have 50 million investors on Seedrs, if you're at 0%, they're not going to invest.

How much time do you think someone has to start his campaign in advance? Let me make an example. I've helped different campaigns in Kickstarter and Indiegogo. Two years ago, we were used to start the marketing a couple of months before the official start of the campaign, building a mailing list, a community, relationship with the bloggers, and so on.

Nowadays in reward crowdfunding, we need to start a campaign at least 4-6 months before it's officially online.

I think in terms of preparation, in crowdfunding for equity, a month's preparation is usually sufficient. And the main reason for that is because unlike Kickstarter, where you're having to prepare the community for and buy into the product that you're trying to sell, on Seedrs you provide an investment pitch.

What you're essentially doing is getting your network lined up for why this is a good investment opportunity, and that takes less time, because you're tapping into people you know, who know you and trust you to build the business, and less actually about the idea, if that makes sense.

Yes. The supporter of a campaign is not a buyer who you should invite into a community, to get to know you and build trust. The supporter is an investor, and if your product makes sense, and the team is good, then that's enough for him

And it's about giving this data to your network . And your network may not necessarily be people you know. For instance, if you've got a new architect software program your network are architects, and it's working out how to get into trade magazines for architects. It's working out how to get database information on architects and so forth. So I think a lot of it becomes preparing the campaign, getting your network ready, and that can actually usually be done in about a month, definitively less time.

I connect to what you just said about trade magazines for professionals, in your example, architects. Another common mistake I see often, is that startups spend so much energy and are so excited to be published in the New York Times or Tech Crunch, while the typical reader of Tech Crunch is a startupper like them, often with no money and no interest in investing in their company.

So sometimes, it's better to be published in a magazine that is not so well known, but is very powerful in your vertical niche, rather than going for the big online magazine that is recognized worldwide .

I think that's absolutely right. And it's less about broad marketing and it's more about focused, targeted marketing. And the main reason for that is, you could feature on some page on the Financial Times, about an accountancy software product that you have, but actually the returns you'll get will be much, much, much, much less than featuring in the UK Accountant's newsletter.

In our example, you're really targeting accountants, and the odds of an accountant who's interested in investing in you reading the front page of the New York Times are going to be much less then the accountant reading about you in the newsletter of his association. So you're absolutely right, targeted is always more effective than broad marketing.

I have one last question that I ask everyone. What advice would you give to your younger self?

What advice would I give to my younger self? The advice I would give myself is to not underestimate the importance of marketing when starting a business.

So you need almost three pillars of any business, which is the tech, the commercial, and then the third pillar is the marketing. And each of those three don't work if you haven't got the other.

It's a bit like a three legged chair, if you haven't got one of those legs it will fall over, and each is just as important as the other. We at Seedrs are very much focused on improving our marketing now, because the other two are very, very strong.

Basically you are following your own advice to your younger self, but right now.

That's very, very true.

So if you're a guy setting up the company and you're the commercial guy, then make sure you've also got a tech guy and a marketing guy sitting next to you. If you're the marketing guy, make sure you got a tech guy and a commercial guy, and so forth.

It may sounds obvious but it's a game changer.

Links

1. Company website
http://seedrs.com

2. Kickstarter
http://kickstarter.com

3. Indiegogo
http://indiegogo.com

Adeo Ressi

Founder Institute

You can't have a good "what" unless you have a good "why." So if you're not sure why you're doing it, then the "what" (the company) will often be flawed.

— Adeo Ressi

If you are part of the startup community, it's very unlikely that you haven't heard about Adeo Ressi. He sold his first company — Total New York — to AOL before graduation. Eventually this first company growth so fast, that "it just was impossible for me to even consider finishing graduation." he said. After that, Adeo started a second company, and a third one, and he hasn't stopped since, even co-founding a space company with Elon Musk that eventually led to Space X.

In the end, he never went back to college to graduate, aligning himself with a long line of famous drop outs, from Steve Jobs, to Bill Gates, to Richard Branson. As he said, "That company became very, very successful very, very quickly. So, it just was impossible for me to even consider finishing graduation".

When the startup community was hit by the crisis of 2008-2009, Adeo decided to start the Founder Institute, a pragmatic startup accelerator based on a simple philosophy: helping the economic recovery by lowering the high failure rate for startups. In his own words, "about 25,000 businesses were started every year by passionate and committed people. And north of 95% of them would fold or die."

The program was indeed successful and soon the goal of the Founder Institute became to "globalize Silcon Valley". Today the institute has a presence across 50 countries, from Vietnam to Columbia. This environment brings some curious consequences even outside the business. Last time I enjoyed a barbecue hosted by the Founder Institute in Palo Alto, I seat on a table with colleagues from France, the Philippines, Iceland and Afghanistan (yes, they have a team building a startup ecosystem over there).

I've a sort of conflict of interest in this interview. I'm a mentor of the Founder Institute myself, and part of Expansive Ventures, their investment syndicate. I had to find a formula for an impartial interview, that's why in the interview you will not find any questions about the success of the Institute.

No matter my opinion, Adeo has been part of Silicon Valley since the mighty '90s, has started over 10 companies and a global community. I am sure you will get useful insights.

The Interview

In this book, I had a chance to interview entrepreneurs and influencers from different countries, and they all brought their different angle. You on the other hand run the Founder Institute with a presence across 50 countries. You can give us an overview of the global trends better than anyone (and with "global trends" I mean politics, investments and/or startups - pick the one you prefer).

Well, I can sort of give you trends in each category, and that might be most useful.

So on the governmental side, governments around the world are becoming quite proactive about helping companies, some of which is good, some of which is bad, but at least they are trying, which overall is good.

So for example, France just launched a startup visa program similar to what Chile is doing. Similar things are happening in Canada.

Pretty much every credible government around the world is taking a variety of initiatives to improve the likelihood of startup success. We have just done some longitudinal studies of our graduates and learned that if a company achieves a great amount of success and progress in the first 11 months of existence, the likelihood of that company succeeding increases five-fold.

So if a government is providing a variety of resources and a variety of programs to help startups, that essentially is helping those startups achieve milestones faster. The data indicates that's a good thing, though I do believe there is a variation in the quality of different programs. As I indicated, some programs are good, and some programs are less good, if you will.

In terms of the funding landscape, I think you're seeing a massive proliferation in funding accelerators and company-builders. For the most part, there's also been a bit of a consolidation happening as well, but the net result is that more and more of funding incubators and more and more company-builders that provide capital are popping up all around the world. That, too, is very beneficial because it's very difficult to raise money at any stage. The angel and early-stage is the hardest of them all. Right?

So angel capital is the hardest amount or the hardest type of capital to raise. Series A is definitely also hard, but a lot easier than angel. Series B is, again, also hard, but a lot easier than a series A. So the proliferation of funding accelerators that have investors sort of locked in, in demo days and many different programs that almost act like they're finishing school for a startup to get their product in good shape and start fundraising, the proliferation of these types of programs is ultimately beneficial for startups because it's just increased the number of startups worldwide that are getting funding.

Probably on the company side, there you have a lot of mixed stuff going on. You have a lot of people entering startups that probably should not be doing so. Startups are sexy and cool right now, and that's drawing greater and greater numbers of people to do startups.

But a lot of times, people who are entering the field of technology entrepreneurship, I call them "tourists", want to come and see for themselves and feel the freezing cold temperature. Then once they do so, they're like, "Oh, wow. That's great," and they go back to their day job.

I think that there's a trend of an increasing number of tourists entering technology entrepreneurship. As a result, you're seeing a lot of people leave the field very quickly, and that's creating some challenges for everyone at every level in the ecosystem. Because everyone wants more stable entrepreneurs. Because more entrepreneurs means that there can be more funding accelerators. More entrepreneurs means that there can be more success stories and more capital available.

Well, this is a common phenomena everywhere. Many wannabe founders have a day job — and that's perfectly fine — but some of them have no intention of quitting their job anytime soon. Their startup becomes a sort of side activity, and as a consequence, the percentage of failures becomes very high. This high percentage of failures discourages future serious potential entrepreneurs. Moreover, it becomes harder to find a good CTO and other professional figures

Part of the reason it's very hard to find those people is because technology entrepreneurship, to date, has been not very sexy. So on one hand, making technology entrepreneurship sexy is good because more people will quit their jobs to do it, but the negative of that is there are also an increasing number of these tourists, which are here by day, gone by night.

Any entrepreneur that has achieved success in their life can tell you that you need to dream big and die trying, in order to succeed. It's not something that you can just try on, like a suit in a mall. You need to really give it your all. You have to try with everything that you have. Otherwise, you're going to fail.

So anyway, it's not something you just try on and be like, "Oh, that was cool." You really need to give it your all. So I think that's one of the challenges for all the programs out there today, whether it be programs that try and inspire people, like Startup Weekend or the Startup Grind conference series, or programs like the Founder Institute that train people to launch businesses.

We have a duty to try and convey the seriousness of the task at hand, in order to ensure that the next generation of entrepreneurs are actually not tourists but, in fact, serious participants.

What area of tech and business do you think are going to be most interesting over the next 2-5 years?

Look. There's stuff that everybody is talking about, but it's not clear that they're going be big. Then there are some things that people aren't talking about, that are already big.

So for example, everyone's talking about IOT (Internet of Things). That sounds great, and I do believe in IOT for sure, but the problem is people don't go and buy new refrigerators every month. They buy them once every two years. People don't go and buy new locks or lights every month.

So I definitely believe that there's going be a big Internet of Things movement, but it's going take a long, long, long, long time for that to come to fruition because the replacement of these devices have quite long timeframes.

I've lived in this house for six years. Not only have I not replaced any of my appliances, but I don't foresee replacing them any time soon.

So it could be, in some cases, many, many years before an Internet of Things refrigerator comes along. By the way, Intel has been talking about the Internet of Things since as long as I can remember, certainly 2000-2002. I went to the Intel CEO's summit at the time, and they were showing off the house of the future. It had basically all Internet-connected devices.

Definitely Internet of Things will be big. I'm just not sure about the timing.

Conversely, there are some businesses that are already very large, like basically all of finance. The truth of the matter is that this is a massive industry that has had little or no disruption happen to it, to date.

You still have a bank. You go to your bank and make deposits. You make withdrawals. The last large-scale innovative banking switch might have been PayPal. Now PayPal is sort of looking to spin out of eBay.

Banks and finance control a large area of our lives. So it's already a multi-trillion-dollar-a-year business, covering everything from retirement planning to investing to everything in between. It's supporting small businesses and loans, everything. It's really had little or no innovation in a long time.

So you're seeing a large number of startups go into what is classically referred to as Fintech (financial technology), and you're seeing multi-billion-dollar companies get built in 24 months, but that's because the entire financial services industry is in the trillions of dollars.

There is also a big interest from investors. I'm based in the financial area of London, and I can say that from the end of 2014, the investment in Fintech has gone through the roof. Probably at least half of the money raised for startups this year was raised in Fintech.

Well, you're starting to see that. Exactly. So that's because you have a number of companies around credit and other financial activities over in Europe that are growing at incredible speeds, making a lot of money doing so.

Basically banks have become so complacent, that they open themselves up to veracious external competition through zero-interest savings accounts. That's ready for disruption, for sure. You've got very high fees on various types of transactions, whether it be moving money or lending money. They can do that because banks are a very small set of competitors that provide very limited service.

But we're talking, still, about trillions of dollars in market size. So it's just inevitable that there's going to be a massive amount of disruption in Fintech.

I have one last question. Actually I have many questions for you, but we'll chat another time. The last question is "What's the one advice you would give to a young person that wants to enter the startup world?" or even better "What's the one piece of advice you would give to your younger self?"

Look. I can actually, quite confidently, say that I did not have an easy entrepreneurial journey. Entrepreneurship is hard, so I'm not unique. Despite how hard it was for me, I was lucky that I basically had mostly success.

So what I would say is that the most important thing for a new entrepreneur— I wouldn't say young, I would say new—is to understand that being an entrepreneur is a process of self-discovery.

If you can start that process in parallel or even before you start becoming an entrepreneur, that's a good thing.

Essentially what you're saying is, "Hey, I'm going to dedicate almost the entirety of my life's energy to a certain vision that I have of the world."

If you're not clear of what your vision is, you're going to mess up. So I like to say that you can't have a good "what" unless you have a good "why." So if you're not sure why you're doing it, then the "what" (the company) will often be flawed.

A lot of times, things that sound logical don't necessarily mean that they are right. For example, I started a space business with Elon Musk that eventually became Space X. I started a video-gaming company that we sold to RealNetworks (A/N Game Trust exited in 2007].

Now I think space is totally cool, but just because I think space is totally cool doesn't mean that space is what I want to do with my life's energy. Just because I think video games are totally cool doesn't mean that I should be running a video-gaming company.

Sometimes things that seem obvious are not. Everybody thinks space is amazing, and I'm excited to work with space. But what happens if once you start working in a the daily routine, you realize, "I really don't like space"?

If you don't like the "what", you can still work hard until you succeed if there is a "why". So it's more a matter of why are you doing this? What's your big vision of the world? What's your big vision for your life, this process of self-discovery? When you go through this process of self-discovery, the business that you eventually pursue should align with your own vision of the world.

Links

1. The Founder Institute
http://fi.co

2. Space X
http://www.spacex.com

3. Game Trust
http://gametrust.com

4. Real Networks
http://www.realnetworks.com

3D Printing. Bones, Clothes and the Third Industrial Revolution

Interlude

If I had asked people what they wanted, they would have said faster horses.

—Henry Ford

How to Predict the Future

The only way to understand what's really going on with 3D printing is to bring Steve Jobs and Bill Gates in to the discussion. At least, this is what I do when we speak innovation with the big corporations or at the startup accelerators; and it always works better than expected.

Our short story starts in 1975, when Steve Jobs and Bill Gates were 20 years old. Interesting fact, the two legendary tycoons were born in the same year (1955) and founded their companies almost at the same time.

Gates founded Microsoft in April 1975, around the same time Jobs was attending the (now famous) meeting at the Homebrew Computer Club, where the idea of Apple was born. Steve Jobs founded his company the same month (April) but in 1976, after dealing for some time with a potential third co-founder. You probably know the story. The original Apple was supposed to be shared between Steve Jobs, Steve Wozniak and Ronald Wayne (who quit at the last minute).

A third but lesser known event also happened in 1975. If you are passionate about tech you probably know about it: the Altair 8080 was on the cover of Popular Electronics, the world's largest-selling magazine for electronics hobbyists. Together with Jobs and Gates, it set the foundation for the personal computer revolution.

The Altair 8080 is considered by many geeks to be the 'first true personal computer'. At the time, Intel's Intellect-8, a computer with an 8080 microprocessor, was on sale for $2,400 ($10,858 in today's money), with the price rising to $10,000 with all the add-ons required to develop software. Adjusted to the inflation, that comes to around $45,000 today.

With the same Intel-8080 microprocessor, the Altair was on the market at $439. It was a computer for geeks, shipped in a kit to be self assembled. Nonetheless, for the very first time many people could have a computer in their home.

Trapped between the too expensive Intel, and the too geeky Altair, the new born PC industry was a joke for the traditional big corporations and government officers. Just one generation before, the president of IBM Thomas Watson, had forecast "a world market for maybe five computers." Today this quote is studied as one of the 10 worst tech predictions of all time, but in 1975 the mass market was still skeptical about personal computers.

Only a minority believed in the future of personal computing. Among them, Steve Jobs, Bill Gates, Larry Ellison founder of Oracle, Gordon More founder of Intel, and they all ended up running multi-billion dollar companies. Ronald Wayne—the third co-founder of Apple—had he kept his 10% stock, he would have been worth approximately $60 billion today.

This is where the 3D printing industry joins our story. Like personal computers, 3D printers hit the market as a joke, and today they are either used at industrial level or by a small (but growing) number of geeks and artists.

This is just the beginning. This week alone there are 3 different campaigns for 3D printers on Kickstarter, and they are all overfunded long before their deadlines.

And it's not just about small customers. In 2012, the prestigious magazine The Economist published a special insert all about 3D printing, by the name the 'Third Industrial Revolution'. Over the next few years we will see a 3D printer in every home. The impact of 3D printers on our cities looks already big; in truth it will be even bigger.

Space the Final Frontier

"A typical F-18 fighter jet is likely to contain some 90 3D-printed parts, even though the F-18 has been in service for two decades — since before 3D printing took off. This is because replacement bits, like parts of the cockpit and cooling ducts, are now 3D printed" (The Economist).

The new F-35 jet has around 900 parts that have been 3D-printed. This data is destined to grow with the growth of the space business. Elon Musk's Space X, Richard Branson's Virgin Galactic, and a group of new companies are aiming to develop transport and business in space.

This business is going to depend on 3D-printing more than any other, because it's extremely expensive to ship anything to space. One single bolt costs hundreds of dollars in transportation, and if it's not used immediately, it would need to be stored in a space station, which is already limited on space. So, instead of shipping the physical bolt, they will just upload its digital representation. If something breaks and the new bolt is needed, they will just need to push a button to print it out in 3D. No shipping costs, no storage costs.

This innovation stimulated by the aviation industry now, and the space industry soon, can be even more profitable in our cities. For a simple repair you can 3D-print the broken piece from my personal 3D printer and install it yourself. If the issue is more complex, you can call a plumber or a technician. As soon as he understands the nature of the problem, he can upload the correct file from the cloud to your home 3D printer and fix the issue without any delay.

No More Shopping

Life in a future city may be a life without shops. No need to go to a store when I can 3D print everything at home. And I truly mean "everything". In May 2015, Kickstarter launched a campaign for Electroloom, the world's first affordable 3D fabric printer.

Eventually shops will be converted into fashion consultant firms, where you can speak with an expert about new fashion trends and the color most appropriate for your skin tone.

Once you have decided what you want, you don't need to buy any new clothing, instead you'll buy the rights to download the file for a new Armani suit (or its non-branded equivalent). You can go home and you print your new pants whenever you want. If they get old or ruined, you can just print them again.

Think about purchasing a MP3 song, and downloading it again and again. Streaming services like Pandora and Spotify will probably hit the market as well. On a Friday evening you just need to check that day's clothing collections, pick and print.

Not Only Leisure

Personal 3D printing is mainly focusing on leisure, making miniatures and jewelry, and trying to make fashionable clothing. But there is much more than that. From an industrial angle, maybe you have watched one of the videos on YouTube with a gigantic 3D printer printing entire buildings.

I am not going to go into a long list of things that can be created by a 3D printer; in this business creativity is the only limit. However I like to point out one case that I found particularly significant. In July 2015, a Chinese researcher from the Southern Medical University of Guangdong charged his (low cost) 3D printer with a mix of rabbit and goat bone powder, 3D-printing bones to be implanted in human bodies.

The project is still in the experimental phase and the Dean, Professor Huang Wenhua, admits that it will take years for the technology to be used in clinical cases, but they can already produce bones in the identical shape and size of an injured patient. Now this is interesting.

3D Printers Will Not Just Change the How but the Where

3D printing will not disrupt only "how" things are built but "where".

In the example about clothing there is no need to outsource the production to China or Vietnam anymore, since everything can be 3D-printed around the corner or even in your home. And it doesn't just cost the same; it may be cheaper as you will save on shipping costs.

Moving the production means moving the jobs. For this very reason, in 2012, President Obama announced a $30 million federal funding of NAMII, the National Additive Manufacturing Innovation Institute, that when translated from bureaucratic language means more or less the "3D Printing Institute".

NAMII is in Ohio, in the heart of the American "Rust Belt", (in)famous for economic decline and population loss. Although to be fair, this state has reduced the unemployment rate from 11% in 2009 to 5.5% this year. The 3D Printing Institute is aiming to make Ohio an innovation power house too.

But Probably Not as Much as We Think

Moving jobs back to the West through 3D printing may be not as easy it seems.

In 2010, researchers at the Irvine University of California analyzed the cost of producing a 16-gigabyte iPad. Of the total cost of $499, they found that the approximate cost only accounted for around $33, of which only $8 was spent in China, where the iPad is produced. That means that approximately 93% of the expenses were not related to manufacturing but to patents, designs, and other costs including, of course, marketing.

With such a small share of labor costs for the overall expense, Apple could afford to make the iPad in the United States. According to research, the low wages are only part of the reason for outsourcing. Shenzhen, China where iPads are manufactured, has been able to create a successful industrial cluster with a complete supply chain of designers and engineers. This might not have been the reason why so many companies moved to Shenzhen originally, but it seems the main reason for staying.

Aside from any political evaluation about the Obama Administration, boosting an innovative industrial cluster with public funding — as China did in Shenzhen with the Special Economic Zone program in the '80s — may be a very good idea.

Links

1. Space-X
http://www.spacex.com

2. Virgin Galactic
http://www.virgingalactic.com

3. Electroloom - The world's first (affordable) 3D printer of fabric
http://kck.st/1HirHsU

4. Southern Medical University of Guangdong
http://www.fimmu.com/english

Hon. Jerry MacArthur Hultin

Former U.S. Undersecretary of the Navy

The traditional university is no longer sufficient. The 21st century university is both a classroom and a birthplace of new ventures, and the head of the university should know both basic research funders and venture capitalists.

—Hon. Jerry MacArthur Hultin

An introduction to Jerry MacArthur Hultin could take an entire chapter by itself. Thus this is going to be a very condensed biography.

Jerry Hultin served in the Navy, seeing action in the Vietnam War. Upon leaving the Navy, he went back to university receiving a J.D. from Yale Law School. During the following 25 years he served in a multitude of areas, including law, technology, defense, health care and the environment.

He was nominated Under Secretary of the Navy in 1997 by the then President of the United States, Bill Clinton. When he left office in 2000, Jerry returned to university—this time as a professor and administrator, eventually becoming president of the Polytechnic Institute of New York University.

Today he focuses part of his inexhaustible energy on the subject of Future Cities and globalization.

The Interview

The readers have been briefed about your career in the introduction, however these are cold hard facts. If you don't mind, I would like to start with a personal question.

You have a J.D. from Yale Law School, and you could have made more money as a lawyer. Why did you choose to dedicate your energy to the subject of Future Cities instead?

With 7 billion people in cities by 2050, cities are best place to combine what people need with new technology—cities are the world's future. This means during the next 30 years, nearly 3 billion more people will become residents of cities.

Never again on this earth will we build so many new or expanded cities for so many people. Once built, we will never do it again. There is no "do-over!"

So well-built, we can have a century of good life for the citizens of the world. A world we would all like to live in.

Done poorly, we have pollution, congestion, and stagnation—a life of misery for nearly 7 billion people. Not a nice world.

So rather than pursue wealth, we decided to seek impact.

Like a good friend says, success is easy, but impact is hard. We've are committed to having impact, even if it's hard.

You served as Under Secretary of the Navy during Bill Clinton's presidency. The Navy's budget at the time was over $100 billion. Entities with such big budgets are always very slow to innovate, and are often afraid of innovation.

Do you think that the quality of our future cities will be determined at government level or by startups developing new technology?

Technology and bright ideas are most frequently the source of transformational innovation. But in the end, you also need to change the culture of government and large organizations—the question is will such transformation come from inside of government—will government have it imposed from the outside.

Often it takes a major, catastrophic event—like the sinking of battleships at Pearl Harbor and the rise of air craft carriers in World War II—to get big organizations to change.

So I see it as a two way street—startups and innovation drive change, but those inside should press for an innovative culture that practices open innovation.

You were the 15th President of the Polytechnic Institute of New York University (where you still serve as President Emeritus). Besides your academic success, I am particularly interested in the economic results of the business incubators of the Institute: over $250 million in economic activity.

I received my education in different countries, including the USA, Italy and Belgium. Sometimes universities dislike generating business. They tend to think that the role of a university is academic teaching. Adding money to the equation could cause to somehow lose their soul.

How do you see this relationship between business and teaching? And what suggestions would you offer the president of a tech university?

The traditional university — which evolved to exceptionally high quality in Europe — is no longer sufficient. Basic research is still essential, but the market place needs solutions. Today's young people are eager to learn how to make a better world — so universities should provide them the skills and resources to do this. In the 21st century university, this means an incubator is both a classroom and a birthplace of new ventures, and the head of the university should know both basic research funders and venture capitalists. Universities can do both at once.

If a university president doubts this, he or she should read Pasteur's Quadrant by Daniel Stokes.

At New York University, we teach people to be innovators, inventors, and entrepreneurs — in engineering and science and also in the social sciences and liberal arts.

This change in what a university does is fundamental to whether China, India, Latin America — and Europe — will build knowledge economies or depend on the United States as the sole source of new technologies and solutions.

You are the cofounder of Global Futures Group an international firm that provides consulting and investment services to maximize the role of the "smart city". Your customers are government, civic, business leaders and non-profit organizations.

I don't think that many governments and business leaders would have appointed a consultant in these matters 10 or 20 years ago. They would have maybe appointed an architect or an urban planner, not a smart city expert.

Do you see a change in the perception of this issue at government level? And what do you think these kinds of customers will require in the near future?

Yes, what has changed is not just urban planning, but new technology has become a driver of new solutions and designs. The physical grid of a city is still important, but the information grid is equally important.

To be a smart city means more than building infrastructure — it means creating learning or feedback systems that use sensors, communications, data, computing, analytics and citizen input to design urban eco-systems that are agile, responsive, and flexible in delivering what people need.

Tech could be expensive. Do you see the gap between cities in rich countries and poor countries growing in the future?

If you gold-plate the solutions with expensive technology, we risk creating a rich / poor divide. But many solutions are not that expensive, indeed may reduce the cost of operation and provide far better benefits and savings.

As our technology for smart cities shifts from hardware to software, costs are reduced substantially. The cloud, ubiquitous sensors, and mobile phones create a way of organizing and delivering services that is less expensive, more ubiquitous, and extremely flexible in the outcome it produces. The smart phone is a good example: the physical network and features of the phone are essential, but the big spike in value comes from the software that turns the phone into a unique, revolutionary source of value for every user.

For example, if you use software (data, analysts, call centers) with ambulances and emergency medical series, as they have in India, you not only reduce cost, you move people to hospitals more quickly and you improve healthcare delivery. For instance, in India this system reduced infant deaths in ambulances by a factor of 5.

Going back to tech, if you had $10 million to invest in startups in future cities, what areas would you pick? What technologies do you think will be in high demand over the coming years?

Transportation and mobility, buildings and energy, healthcare, and education. But don't overlook some smaller, but high potential opportunities in tourism, governance, security, and citizen input

Fortunately, more and more investors — like social impact investors and clean-tech investors — who are focused on a triple-bottom line of social, environmental and financial returns.

Last but not least, what advice would you give to a young man/ woman who wants to open a tech startup in the area of future cities?

Start local and solve a problem or provide a service that benefits citizens in their city. Invent an approach that significantly reframes the way services are delivered. Take advantage of local data, citizens, and other entrepreneurs.

Then, think lean!

Read a good book on entrepreneurship like The Startup Owner's Manual by Steve Blank and Bob Dorf or Disciplined Entrepreneurship by Bill Aulet at MIT.

Is there anything else you would like to share?

I challenge mayors and urban leaders around the world to stand up and seek innovative new ways of meeting the needs and desires of their citizens. If they do, within a decade their cities — and the world — will be a better place.

Links

1. Global Futures Group
http://globalfuturesgroup.co

2. Polytechnic Institute of New York University
http://engineering.nyu.edu/

3. Download "The Startup Owner's Manual"
by Steve Blank and Bob Dorf
http://futurecitiesbook.com/109

4. Download "Disciplined Entrepreneurship: 24 Steps to a Successful Start"
by Bill Aulet
http://futurecitiesbook.com/110

5. Download "Pasteur's Quadrant"
by Daniel Stokes
http://futurecitiesbook.com/111

Kyrill Zlobenko

Ecozy

A startup is like being on the waves in a small boat. Nobody really sees you, but you are there working as hard as hell, while the boat goes up and down on every wave.

—Kyrill Zlobenko

What you are going to read is a true startup story. This company—eCozy—works with the Internet of Things and produces a smart thermostat. They have teams in two countries and aim to be the "European Nest"—the company acquired by Google for $3.2 billion.

However, this is only part of the story.

Let's go back one year. At that time, eCozy was planning a crowdfunding campaign and their COO Kyrill Zlobenko downloaded my eBook—*Kickstarter UK Handbook*. We met on Clarity, a service that provides online brainstorming, and eventually we opened their local branch, again online.

Do you see where I am going with this?

Shortly after our meeting, eCozy launched a campaign on Indiegogo, which is an online fundraising platform, and I was one of their online backers.

In the last twelve months, we have exchanged emails and had a couple of Skype conversations. I haven't got involved in the business again—they are doing an excellent job by themselves—but we keep in touch.

We have never met in person.

Maybe one day we will meet in the same city, but I have already collaborated more with them than with some clients of my old firm, when people were used to meeting in an office.

Today I'm going to interview Kyrill for this book. As soon as we finish our call, the recording will be sent to the Philippines to be transcribed while I sleep.

When I wake up tomorrow, I'll find the transcription in my email and I will smooth the text into a written interview. I will probably finish just before my proofread wakes up in the United States. Me, my virtual assistant and my proofread work together through UpWork and Slack — two online platforms.

In the last ten years, many consultancy services moved online. Virtual assistants and programmers first. Lawyers and consultants later. Over the next few years, the management of cities and buildings will move online too. Smart thermostats are proof that this is already happening.

The Interview

Hello Kyrill and welcome. Let's start introducing yourself to the readers.

Sure. My name is Kyrill Zlobenko, and I'm the COO of a startup called eCozy. We produce smart thermostats for the European market, and we will eventually become the European Nest. The heating systems in Europe are different than in the United States, so we can serve our market better than any US company. Europe has 740 million citizens, the USA just 320 million. When investors do the math, they see a huge potential in our business.

A bit more about me. My background is in economics. I was born in Kiev, Ukraine, and I'm 29. I have lived the last seven years in a lot of countries: Germany, Italy, Sweden, and Austria.

Did something specific happen to convince you to move abroad? An external event that made you take this decision?

I love challenges — all entrepreneurs do. One of the most exciting challenges is to learn and live in a new culture, so in a way, I was destined to go abroad.

Eventually, I ended up in Germany. But the roots of this decision grew in another country: Austria. I spent four years in one of the most beautiful cities in the world: Vienna, the Austrian capital. The language is basically the same as that in Germany.

Vienna offers a full social life with coffee shops and long walks in the historical downtown. You don't want to miss all of these opportunities because you don't know the language. So you learn very fast.

Can we say that you moved for business but you stayed for the quality of life?

Absolutely true. The quality of life in a city is more than ever a strategic element to growing a tech ecosystem. Don't you think?

I think that quality of life has always attracted people of talent, but the impact of those people was limited when the economy was based on factories. On the contrary, our economy is based on knowledge, and one talented co-founder can make the difference between success and failure.

Some politicians start to understand, you don't create a startup ecosystem just with tax cuts or public funding. They have to make our city liveable and talent will come.

I met Julian Castro, the mayor of San Antonio, Texas, at the Google Campus in London. His pitch was entirely about making his city a better place to live, and leaving the rest to the entrepreneurs. Every geek in the room fell in love with his vision.

Anyway, better not ask me about cities and culture because I am very much into this subject. This is your interview, not mine.

Having learned German in Austria did you then move to your current location, Munich?

Not directly. I had an experience in Malmo, Sweden, and then moved to Trento, in northern Italy.

For the sake of the readers, Trento is in Italy but the region was ruled for a long time by the Austrians, so German is a common language. It's an interesting phenomenon. An Italian region, under Italian law, but you can go to court and litigate in German.

Indeed. And living in Italy is always a great experience. The area around Trento is very productive and business-oriented. A good mix of work and pleasure.

And now I'm in Munich, where I joined eCozy. As a Chief Operational Officer, I help the team outline operations. In practice, on top of that I do a lot of interesting stuff.

You know with startups, especially in the early stages, you have to do pretty much everything. We're not such a big team yet—just 10 people—and the majority are engineers, and three are in management. So, we do pretty much everything.

You speak about Munich. I've been there but I'm not going to say what I think because I want to know what you feel about the city.

Munich is a pretty interesting town. It has some pros and cons, like every city in the world. I would just say that Munich has been named as one of the main tech hubs in Europe.

It might seem funny to some experienced entrepreneurs who are all about Silicon Valley, New York and London. The rating doesn't depend just on the number of successful enterprises but also on the access to education and work and, again, on the quality of life.

In any case, Munich is a pretty cool city—not so big, not so small, about 1.5 million inhabitants. It's growing. It's not the cheapest city to live and build a startup in, but the salaries are good, and the city services are excellent. So when you find a job, you have a very good standard of life.

On top of that, Munich is a very green city, it is friendly and there are lots of international people living here.

What about the team? Can you tell us briefly about them and whether they enjoy living in Munich?

It all started two years ago, when the cofounder, Andre Kholodov, had the idea to produce a thermostat for the European market.

Thermostats don't sound like a sexy business. But when you add in the Internet of Things, it's definitely hot. You can control the temperature of your house from your smartphone, reduce energy consumption, save money and be environmentally-friendly at the same time.

You can adapt a different temperature to each room based on the people in it. You can switch the heating off when you are at the office and switch it on again when you leave the office. So when you arrive home, everything is perfect, including the bill that is much cheaper.

And everything requires just a few taps on your smartphone.

This is made possible by a team of six engineers based in Ukraine, and a management team based in Munich.

The cofounder, Andre, is what I call a serial engineer. He had worked for impressive companies like Linda. His background is extremely useful for making things happen.

When we met about a year ago, you were planning to fund the company through crowdfunding. You had a successful campaign on Indiegogo. I receive your updates and I see that you are growing.

What was your experience? And can you provide any actionable suggestions for startups that want to do their own crowdfunding?

Crowdfunding is especially good for teams who are in the idea concept stage to test their ideas and to bring them to the first users. To be successful on a crowdfunding platform like Kickstarter or Indiegogo I strongly believe that you don't really have to have a product yet.

It's really great if you have a product of course. But it could be even better to not have a final product and to use the campaign to understand what people really want and adapt your product accordingly.

This is my feedback about my experience; it's also a suggestion. Use the campaign to interact with your backers and ask them what they want from your product.

The cost of entrance into crowdfunding is pretty low. You just have to have a solid team and a good idea that really solves a problem. And you have to present it in a nice way that convinces people to pre-order it.

What's the main challenge in a campaign for you?

I think that the major challenge is not in the campaign but it starts when you successfully close your crowdfunding. At that point, you basically owe the customers a product that you don't have yet.

And this is what entrepreneurs underestimate. It's not about raising money on crowdfunding. Money is a commodity and you can always find it. Maybe you have to move to another city or even to another nation, but if you believe in your project, you can find funding. The challenge is about building the product and delivering it.

And about building your customer base?

Right. Totally. That's a great point. What crowdfunding has taught us at eCozy is that we would have probably been more successful if we had developed our early adopters before starting the campaign.

This is my second strong suggestion to whoever wants to do crowdfunding. You should start working on your campaign many months before your Kickstarter or Indiegogo page goes online.

I would strongly advise every budding entrepreneur to talk with your customers from the first day, even if you don't have a product yet. Show prototypes and start to build a customer funnel from day one, when you just have an idea.

Can you provide a number of how many months in advance?

As far in advance as possible. It depends on your timing. Entrepreneurs can't be too relaxed with time. There is always a window for every product.

Many studies have provided evidence that timing is the number one reason for success or failure.

Let's say that unless you are forced to go to market immediately, it doesn't hurt if you start planning today and launch your campaign six months later. But in these five or six months, you have to work on developing your customer base, fans and evangelists. You can't just build the product because when you launch, you have to be sure that a lot of people are going to support you.

I am totally with you. When I published my book Kickstarter UK Handbook, we were used to starting a campaign two months in advance. There was less competition and because crowdfunding was a novelty, it was easier to access journalists and get your project in the news. Now I would say that four to six months in advance may be a must.

If I may move to a more personal question. You have been in eCozy almost since the beginning and before the crowdfunding campaign. What have been your best and worst moments so far?

That's a good question. It's a startup, right? So you have ups and downs basically every week, every month, and sometimes even during one day, you have ups and downs. The day can start exciting and finish with nothing. Or it can be the opposite.

What I would say is that you definitely have to be passionate about what you do because eventually it helps you to get up in the morning. If you are not passionate, these ups and downs are eventually going to put you out of business.

Passion can turn these ups and downs from depression to adrenaline. I can tell you that people who have experienced a startup, no matter if the startup is successful or fails, they most likely will go into another startup.

A startup is like being on the waves in a small boat. Nobody really sees you, but you are there working as hard as hell, while the boat goes up and down on every wave.

Sounds like a powerful example. What's your suggestion to avoid "seasickness"?

The team. A small but strong team that is supportive. A team that is well-rounded is the key to overcoming most kinds of struggles that you may have. Going back to the example, they are in the same boat. When you have a down moment—and you will—they understand you and bring you up again.

But the team is nothing if you don't have customers. So you have to work on your customers.

In our example, the customer is Poseidon, the god of the sea. He's going to decide if you're going to be dead or alive. So you have to make sure you have enough customers. Not just any customer, but good customers who are not rooting for a product just because it is

10% cheaper, but because they trust you.

This feeling of living on a rollercoaster, what you have described as a small boat, is the most common characteristic in my interviews with startup entrepreneurs.

When I interview managers from big companies, they always remember a best moment and a worst moment, with stability in the middle. On the contrary, in startups, it's a continuous shift from one to the other. The interviewees don't focus on reaching a good moment, but on learning to enjoy this rollercoaster ride.

Indeed. There is a good book that recently came out, and I am sure you've either heard of it or read it: The Hard Things about Hard Things written by Ben Horowitz. This is a read I suggest to every person in the startup business and even to anybody who is thinking to quit a company to open his own startup.

It's exactly like Horowitz points out. When it's low, it can be really low and dark. When it's good, it can be really great and high. You constantly experience this feeling, and it can be really intense.

What's your grand vision for your company and future cities in general ?

That's a grand question [laughs]. I'll try to reply with how I feel personally.

Cities are very different. We talked about Trento and Munich. We didn't talk about other cities where I have been, but just think about London where you live. They are all different.

Today, the big cities are packed with information; the smaller cities are not. I think that eventually all the cities will become like bigger computers themselves. Spotlights inside a bigger global Internet of Things. An Internet of Everything community.

Another interviewee stressed exactly the same point. Jerry Hultin, former US undersecretary of the Navy, points out that cities already have the data but they don't know how to use it.

We have the input, but not the output yet. The goal over the next few years is to learn how to use this data and to improve the quality of life for the citizens.

Right. We have no clue what to do with everything we have.

What's the practical impact of this condition on day-to-day business?

In the next ten years, we will see more of what Ray Kurzweil calls "singularity", or changes in a big leap. The companies that will be successful will present solutions that are sustainable on the business side but also sustainable on the social side. They will be forced to think further ahead than just earning money.

In the past, a company with a strong market position and the cash flow to buy TV commercials could stay afloat for 20 years without innovating. Today, you can lose your market in 2 years. Tomorrow, you could lose your market in a matter of days.

Do you think we should be scared or excited by this?

I think it's definitely an exciting time. We meet other startups every day, and you can see how the generation of people who are under 30 years old were born into an interconnected world. They are all thinking about building more sustainable startups than ever before.

Technology is cheaper than ever. So I think it's the best time to build a company.

Last but not least, you are relatively young—you are 29—but you already have experience with three startups in different countries. What advice would you give to a young guy or girl who wants to open a startup after the university? Or after dropping out if this is the case?

The one thing that I would advise, and I would advise it to myself as well if I had been six or seven or eight years younger than I am now, is this: Just do it; don't think about it. The best way to start something is actually to start something.

Together with the rollercoaster, this is the other most shared characteristic among startup entrepreneurs.

That's because when you're in your twenties, you don't have really anything to lose. Of course, you risk losing time, but this is something you can afford at this age.

I don't want to encourage people to drop out. Everybody should decide for themselves on this point. But once you have finished university, an experience in a startup that fails could be more exciting and educational than a job in a big company.

Also, you will understand if you like it. Being an entrepreneur is not for everybody. If you live with regret, you will eventually be unhappy or quit a big company later in life. You want to find out that being an entrepreneur is not for you as soon as possible. The hit can be hard later in life.

Speaking about sharing experience with younger folks, can you name a person, dead or alive, who inspired you or your company?

We are lucky because in the startups ecosystem, we don't have one person to inspire us but many. Andre, our CEO, talks about how he was inspired by Steve Jobs at the beginning. If you wonder why our thermostat is so beautiful to look at, it's because of the influence of Steve Jobs.

Now we have new inspirations. There is Tony Fadell and Elon Musk and many others regularly come onto the scene. You see a regular stream of amazing people that were on a small boat some time ago, to again use the previous example. They are living proof that you can grow your small boat into something bigger and make a difference. It helps you accept the rollercoaster.

Fair enough. Anyway, you always sound passionate about startups. If I may ask, is there something that bugs you about this world or is everything fantastic?

Yes there is. I'll tell you one story.

There is a really cool startup now, a fast growing company called Freeletics. It's an app for IOS and Android, where you have your personal training videos and trainer. Huge growth rate, basically a rocket.

The media talks about their success and how lucky they are. It seems that they just caught a trend, because everybody wants to be healthy.

But in fact, I found out in Berlin a couple of months ago that the founder has been in business for the last six years building the app. They are all very much into sport and that's their passion.

First it was a website. Then they built the app. They have been pivoting all the time. They just had a strong vision and a motivated team. They have been bouncing off the walls for years.

You have to be prepared as a startup founder or co-founder to accept that it can take you three, four, five years to succeed.

So what makes you mad in the startup world is the myth of overnight success.

Indeed. In Ukraine, we call this kind of media the yellow press. They focus on the hype; everything is a dream or a nightmare. The unsexy daily hard work doesn't exist for the media because they need to sell page views.

This is a trick I have learned working on multiple startups. Don't listen to these stories. Don't even read them.

Of course, you have to understand where your industry is moving. But if you read about it constantly, if you read Facebook, if you start your day with a coffee and an online magazine, eventually, you won't get anywhere, because what you have to do as a startup is the really unsexy things: working day by day to build a product and your customer base.

Reading these overnight success stories makes me a little jealous and very unproductive. It's not my story, right, and it shouldn't be your story either. Your story is to build a great company that will be a scalable business that will eventually change the world, even if just a little.

Links

1. Download "Serve To Win"
by Novak Djokovic
http://futurecitiesbook.com/107

2. Download "Kickstarter UK Handbook"
By Stefano L Tresca
http://futurecitiesbook.com/112

3. Clarity - On Demand Business Advice for Entrepreneurs
https://clarity.fm

4. Freeletics - Individual training plan
https://www.freeletics.com

5. Singularity University - Solving Humanity's Grand Challenges
http://singularityu.org

6. Slack - A platform for team communication
https://slack.com

7. UpWork - Find freelancers to tackle any job
http://upwork.com

Sex and Robots: Do Humans Dream of Electric Mates?

Interlude

At present machinery competes against man. Under proper conditions machinery will serve man.

—Oscar Wilde

One person in ten would have sex with a robot, according to a poll by YouGov. If you are amazed by this number, you would be shocked by the real data.

Let's consider similar surveys. About 15% of the population admit to watching porn on the Web, but the internet providers reveal a more realistic 70%. About 9% of the population admit that they would have sex with a robot. Do the math and you can forecast the real market for the 'Sexbots', as they call the sexual robots.

In just five years, this may become a very disturbing phenomenon, or a great business. On second thought, it will probably be both.

Would you like more examples?

An Illinois startup in this "market" raised 622% of their target funds on Indiegogo, the popular crowdfunding platform. I'm not going to describe their product in detail, because I want to save this article from censorship. However, the name of their campaign - 'AutoBlow2' - is probably enough to understand what the product is about.

In a 67-page white paper on "Robots and the future of jobs", released by the prestigious Pew Research Center, the experts are split into two factions, for and against robots in the workforce. While they were not able to decide on the impact of robots on jobs, almost all of them agree on one point: by 2025 "robotic sex partners will be commonplace."

The Future Is Already Here. It's Just Not Evenly Distributed

William Gibson used to say, "The future is already here; it's just not evenly distributed." Let's have a look at what's already here in this industry.

Japan is definitely the market leader. And we are not talking about a couple of obscure research centers. Well-known Japanese mega corporations like Toshiba are investing billions of yen to develop the perfect robotic sexual partner. Not long ago, at the Consumer Electronics Show in Las Vegas, they released an Automata, an android with human resemblance. "Her" name is Chihira Aico.

To be fair to Toshiba, Aico isn't designed to be a sexual toy, but a perfect housekeeper and employee. On the other hand, this may be one of the best lines of defence in the modern history of PR. "This is not about sex; this is just a housemaid and secretary at your complete disposal." I can already see a very long queue of male consumers waiting for Aico to go mass market.

At the moment, Aico smiles to the crowd and can perform minor interactions. But it doesn't take much thought to guess what other features may be available in future releases.

Although these androids are built to provide many different services, the fact that they are all designed as females may seem suspicious. There is a female android to train dentists (the Simroid Series), and a female android to work as a receptionist (the Asuna Series).

Even China developed a competitor a few years back, of course female - the 'Dion' - designed to be the perfect companion for your karaoke nights.

The Web reveals such an appetite for sexual content that it's easy to imagine a similar growth for sexual robots.

A Second Alternative Future

Sexbots aren't the only possible future. A few months ago I was brainstorming with a startup about the possible use of their technology, and robots was one of our bullet points.

"Customers will not be interested in having sex with robots," said one of the engineers, "it will be cheaper to have sex in virtual reality."

Well, this is … reassuring, right?

In the meantime, I've registered Botsder.com, 'Tinder for robots'. If I get a call by a venture capital firm, you'll be the first to know.

In the meantime, I've registered Botsder.com, 'Tinder for robots'. I am very curious to watch the reaction of the venture capitals.

Rohit Talwar

Fast Future Research

People should stop getting obsessed with what technology can do and building apps that get downloaded but never get used. Instead, they need to start really thinking about what should happen, and what kind of cities we want to create.

—Rohit Talwar

If you are somewhat interested in the future, there is a chance that you already know of Rohit Talwar. I've had the pleasure of enjoying his regular meetings in London, with guests of Jim Clark's caliber, but you could meet him anywhere since Rohit has given speeches in more than 70 countries.

His latest book "The Future of Business" is the coordinated effort of 60 futurists from 21 countries, and anticipates what is going to happen over the next few years. I'm very much sure that you will enjoy his interview.

The Interview

I've already introduced you to the readers, and they may even know you already. Still I would like to hear it in your own words.

Sure. Hi, I'm Rohit Talwar. I'm the CEO of Fast Future Research and Fast Future Publishing. I'm a global futurist advising clients around the world on the ideas, the forces, the trends, and the developments that could shape the next 5 to 50 years. I'm particularly interested in how you bring exponential thinking to business and helping clients use exponential principles in the design of their organization.

Most recently, we've brought exponential thinking to the publishing industry and our first book on the future of business has contributions from 62 authors from 21 different countries (A/N "The Future of Business"). The whole project was completed in four and a half months.

By the way, the link to the book is at the end of this interview. What are your thoughts about future cities in general? What's going to happen in the next 5-10 years?

There are two different views here. One is what should happen and could happen, but then there's what seems most likely to happen.

I think what should happen is that people should stop getting obsessed with what technology can do and building apps that get downloaded but never get used. Instead, they need to start really thinking about what could happen and what should happen, which is that we use this as an opportunity to think deeply about what kind of cities we want to create.

How do we want people to live there? How do we want to make sure they're livable, breathable, viable cities? What's our vision for the kinds of experience we want people to have of our city and in our city? What kind of industry mix do we want for the future? What kind of jobs do we want to create? What kind of transport systems? What kind of social welfare, education, and healthcare provision?

Really use this as an opportunity to visualize where cities are going in a world that's changing so rapidly. Then you can start to think about how you deploy technology within that. Simple applications like Smart Parking, etc., yeah, they're great.

But unless you really have a sense of where you're going, I think we will end up wasting a lot of time and money putting in place applications that don't work.

That said, I think there's some fantastic potential around intelligent management of buildings, around the entire city value chain, starting in the home through to the street level to the district level to the citywide level, to start to build intelligence into the fabric of our infrastructure to manage our transport systems, our energy systems, our communication systems in a smarter manner.

I think all of that is possible, but you need some of that thinking going on at the top level about what you're really trying to create for the city before you start spending the money on these infrastructure projects.

This is very true. You need some of that thinking going on at the top level, but who is this "top level"? This is not easy in the smart cities market.

Let me give a quick example. One area of my specialization is Fintech (financial technology), a market with a clear process. You go to a bank and you show them an interesting startup. They are a private institution with a more or less clear hierarchy. They can be conservative and refuse change for some time, but in Fintech you know who's the "top level".

With cities, it's not so clear who's in charge. There are many entities involved, and they are usually government bodies who are often not very practical.

Well, there's a difference in terms of how you can drive the commercial viability of the two different types of ventures. For Fintech, I can go to a bank and try to raise the money. And quite often, the banks lack the vision or may lack the vision to understand the potential of these technologies.

I think it's changing a little bit, and more banks are investing in Fintech startups. But the great thing about Fintech is if you can find an investor who's interested, you can actually go directly to the marketplace and to the community and say, "Use these services," for activities like person-to-person lending, invoice discounting, and equity raising.

As a new venture, I can now bypass the banks with my mechanism to get to market, so I don't have to have the bank's support.

On the contrary, in the case of smart city or intelligent city solutions, I can come up with great tools but if they're related to energy infrastructure, transport infrastructure, or citywide solutions, I have to have the relevant city authorities on board.

Where I can still succeed is where applications help a neighborhood communicate. You're seeing a variety of these. When neighbors can communicate with each other, can share information with each other, if they work, then you might see a city get on board and use those platforms to communicate with neighborhoods.

So where you can start from the ground up, I think that's great; and individual investors or early-stage investors might back them. But where you need city-level solutions, then you have to have a political change mechanism in place.

To do some visioning, you have to engage the energy company, the education system, the health system, the water and sewage system. There aren't many players, but there are enough of them that you have to really engage at a citywide level to say, "How do we make this happen? How do we create a more intelligent, livable, viable city for the future?"

This is working in a few cases. So for example, in a totally different arena, for the Olympics in 2012, London & Partners, who are mainly the agency for attracting tourists to London, actually took on the responsibility of bringing together government, transport, infrastructure players, airports, airlines, and everyone else to work together in saying "How do we create a brilliant experience for visitors?" And from that came many developments that really made a seamless experience for those visitors.

So we can convene the powerful players, and in smaller cities it's easier to pull them together sometimes. But I do think if you're trying to do citywide solutions that transform some aspect of city services or the city experience for the individual citizen, then you have to have political buy-in from the top, and you have to have that vision of where we're trying to get to in order to make it possible.

The other thing, I think, is that this requires a fundamental shift in how city governance sees itself. In the past, it saw itself as making decisions on behalf of the populous and having an election once every few years if it was a democracy, but basically the public were allowed to have a say once in a while.

Now, we're beginning to understand that cities have much more of a convening role, and their role is to actually facilitate public dialogue, to educate the public about what's changing, to help them understand the options and the process of moving from decision-making to action, and then to bring the public into the decision-making process and the dialogue around what we want for our city and how we make it happen.

A lot of cities are beginning to see that, but there's a big step from seeing it to actually making it happen.

The Olympics is a fantastic example because when a city has a special event and good administration, then things happen.

One of the startups in our accelerator Level39 is Asset Mapping, and they were born, essentially, during the Olympics. Now they can focus on growing and acquiring customers, because they have already achieved the proof that their concept works under the duress of such an important event like the Olympics. By the way, they are one the interviewees in this book.

Just one thing on that; I think there are ways of making this happen without the city buying in. If there's enough potential to bring in individual customers, whether it's citizens or businesses, and it's creating city solutions like Asset Mapping, then you might be able to do it without the city being involved to start off with because you might create a groundswell.

If enough people buy in to intelligent heat mapping of buildings or smarter recycling of resources amongst players in a city, you could see that happening, setting up platforms for car sharing, and other kinds of resource sharing, sharing our drills, sharing our garden mower, that kind of stuff.

Then you could see that, actually, the city might buy into them at some point and say "Yeah, let's use this." But for the things that really change the fabric of the city you've got to have political buy-in, and you've got to have an integrated sense of where we're trying to get to in order to guide the resulting choices.

What's also interesting in some big cities is that some areas may be managed at a practical level by private companies. London is a good example. The entire peninsula of Canary Wharf is mostly managed by the Canary Wharf Group. And they are a private company who are very interested in innovation.

So a startup can pitch their idea to one private entity, like the Canary Wharf Group, and make thing happen very fast.

There's another issue. A private corporation is great when it's managing physical aspects. And the things that Canary Wharf can do are great. But there are some broader societal issues where I think people might be uncomfortable handing those over to a private corporation to take responsibility for.

So you might have the private corporation take responsibility for the execution of a strategy, for example, for education or healthcare, but you would be more nervous about them defining the curriculum and the overall objectives.

And that's where I think we're entering some very interesting territory with the public-private boundary. Everywhere we go, everywhere we look, we can see that we're in relatively uncharted territory as we start to bring the private sector into the management of cities.

Part of your role is consulting for big companies and government about what's going to happen in the next few years and how to deal with it.

But what do you think a startup should do? Looking at the question from another angle, if you had $10 million to invest in startups in future cities, based on your experience and your feedback from your bigger customers, what are the areas you will choose?

I would not pick things that require essential support from government because they usually take too long to buy into change, unless you get lucky.

I would focus on the applications where you could target the individual citizens or the individual businesses in a city and show them that there's some significant benefit.

Some areas, and this might have already been picked up, are things that help you use your assets in a smarter way, sharing your resources, your cars, your home improvement equipment, books, etc. that start to allow us to share and recycle assets and save money because we no longer have to buy everything.

We can share and recycle within our postcode, within our neighborhood. Secondly, I think we'll see growth in demand for things that start to allow us to, if you like, quantify and compare our lives; so information about energy prices, transport prices, things that just allow us to compare prices and see who the best providers are in our neighborhood.

A big part of the value of the projects you are suggesting seem connected to Big Data.

Sort of, yeah, big data, but you don't have to have that much data. You can do it at a relatively small level and start to make it work.

The third is the person-to-person or business-to-person solutions where you can start to create marketplaces around spare capacity. So Uber kind of does that today. Depending on what time of day you go on Uber you'll be charged a different price for the journey.

So what we could have is citizen-level platforms where if I'm buying a haircut, I'm buying someone to fix my fence, paint my house, cook my dinner, we could have city-level solutions or district-level solutions where you can basically reverse auction your requirement and choose not just the price but also the creative option that best fits your need.

So I could say, "I'm having a dinner party for 12 guests. I want a themed party that blows their mind, gets them thinking very differently. My maximum budget is 50 pounds per head. Give me some suggestions, and give me a possible price for doing it."

And that then become something where, whether it's giving me a customized dinner for my friends or organizing my travel, or managing my finances, it's a whole range of things where within the city, you could bring people together within neighborhoods to serve each other in very different ways. And that saves money. It creates opportunity. It gives the businesses a route to market.

And then another area that I think will be interesting is a lot of people have a lot of excess stock. Shops, warehouses, factories, they produce more than they need.

So you could create platforms that allow people to purchase that extra stock, so rather than throwing the food away at the end of the day, you can have a bidding process where people can just go online and buy what they want and then collect it from the store. Similarly, I've got too many TVs.

Rather than deliver them to you from my warehouse, you come and pick them up, but you reverse bid on them. So I've got a minimum clearing price. You could create a whole range of those things that add value for both sides, that, I think, starts to change the way the city operates.

And then finally, I think there are applications that aren't necessarily big money makers but they're very important in terms of civil society, like connecting people with voluntary opportunities. So you've got thousands of charities and volunteer groups who always need help, and then you've got individuals who are willing to give time to that process.

I think simple solutions that map you to those needs at the city-level or the district-level, could be very effective. Imagine I've got a Sunday where I'm not doing anything and I think "Hey, I'd love to do something to help."

I could go online and find something I could do that day, go and give some help, and that would be it. I think that would be a great area in which to develop apps. I don't think it would make a lot of money for anyone but it would be a very important part of civil infrastructure.

What about the rest of the world? Some of these issues we're discussing are, in a way, first world problems. In 15 years the largest number of mega cities will be in Asia and in other parts of the world that today we call "developing countries".

Well, those are the ones where I think these kinds of things work best actually, because you've got big communities who are going online, and they're already used to operating in a community basis. This just makes it easier.

So if you look at Grameen Bank and all the other similar agencies, that's kind of how they work. Helping me find the best price for my products in the marketplace. It's those solutions that make life easier for the citizen and cut the cost of doing business. Wherever you've got to have the city involved, it's harder. But I think all those local-level applications are great, like ride sharing.

You take somewhere like Mumbai. A lot of people still don't have cars, but if someone would offer them a ride, that might make their life easier. And you can save a bit of money, and the driver of the car can make a bit of money. So I think it's in those applications where you could see some of the biggest benefits, rather than in the more mature and developed economies.

Your suggestion to start from the bottom works very well when the government is involved—and they usually are involved in future cities tech—because you can bypass the government bureaucracy. But there are some areas where I think this is not possible.

In some areas the customer is not the government and they are not the final consumers. For instance, in this book I've interviewed startups from our Cognicity acceleration program. Polysolar produces windows that are also solar panels. SeAB produce a recycle bin to transform large masses of wasted food into energy. Pavegen produces flooring tiles that transform footsteps into energy.

None of them can be sold to an individual consumer. They need to convince the owner of the building, therefore the sales process can be very long.

The examples I chose were really mass-market solutions where the individual has a very low cost of entry to become a customer to these things, and there's a very low overall impact on them.

Selling solutions to buildings, like effective building management solutions, smart windows, self-cleaning structures - all of those things are great, but as you say, there's a long selling cycle. However, I think innovation is happening, and lots of great ideas will come to market.

The trick is building the right ecosystem in your business, having the right group of non-executive directors and advisers who have routes into construction companies, building management companies and the people who can say yes or no to these new services, so you don't have to do a lot of cold calling to get to the owners of buildings.

But if you've got a direct route into a construction company, then you can say "Great, let's talk about this thing, and let's work with you to prove its value."

And I think the key is being smart about the design of your business, not just having a good idea, but surrounding yourself with the right investors, non-exec directors, and advisers who can open doors and who can help you think about what is coming next and how you can get to market.

Because we can develop cheap technology for the masses, do you think the gap between rich cities and poor cities will be reduced in the future? Or vice versa?

You've got two different sets of challenges here. In the rich cities, or the so-called rich cities, you still have extremes of poverty and wealth, but what you've got a real lack of is attention.

So getting your solution across is very hard because people are so time-pressed. So you've got a different challenge. It's a marketing challenge. People aren't so price-sensitive about the cost of it.

In the developing world, everyone's hungry for things that can work for them, save them money, make them money, help them achieve more for their kids, their family, or whatever.

So there are some massive megacities on the radar, cities of 10 million plus. Here you can get attention if you get the right low-cost solution. I think there is huge potential developing solutions for the emerging markets, whether the solutions are for Dakar, Dar es Salaam, or Nairobi.

If we can get solutions that work at low-cost, that serve a lot of people, I think actually with a lot of these things, we'll get them working there first, and then you'll find them transferring to the rich cities in the developed world.

And you're already seeing that. So, the $25 computer, the $10 insurance policy, the $2,500 car, these were all developed for emerging markets. But now people are bringing those same ideas to the West or to the developed world and saying "Hey, this is working now. We've proved it, and this is something that could work for you."

And as people's incomes get pressurized, and I think they will do, then you've got some real challenges. What we can see is a massive rate of automation in businesses; a forecast of anywhere between 50% and 80% of all the jobs that exist today could be automated out of existence.

The question is how are people going to live? How are they going to find new jobs? Are they going to have the same amount of money? So local solutions are going to be critical. Pioneering them in the developing world may be the way to go, and then bringing them back to the developed world when the developed world is then aware enough that it needs a different approach.

This is an interesting point. In fact more technologies than we think originally come from developing countries, especially in Fintech and Future Cities tech. Prepaid meters to pay for electricity are an example. They are becoming very popular in the UK but they were born in South Africa. The most popular mobile payment system — Mpesa — was born in Kenya.

I think you'll see that more and more, because there are lots of these innovative ideas. Resources are cheaper. People can develop solutions in the emerging markets in very creative ways.

I think one of the things that I'm always amazed by is how, because of bureaucracy, because of complexity, because of a lack of availability of everything you need, people there can be very innovative.

They learn to behave like water and get around any obstacle. And they create these truly imaginative low-cost solutions that work. And then we in the developed world go "Wow, isn't that clever?" And then somehow we don't quite transfer the idea in quite the same way.

There's a whole theme now in academic circles around what's called frugal innovation or *Jugaad Innovation*, which is looking at these solutions that work there and how you bring them to the West.

The one example I love is of hospitals that can do open-heart surgery for about 4% of the cost that it is done in for the West. Or of the guys doing cataract surgery where they actually have six patients sat around them in a circle and they literally move from patient to patient and rotate back again, going around the circle, doing what they have to do and then dealing with the next patient.

But they do the surgery at a fraction of the cost. These are genuinely smart solutions for that world. And actually, everything they're doing is transferrable to the developed world, but somehow we have an unwarranted and heightened belief about our own importance. And that stops us from embracing some of these things.

Last but not least, what advice would you give to your younger self?

I'd say "Look around. Look for ideas that interest you." And look for points of pain or look for opportunities for creating pleasure. Where is there a pain in someone's life or in their business? Where is there a point where it's excessively complicated or there's an issue for them? What innovative solution could you create for that? And then look for new areas where you can bring pleasure, where you can simplify people's lives, create new services.

Look at Uber. One of the biggest benefits of Uber is a kind of guarantee or a rough guarantee of when the car will arrive and the fact that I can pay by credit card so I don't have to carry cash.

I get to rate the driver. The driver gets to rate me. The cars are, therefore, very clean. There's a totally different proposition there that's taken away some of the pain of riding a taxi and created new pleasure around it. So it's looking at, in different walks of life, where are those problems today, or where are those opportunities?

And really starting to look for simple concepts that you can then enable, whether that's through people or technology or some combination of the two, that can really solve these problems in innovative, creative, and elegant ways.

Basically your position is that there are not specific areas to focus on, but really you can succeed if you find a pain and fix it. You don't need to focus on hot topics like environmental services, energy or transport or something else.

No, because in all these sectors there are a lot of players going in, so there's a lot of competition. I think finding genuine solutions to issues is the thing to do.

I'll give you one simple example. There's a new service launched in the States called DUFL. It's very simple. You pay $9.95 a month as a subscription. They send you a suitcase. You fill it with your clothes that you use when you're traveling. They take those clothes. They photograph them all. They put them on a webpage for you.

Then when you're traveling, let's say you're going from New York to Milwaukee, you tell them which hotel you're going to and on what date. You choose which clothes from your collection that you want in the case. They pack and deliver it to the hotel for you. It costs you $99 each time you do that, plus the $9.99 monthly subscription.

When you leave the hotel they collect your case from the concierge. They dry-clean your clothes. And then you're ready for your next trip. If you want to send them two suitcases worth of clothes, you can do that. And basically, you take away any issues of luggage, and they take on that responsibility for you. Now, that's just spotting a really interesting gap in the market and saying, "Here's how we can tackle that."

Links

1. Rohit's Fast Future Research
http://fastfuture.com/

2. The Future of Business
By Rohit Talwar and Others
http://fob.fastfuturepublishing.com/

3. DUFL : Changing the way the world travels.
www.dufl.com

4. Download "Jugaad Innovation: Think Frugal, Be Flexible, Generate Breakthrough Growth"
by Navi Radjou and Others
http://futurecitiesbook.com/113

Tom Samodol

PayProp

My favorite startup advice to anybody, young or old, is from Howard Aitken. "Don't worry about people stealing your ideas. If your ideas are any good, you'll have to ram them down people's throats".

— Tom Samodol

In this article, the introduction is at the end. You'll find out the reason why when you get there.

The Interview

Welcome Tom. Can you introduce yourself and your company?

Hi everybody, this Tom Samodol, Director of Strategy & Corporate Development at PayProp.

We are an automated cloud-based platform for the property management industry. That means that you can collect payments, manage your properties, organize your tenants, and every other action required to run your real estate portfolio, big or small, directly from your smartphone or tablet.

Johannes and Jaco van Eeden started PayProp in South Africa, and now we are sharing our services with the UK and Europe in general.

What's your situation in terms of fund raising?

We are in the enviable situation of not needing a funding round.

PayProp already generates profit, and international expansion is self-funded. At least in our area, you don't need to give your shares of the company to investors, when you have happy and satisfied customers.

This is sometimes called "customer-strapping" in investor circles, and is especially sought after. Going back to you, how did you decide to join a startup from another country?

I was working in Technology Corporate Finance at Dresdner Kleinwort (Commerzbank), a huge organization. While at that job, we also incubated, scaled and exited several Fintech startups, and I had a chance to play a major part in many of them. Having been sitting on the fence to the entrepreneurial tech world for a while, it was just matter of time for me to take the plunge.

Why PayProp specifically? Because we are solving a major headache in an enormous market, worldwide. I knew the PayProp team for over 5 years, and I was very impressed with what they had done in South Africa. So we teamed up to go after the UK and European market first, before going globally.

In the UK alone, £50 billion ($78 billion) of private rentals are transacted every year and this is expected to increase to over £ 100 billion in 2022.

Aside from the potential, the key point that attracted me is the focus. We are an all-in-one platform, and that may seem broad, but in reality we do only one thing: we process payments and tenants for the real estate market, and we do it really, really well.

Last but not least, what would be your advice to your younger self?

My favorite startup advice to anybody, young or old, is from Howard Aitken. "Don't worry about people stealing your ideas. If your ideas are any good, you'll have to ram them down people's throats".

An Introduction

Tom Samodol has a secret. That's the reason why the introduction in this chapter is not at the beginning but at the end, to avoid spoilers.

This secret is the location of the company's headquarters. And I'm not talking about the legal address of the company, split between South Africa and England. Instead, I'm talking about the real headquarters where the majority of the team is based. This place simply doesn't exist.

You have almost certainly heard about big companies outsourcing their software development to India, or about smaller companies outsourcing their customer care to the Philippines. But these are examples of businesses born in one place, and then 'externally' outsourcing one or more functions to another place. PayProp is different as the entire 'internal' team is divided between multiple countries.

When a colleague at PayProp says "Let's chat over a coffee", the two cups of coffee can be 9,000 miles away and the chat happens through Slack, Asana or Skype.

This is a reality quite familiar to multinational corporations, but it's becoming more common for companies of any size. Take as an example Basecamp, formerly known as 37Signals. They proudly announce on their website "Our office is in Chicago, but everyone at Basecamp is free to live and work wherever they want".

To date Basecamp is a company with just 47 employees spread out across 26 different cities around the world. With this organization they have attracted investors of the caliber of Jeff Bezos, founder of Amazon. Not having traditional headquarters doesn't mean that they are a bad company, or a fake company. On the contrary, sometimes the company performs quite a lot better than their traditional competitors.

Back to PayProp, thanks to their 'spread out organization' the team speaks 16 different languages, and can provide 24/7 assistance without extra costs. In the full interview Tom says "We go through great lengths to have all team members use Slack, Asana and Skype from the outset, and put lots of emphasis on any new hires to be on-boarded on all communication tools from day one."

As you can see, PayProp's 'secret' is not kept hidden. They are proud of their unusual organization and they share this fact with their customers.

We have the technology to transform almost every company into an organization similar to PayProp or Basecamp. This doesn't mean that we'll see more workers moving to a beach in Thailand. In fact, the trends show the opposite.

Over the next 10 plus years, more people will decide to live in a city, to have access to the community and the knowledge that only a city can offer. But they don't have to be the same cities anymore. Tom lives in a city (London), Johannes and Jaco van Eed who started the company live in another city (Stellenbosch in South Africa), and other members of the team live, for the most part, in other cities in the world.

Maybe this is not your situation right now, but it could happen to you in the very near future. You could decide right away to get a job in a small company with a great, friendly environment and to move to a new city every year. To keep your job, you just need to log onto your computer, no matter where you are.

You don't have to be a programmer, as remote work is becoming business as usual for every kind of job, from customer care, to accountancy, to marketing. If you are interested in these kinds of jobs, or are just curious enough to have a look, you can check a website like WeWorkRemotely.com or a startup job offer board. They are more common than the majority think.

Links

1. Company website
http://payprop.com

2. Basecamp
http://basecamp.com/about

3. We Work Remotely
http://weworkremotely.com

What Is a Smart City?

Interlude

Cities have the capability of providing something for everybody, only because, and only when, they are created by everybody.

—Jane Jacobs

I get this question all the time—What is a Smart City?—and I like to start with an official answer. Cities are "smart" if they cover at least five out of these eight smart parameters:

1. Smart Energy
2. Smart Building
3. Smart Mobility
4. Smart Healthcare
5. Smart Infrastructure
6. Smart Technology
7. Smart Governance and Education
8. Smart Citizens

This is not the only definition of a Smart City, but it's a good place to start. Its creator—Frost & Sullivan—is one of the biggest consulting firms in this area.

According to these principles, there will be around 26 Smart Cities in 2025, 50% of them in North America and Europe. The value of their market is estimated to reach $1.56 trillion by 2020.

This Is Sparta!

To make sense of this cold hard number, let's imagine that Hollywood decided to make a movie set in the near future where smart cities declare independence—an era of City States such as Sparta and Athens, but with modern technologies.

In this scenario, the market size of the smart cities would be the 12th largest GDP in the world, sitting above primary nations like South Korea and Australia, and double that of Saudi Arabia.

Top 20 Countries by GDP

1. United States $17.42 trillion
2. China $10.38 trillion
3. Japan $4.62 trillion
4. Germany $3.86 trillion
5. United Kingdom $2.95 trillion
6. France $2.85 trillion
7. Brazil $2.35 trillion
8. Italy $2.15 trillion
9. India $2.05 trillion
10. Russia $1.86 trillion
11. Canada $1.79 trillion
12. *Smart Cities $1.56 trillion <=*
13. Australia $1.44 trillion
14. South Korea $1.42 trillion
15. Spain $1.41 trillion
16. Mexico $1.29 trillion
17. Indonesia $0.89 trillion
18. Netherlands $0.87 trillion
19. Turkey $0.81 trillion
20. Saudi Arabia $0.76 trillion

The complete list by the International Monetary Fund includes 188 countries.

Officially Smart

Having an appropriate number of parameters makes your city "officially" smart, however your life may still be miserable. From the point of view of citizens like me and you, what really matters is the quality of life.

In the next five years many cities are going to embrace smart technologies. They will not be "Smart Cities"—not officially—because many parameters require the intervention of the government, and five years is a short period of time for any bureaucracy.

Yet we are going to see many changes from bottom to top. Citizens will use existing technologies to organize their neighbourhoods. Startups will develop platforms and small home hardware products that have a direct impact on our lives. Your building might still be dull, but your flat could be very smart!

The Game

Shaping cities has always been a governmental game. Citizens can't decide to build a defense wall or a water system; this was a matter for kings and other powerful figures.

This is why the official definition of "Smart City" encourages a passive attitude. We—the citizens—can't build smart infrastructure by ourselves. Our city can be smart or not. Rich or Poor. With a good transport system or a bad one. This is the world we are used to living in.

Well, this bipolar world is over.

The new goal is to improve the quality of life one step at a time.

In business, this attitude has generated the concept of the Lean Startup. It is not simple with a city, but this is the trend. Citizens can directly impact two to three parameters of a Smart City.

I'm not saying that it's easy to be part of the change; I'm just saying that it's worth it.

If you ask me, "What is a Smart City?" may be the wrong question. "What smart changes do you want to see in your city?" is definitely more interesting.

Links

1. Frost & Sullivan
http://frost.com

2. Complete list of countries by GDP (by Wikipedia)
http://futurecitiesbook.com/114

Jimmy Garcia-Meza

Investor

Having the wrong investors will destroy your company and part of you will go with it.
— Jimmy Garcia-Meza

I will be very brief in this introduction, not because Jimmy Garcia-Meza has a limited resume — in fact the opposite is true — but because the main points of interest are in the interview.

In a few words, Jimmy started his career at Sun Microsystems, moving his way up the corporate ladder to the position of Worldwide Director of a 1.7 Billion Telecom Line of Business. He's a serial entrepreneur, with an exit to IBM, and a former director of Index Ventures, the venture capital.

On a personal note, his personal mantra is "Focus on one thing, and do it really well", which he repeats over and over to the young startuppers who he involves in his journey. In fact, it's more than a suggestion; it's Jimmy's way of life. I've seen brilliant but unfocused programmers become laser focused and effective when Jimmy is around.

One last thing, if you have a chance to meet him informally, ask him to share the story of the Two Kids and the Pony. I am not going to spoil the surprise. Believe me, it is pure philosophy.

The Interview

Welcome Jimmy. I would like to use the first question to share your market knowledge with the readers. You have played different roles in your career: Worldwide Director of a Telecom line of business at

Sun Microsystems, venture capitalist for Index Ventures and serial entrepreneur with an exit to IBM (A/N FilesX acquired in 2008).

Now you are back with a new startup — CloudPlugs — a lifecycle automation platform for the Internet of Things. Not only you are Co-founder and CEO, but you have invested your own money in the company. Buildings, cities and infrastructures are one of the main focus of this platform.

With your contacts and experience you can pick and choose any market. Why have you decided to invest time and money into a business connected to cities and buildings?

The best place to start is always from the market data. The Internet of Things is expected to be a 7 trillion market for solutions by 2020 with over 50 billion connected devices. Much like networking transformed the face of computing forever in the 80's and 90's yielding across the board gains in productivity; a world of connected devices will dramatically increase efficiency, reduce costs and enable better customer interactions.

While Home Automation solutions will deliver better comfort, security and control for individuals, advanced facilities management and smart city services delivered by a new generation of smart, connected devices based on open technologies will enable organizations and municipalities to manage the use of critical resources like energy and water more efficiently without sacrificing comfort.

Smarter, faster computers have transformed the world in very few years. Smarter, connected devices using lower cost open technologies and open networks like the Internet will open a new world of possibilities to continue to innovate in all disciplines.

At CloudPlugs, we hope to contribute to the creation of this upcoming wave of innovation by providing the technology and tools that will enable businesses and governments to embrace and adapt to continuous change.

Let's go back a few years. You started your career in a major company, Sun Microsystems, moving your way up the corporate ladder to Worldwide Director of Sales. Then you become an entrepreneur.

This was the common path among many successful entrepreneurs, with drop outs like Steve Jobs being an exception. This is not true anymore. Many young entrepreneurs start their own company directly after graduation, even before that sometimes.

What are your thoughts on this subject? Do you think the new startuppers may be missing something?

And would you suggest a young entrepreneur gets some experience working in a big company first?

I find it admirable that many students can transition directly into entrepreneurship and some are able to build sustainable, large businesses that have created new industries.

Yahoo, Google, Facebook and several others are good examples. However, as impressive as those achievements have been, we do not hear the tales of all the failures.

In technology, the odds are stacked up in favor of very, very few bright minds that flourish and are extremely successful. Most startups fail, and very few make it on the second try.

The start-up world is tough and it requires a lot of personal sacrifices and experience to learn how to navigate the growing process.

Employees of large corporations that end up being successful entrepreneurs are typically those that work in organizations that stimulate innovation and give their employees the freedom to dream, create and deliver projects successfully.

Basically you are saying that this is not a competition between sizes — with startups on one side and big companies on the other — but between cultures. Startups and big companies with an open mind in one corner, and the rigid companies in the other. Correct?

Exactly. Large companies with rigid career paths and formal processes for everything and that are very conservative are not a good place for entrepreneurial minds. I was lucky to work for Sun Microsystems and to be part of organizations that gave me a lot of freedom, and as long as I produced results, I was able to climb the corporate ladder quite fast.

Sun was a company with a mission. I used to wake up every day not thinking how much I was going to sell that day, but thinking how we were going to change the world of proprietary closed systems and central computing to a world of open network computing. That thought of democratization was a really powerful driver for me and for many people inside the company.

There is a saying that says: "Managers light a fire under their employees feet. Leaders light a fire in their employees hearts." This is what Scott McNealy and the top management did, and it was a great lesson to learn.

Many Sun employees have built successful companies and the experience at Sun was truly invaluable. Working with really smart people is a great learning experience, seeing mistakes that are not going to cost the whole company gives you new perspectives, working with all kinds of people and dealing with politics and problems prepares you well.

Much of what I learned at Sun I applied to build Silicon Image's business from $40M/year to $190M/year in two and a half years, to build up and sell FilesX and to build CloudPlugs today.

I'm sure that your network of contacts is quite helpful for your startup. What about the rest of your experience? How do you use your Sun background on a daily basis?

The experiences of working for large companies are invaluable. That is why many venture backed entrepreneurs end up surrounding themselves by people with corporate experience. The Google founders got Eric Schmidt who was the CTO of Sun for many years and then ran Novell. The examples are countless.

I am on the board of advisors of two other companies and one of them greatly benefited from contacts I had, employees I helped hire and strategic industry advice in dealing with global standardization processes and M&A.

The other one requires to date, hands on help with operations reviews, strategic matters, sales matters, employee issues which are sometimes complex and a pair of experienced eyes can help reduce complexity and to make better decisions. There is always a lot of advice required in internal and external investments and M&A matters.

On the other hand, many managers I worked with simply don't enjoy the freedom of a startup.

While there are always exceptions, I believe that having experience in a fast growing, game changing company is a great boot camp to start and build a successful business. If someone starts a company right out of college, he or she should hire a few people that have been successful entrepreneurs, and people with successful careers next to them.

While there is not just one formula for success, and many corporate people do not do well in start-ups, having the advice of someone who has been there is very important, as is getting advise from other entrepreneurs.

Moving on to something different. Last time we met, we watched the World Cup in a pub in London. This is not unknown territory for you. You also built Sun's telecom sales practice in Europe. Indeed you have quite a wealth of experience in different locations.

Your main background, as an entrepreneur, is in Silicon Valley and—for your last exit FilesX—in Boston and Israel. Yet you live in Washington D.C.

What are your thoughts on location? Do you think that startups should move to Silicon Valley at any cost?

If not, what location do you see high potential in for a startup, especially in the Future Cities business?

Startups should be able to grow and flourish everywhere. Unfortunately, the truth is that the conditions to promote entrepreneurship and innovation are not available everywhere.

There are multiple tech hubs in which to build companies, even in Washington D.C. which was a tech corridor during the heydays of AOL. When I joined Index Ventures, in Geneva I did it because I wanted to help create an environment that would provide entrepreneurs with a platform for innovation in Europe.

There are many companies that get funded in Europe, but we do not hear of big, world-changing successes such as those from the Valley. I am very biased, and I believe that to do Tech right, you need to do it in the Silicon Valley.

The energy, the vibe, the number of really smart people trying to change the world is incomparable there. If you want to do deals or partnerships, the people you want in your camp are pretty much all there.

If you are an ethical, hard working person that treats people right, you can build a strong network of people who will continue to want to work with you even if you have not seen them for years.

Does Silicon Valley have its negative aspects too, or can we assume that everything is great?

The challenge with the Valley today is that it is expensive; it is very competitive and difficult to hire and to retain engineers. In my view, if you can access good engineering talent in another location, keep your R&D there, yet still put your headquarters in the valley.

What about Europe instead?

When it comes to Smart Cities, many European countries are putting in place incentives for young companies to participate in European projects and contribute to the path towards energy efficiency, sustainability and connectivity.

London is becoming an attractive hub for entrepreneurship, and while expensive compared to other countries in Europe, most U.S. VC's have offices in the city, facilitating links with Silicon Valley.

You know that I am a big fan of London. I decided to relocate there after all. But if you could share a practical suggestion with younger entrepreneurs, a step by step path to success, what would you tell them?

For a European startup that is interested in a global business, if resources and the team allow it, I would suggest to build the operation in Europe, get the first customers to prove your product and technology, and establish a foothold in the U.S. to gain exposure with the movers and shakers in the target industries.

In terms of the Internet of Things, Europe is a fertile ground for projects, yet most companies move at a much slower pace than in the U.S. Hence my bias towards building the mid and long term business in the U.S.

I don't completely agree, but I love to hear these practical answers. They are extremely useful for me and the readers. Let's share another actionable suggestion if you may.

If you have to invest $10 million in startups in future cities, other than your company, what areas would you pick? What technologies do you think will be in high demand over the coming years?

To build real companies that can handle a future city project, the investment is probably in the 100's of millions. Getting people started is one thing, getting the companies to profitability is a different thing and given that smart city projects and smart building projects have long development and deployment cycles, the investors will need to stay on board with their companies for the long haul.

Short, quick hits are not going to be the norm in this space. The technology for smart cities needs to be reliable, scalable, it needs to interoperate with all kinds of legacy and new devices and systems. The amount of data to be processed for really smart applications is huge. Most solutions required to create smart cities are infrastructure related and they require important engineering and financial investments.

I am totally with you on this. At Level 39, we have an acceleration program dedicated to future cities tech, and backed by one of the most prestigious property companies in Europe, the Canary Wharf Group. The common issue I hear from the startups is the amount of money required and the long sales cycle.

This is a characteristic of this specific market and it can't be erased. But through your experience, can you suggest a useful way to at least reduce the problem?

It is such a vast space, that I would advise thinking in simple terms: "Doing more with less." If you can provide solutions that do more with fewer resources, then you have a chance to succeed.

For example, designing a new range of low power, yet powerful processors will enable the deployment of millions of battery powered devices across cities.

Wireless sensor networks that are reliable and have wider ranges are important to connect devices.

Reliable, lightweight protocols need to be developed.

Simpler methods for efficient data transcoding that enable tens of thousands of devices to interact independent of their own communications protocol are important.

The ability to use the population and their smartphones as human sensors may prove valuable to smart cities.

Fast, pattern-matching algorithms that can be used for predictive maintenance and other services are important. Data analytics tools are always a key component and, related to that, systems that can correlate data quickly are going to be critical in smart city applications.

New generation smarter RFID and beacon control and asset location systems are definitely going to be part of the infrastructure.

On top of these infrastructure systems, specific applications for safety management, energy management, lighting, security, transportation, are important.

On a lighter note, social media applications that can be used to bring awareness to situations and problems will play an important role.

Most of the smart city infrastructure requires high core, well tested, reliable, secure and scalable technology.

Only companies that understand the requirements of a complex enterprise will be able to provide some of the core solutions and potentially compete effectively against the big systems integrators and technology companies that also want this business.

Last but not least, what advice would you give to your younger self?

I would say, find an important area which you are passionate about, focus, and build the best solution available in the market.

Before starting your project make sure that you do your homework and that there will actually be a market for the product you are building. Build it in steps making sure you can create proof and validation points along the way to ensure you are on the right track and that your product will actually solve a problem that people care about.

Make sure that you protect your ideas early on.

Seek advice from people that are in the industry and that can help you open doors.

Make sure that if you take money, you take it from honest people that will really be behind you. Having the wrong investors will destroy your company and part of you will go with it.

Build a systems integrator partner network. In most cases smart city projects are too big for start-ups and the solution will need to be proposed and delivered by a well established company.

Is there anything else you would like to share?

I would encourage everyone to pursue their dreams and take chances while the burdens of life do not become constraining factors.

I would also hope that governments create more incentives for entrepreneurial minds to have a shot at contributing to the transformation of cities into smart hubs of great services and innovation. Some of the great innovations come from small companies and we must give them an environment that will enable them to flourish.

Links

1. Canary Wharf Group
http://group.canarywharf.com/

2. CloudPlug
https://cloudplugs.com/

3. Cognicity
http://cognicity.london/

4. FilesX
Now IBM

5. Index Ventures
http://indexventures.com/

6. Level39
http://level39.co

7. Sun Microsystems
Now Oracle
http://www.oracle.com/us/sun/index.html

Simone Tarantino

Inspect Manager

I moved to New York for the love of a girl. I ended up staying because I felt in love with the city.

— Simone Tarantino

"Do good but play greedy; pure good doesn't sell." This may be Simone Tarantino's secret to a successful business. Simone is a entrepreneur who moved to New York for the love of a girl, and—in his own words—ended up staying because he fell in love with the city.

Simone's startup—Inspect Manager—removes the need for paper and pencil during public inspections. Four billion trees are cut down every year to produce paper, that's 35% of the entire deforestation statistic. But doing good alone is not enough. So Simone's sales pitch to me is all about saving time and money through their platform. This may sound obvious to many entrepreneurs out there, but for a self defined 'former naive and idealistic tech guy' it is a big leap forward.

When in New York, do as the New Yorkers do. Not by coincidence, Simone has launched a startup with a community angle. New York is the startup powerhouse of the United States together with Silicon Valley.

Etsy was founded in New York, and so were Tumblr and Digg. Once upon a time, when the Internet was young, AOL was also born in New York. Mashable was founded in Aberdeen Scotland, but moved to New York when it reached an advanced early stage. New York may be less techie than Silicon Valley, but it's definitely great for media and social ventures.

"You move to Silicon Valley because it's a cool place to do business. You move to New York because it's a cool place to live AND to do business." There is always a mix of passion and pride when you interview startups from New York City, and Simone is definitely one of them. A paperless bureaucracy isn't as glamorous as robots, drones or 3D printers, but it's a big part of a smart city. Technically it's more or less already possible, but culturally it's going to take some time to change the mindset of public offices around the world. And I use the word 'public offices' not 'public officers' on purpose, because I've spent enough time working with institutions to swear that many officers are smart and ready to innovate. The bureaucracy, on the other hand, often acts as a self conscious entity separated from its own men and women.

Simone talks about the current state of Environmental Inspections with a kind of naughty pleasure: "The inspections are still performed with pen, paper and a clipboard. Photos are taken with a portable camera, and clipped onto a paper floor-plan. These notes are shipped back to the office, where a clerk has to interpret the inspector's handwriting, which can be an unpleasant experience in itself, and copy them manually into an Excel spreadsheet or Word document - or even both sometimes, often with typos and other frustrating errors. Out of that messy content, they have to add company and customer information, licenses and several other pieces of data, and aggregate all of that into a report."

This is Simone's rule for running a startup – "Listen, learn, repeat". When you finally spot a inefficiency, that is both producing a big pain and a big market, then and only then, can you create a solution.

"Inspect Manager solves all these painful inefficiencies with an easy-to-use tablet app. All the data is aggregated in the cloud, and transformed into a report, thus removing the pain of manual labour"

And saving the lives of a couple of billion trees, I add, to draw out Simone's idealistic side, but he doesn't fall for my good natured trick. What he can't hide is his pride at having an international team. It's a good list: Andrea Esper, Mark O'Brien, Don, Jaime Sayers, plus a group of investors who believed in his idea to the tune of an initial round of $1 million.

And yet, as it happens as with many successful immigrants, the link with their past is never completely broken. The last name that Simone quotes at the end of the interview is Enrica Fortunati, his first boss at Intel back in Italy. "Leukemia had the best of her, but she believed in me and put me on the right path".

For me, the interviewer, this is a delicate subject. I lost my mother to cancer, and on top of that talking of a passed away mentor is always at risk of cliché. Still I would like to share what was my first thought; I didn't know Enrica Fortunati, but if an entrepreneur like Simone projects the future, lives in another country and does a completely different job, and after so many years mentions her name as soon as we talk about inspiration and success, she must have been a hell of a mentor.

Links

Company website
http://inspectmanager.com

When the Police Invented the Radio. A Short History of the Mobile Network

Interlude

When wireless is perfectly applied, the whole earth will be converted into a huge brain.
— Nicola Tesla

In 1922 the Detroit Police Department launched "KOP", its own entertainment radio station, playing music from the frequency 1050-AM. The song *My Man* by Fanny Brice was at the top of the U.S. chart for 9 weeks, and the nation was in the middle of the Prohibition era; the statute that made alcohol illegal in 1919.

To understand why a police department created a radio station you need to meet their Commissioner, William P. Rutledge. Today we call this kind of man a "visionary" or a "first mover" however at that time he was just "peculiar" for some, and "weird" for others.

In 1922 radios were huge, bulky objects but a radio enthusiast from Philadelphia named W. W. Macfarlane had recently set up a portable system that allowed communication between two moving cars. Macfarlane is officially considered the inventor of the mobile radio, the great grandfather of the mobile phone.

In this invention Rutledge saw the opportunity to boost the efficiency of his police force. He installed one of these portable radios in each car, creating the first radio police dispatch system. And because having a radio station without a Federal Licence was illegal, Rutledge had to get one of those too. Station 1050-KOP-AM was used to play music in between official police announcements to comply with its federal licensing as an entertainment radio.

Seen from another angle, the entertainment radio was just a front for a different operation; an activity that would have been probably considered illegal by the police if used by anybody else. George Bernard Shaw used to say "The reasonable man adapts himself to the world; the unreasonable one persists in trying to adapt the world to himself. Therefore, all progress depends on the unreasonable man." Rutledge was definitely one of these men.

From the Mobile Radio to the Mobile Phone

By 1940 Motorola had improved this portable radio to be a device that could be carried in a soldier's backpack. Europe was in the middle of World War II and in case the United States had to join the conflict, a portable radio would have been a disruptive technology.

If we think about it, the first radio police dispatch system was created in the middle of Prohibition, a kind of war between the police and newly born organized crime, and truly portable radios during WWII. And that says a lot about human progress.

After the end of the war the technology was adopted into civil society, as often happens. In 1946 AT&T launched the first US mobile phone network in Saint Louis, based on the technology first used by Rutledge in Detroit. In 1980 Motorola launched their mobile phone (the size and shape of a brick, and almost the same weight).

From this moment, technology sped up. New government licenses and more frequencies hit the market across America and Europe, and new mobile operators and mobile telecom providers joined the industry, reducing prices and improving performance.

At the end of the '90s, I had an opportunity to be part of this fast growing market. The starting salary was really bad, but the newly founded telecom company that I joined as employee no. 8, eventually raised an impressive amount of money and grew to 6,500 employees.

In order to increase the level of competition, the military's radio frequency was opened to the private sector in a project named "Marte" (Mars) not because of the Red Planet, but for the name of the Roman God of War. And this is an excellent example of the creativity of military and government officers.

From the end of the '90s the international mobile networks capacity has grown exponentially every year, and has also gained the support of another network: Wi-Fi. In truth, Wi-Fi technology was launched in 1985, but it only started growing in 1999 when the universal standard IEEE 802.11b was agreed in the industry.

The Next Generation

No matter how fast the mobile network grows, it's often due to consumer request. When Steve Jobs introduced the first iPhone on 29th June 2007, access to images and videos saw a spike and it has grown exponentially ever since.

In the next 5 years a second spike is estimated to hit the network, due to the growth of the Internet of Things. Billions of gadgets, kitchen appliances, buildings and transport talking between each other need a network capacity never seen before.

Check Kickstarter or Indiegogo, the popular crowdfunding platforms, and you'll see new startup companies joining the market with one of these gadgets. The big corporations are in the game too, starting with the Apple Watch, although the bigger hit will probably come from the Internet of Things at business level, with connected buildings, transport systems, and more.

I bet that while thousands of new companies will fight for the gadget market, the real money will be made by the one startup that finds a system to grow network capacity or use existing capacity more efficiently. To close with another quote, "During the gold rush it's a good time to be in the pick and shovel business".

Eric van der Kleij

Level39 / Cognicity

What's their game? Their game is mostly about the data.

—Eric Van Der Kleij

"I am at the center of the center" said Salim, brother of the leading character in the movie *Slumdog Millionaire*. Salim and Eric van der Kleij have nothing in common, but I think about Eric every time I hear this quote. To understand why, let's go back a few years.

In 2010 the United Kingdom was trying to create their answer to Silicon Valley. They launched an entity called Tech City in one of the oldest areas of London, and Eric was appointed CEO. The majority of my friends in Silicon Valley branded this idea as a crazy European idea and a project destined to fail. A healthy startup community can not grow in an old area in an equally old city — they said — and it can not be connected to the government.

Well, the majority was wrong. In just a few years London has become one of the hottest centers in the international startup community, and Eric was at the center of this center.

After a couple of years, Eric left Tech City to co-found Level 39, a startup accelerator specializing in Fintech and Future Cities tech. Guess what? For the majority this was a project destined to fail. First of all, accelerators perform better in an area with a strong startup community, but Level39 is based in Canary Wharf, far away from the traditional startup district of Shoreditch. Secondly Level39 is designed to please both bankers wearing ties and coders wearing hoodies, and the common rule says that you fail if you try to please everyone.

So when I was invited by Eric to join the project as one of the initial 39 members, the general consensus was that Level39 had no future. Of course I accepted. I like challenges, and I love to prove the majority wrong.

Well, the majority was proven wrong (again). In just two years Level39 and Canary Wharf have become two hot spots on the international map. Level39 is the biggest accelerator in Europe in the area of Fintech — financial technology — and Fintech is one of the hottest markets for startups. We are "at the center of the center" and it feels very good.

The leadership of Fintech isn't just another crazy European idea. Check out the interview with Adeo Ressi, founder of the Founder Institute and a legend in Silicon Valley, and you'll see what I mean.

This year, Eric and his business partner, Claire Cockerton, launched a Smart Cities program for the Canary Wharf Group: Cognicity. This interview is particularly short because of this program, as we are in the closing week between startup pitches and introductions to the investors. And yet this is reassuring. If Eric has decided to invest so much energy into the subject of Future Cities, you can bet that it's going to become the hottest topic in town.

The Interview

So Eric, you are the CEO of both Cognicity, a Smart City accelerator program, and Level39, an accelerator/incubator specializing in Fintech and Future City Tech. You have access to both startups and big companies. What's the most important trend you see in smart cities?

One of the most important trends in recent times has been the move by huge technology companies, such as Google and Intel, either expanding their activities or entering this space. For example, Intel, through their substantial support of the Cognicity Smart City Programme, and Google entering the "urbanisation" sector through their recently announced Sidewalk Labs initiative.

The most important thing to remember about these players is that they do not come with very much built environment experience. So what's their game? Their game is mostly about the data.

If you think about what an amazing business Google made from just helping us find out what we want to know about, can you imagine what kind of businesses they will enable by knowing about what we all do, where we do it, and for how long, not just for a few seconds as we type into a browser but all the time?

And with players like Intel focusing on the Internet of Thing (IoT) and Internet of Everything in the built environment, we start to see a whole new world of sustainability and consumer convenience, within which the many-faceted concepts of smart cities exist.

The other big trend is, of course, the secure access and ethical custodianship and use of all this new data. It's going to need a whole new set of security, interoperability methods and adoption of new standards, such as the UK's Hypercat standard. So I think standards will also play an even more important part of these emerging trends.

If you had $10 million to invest in startups in the smart cities space, what areas would you pick?

IoT security, community cohesion and engagement solutions, also healthcare or mobility in cities. We know we really are facing such a rapid rise in the growth and density of cities, it will become even more important to facilitate a "rediscovery" of community to allow hugely dense communities to coexist less anonymously, in a way that they care about each other and help support, problem solve and trade together.

These are the kinds of solutions that help prevent civil unrest and actually can create powerful micro-economies within the densest urban environments, by curating interdependent microeconomics. Interestingly, none of this is new. This is in fact original "village" and "market square" theory, but now curated by technology and mobiles within a densely populated environment. Imagine any city region that could convene a self-reliant, collaborative and peaceful community by sponsoring a technology-assisted solution to curate such a phenomenon. Priceless!

Technology can be expensive. Do you see the gap between cities in rich countries and poor countries growing in the future?

I have always held the belief that technology-led innovation that becomes popular and scales within affluent countries must help commoditise costs and simplify user experience, making it much more accessible to developing countries.

Fantastic examples already exist, such as the outstandingly simple but highly economically important mPesa in Africa. I do, however, think we need more entrepreneurs to enter this sector of what we like to call "leapfrog" technologies that can often operate without traditional infrastructure, but often need just a little more connectivity or *infostructure*.

Also related to this topic, it is encouraging to see the bigger technology players investing in more ubiquitous and accessible connectivity such as Google's satellite project, which will start to level the playing field, and frankly if they can do this where traditional industries have yet to succeed, then they deserve both the credit and to share in the data of emerging businesses that blossom from this kind of upgrade.

Links

1. Cognicity - Smart City accelerator program
http://cognicity.london

2. Tech City UK
http://www.techcityuk.com

3. Level39 – The Biggest Fintech and Future Cities accelerator in Europe
http://level39.co

4. Hypercat - A consortium and standard driving secure and interoperable Internet of Things (IoT) for Industry
http://www.hypercat.io

Domenico Colucci

Nextome

Being an international company doesn't erase your national origins.

— Domenico Colucci

There are two reasons for this interview: a good one and an excellent one. The first reason is the persistence of Domenico Colucci, the co-founder of Nextome. Through multiple direct messages on social media, he shared the story of his company bit by bit over a long time. So when I decided to write this book, Nextome was as fresh in my mind as much bigger companies that are regularly present in the media.

This is a lesson I have learned working with venture capitals. There is an added value in sending small regular reports to investors and journalists. It works much better than a lengthy press release sent at the very last minute before the launch of your fund raising campaign.

The only back draw of this tactic , is that you are forced to be honest. You can't talk about almost having a million customers, if in the next update you don't have those million customers in reality. If you send regular updates, and you promise something, then you have to deliver. This is one of the reasons why many investors and venture capitals prefer to establish this long term relationship quite some time before you need money.

The second reason why Nextome is an interesting case study for any book, is in their origin. This startup was born in Southern Italy, an area (in)famous for the high unemployment rate and the lack of major companies. Italy in general is seen as one of the most bureaucratic and less entrepreneur friendly countries in the European Union.

Despite their origins, or maybe because of their origins, Nextome was born as an international company. They are relatively small, but they have won awards and closed deals outside Italy, including in the USA, and have on their board of directors Marco Bicocchi Pichi, one of the few Italian angel investors with international experience.

Southern Italy has an history of young graduates looking for a regular job within a public company or in local politics. So what has changed?

The answer sounds obvious (once you know it): you can't code in Italian. Tech and startups are forcing an entire generation of Italians to become international. I've seen the same phenomena in Spain, in Portugal and in Belgium, and I guess that it's happening in many other countries.

The word "startup" is used and abused by the media, but in the long term they deserve the hype. Startups are forcing many countries to open up to the world without much help from their government, and often despite the government.

Every startup declares that they "will change the world". We know that the reality is different. The majority is going to fail, and even when they survive, they usually don't change our lives very much. In most of the cases, they will deliver just another funny gadget or another leisure app. Only a small number of startups will be truly disruptive, and yet "The Startups", as a collective phenomenon, are already changing the world, they are forcing young graduates to learn English, to open to the international market, and forget a traditional secure public job for life. Now this is interesting.

The Interview

Domenico, let's start with a brief introduction of yourself and the company.

Sure. My name is Domenico Colucci, co-founder and CFO of Nextome. The company was founded back in 2012 by 3 university colleagues: me, Vincenzo Dentamaro, CEO, and Giangiuseppe Tateo, together with our first adviser and angel investor Marco Bicocchi

Pichi.

Did you have a Eureka moment that gave birth to the idea of Nextome, or it was more due to rational market analysis?

Indeed we had a specific event that gave birth to Nextome, but it's nothing like these stories that you read in the media. I'm not sure that you want to share something so weird with your readers.

At the time, Vincenzo and I were in Milan. We used Google Maps to find the Rinascente, one of the most famous shopping centers in the city, but at one point Vincenzo had to go to the restroom and Google Maps doesn't work indoors (A/N This is an unusual discussion but it's true. I lived for one year in Milan and this mall is famous for only having one very hard to find restroom over 6 floors. That aside the mall is one of the city's top spots for shoppers).

So Vincenzo and I started joking about creating an indoor map app for restrooms, but being the geeks that we are, during the chat we noticed something really interesting. The Rinascente is one of the top malls in the country, with a very professional team of interior designers and planners, but still, they didn't have any tools to track customer behaviour.

What clothes were people looking at but not buying? Why? Was there something that the customers were missing? Why? How can you help the customers to have a better indoor shopping experience ?

We forget to go shopping and started sketching notes in my notebook and on a dozen napkins from the mall cafeteria. And this is how Nextome was born. There was no illuminating journey to India, Steve Jobs style, no dramatic night of coding like in the Facebook movie, just a geeky passion to solve a real problem.

Maybe it's not dramatic, but it sounds like quite a story to me. We should keep it. What does your company do exactly?

Nextome is an accurate indoor positioning and navigation software for smartphones that allows people to localize precisely inside a building and access services connected to the user's position: search and reach for places or products (imagine in retail), access advanced location based services and pedestrian flow analysis.

In exhibition the user can find anything and anyone, no matter how huge the crowd or the building are.

Tell me about your secret sauce. What makes you different?

Nextome is different because of the accuracy and its scalability: the localization algorithms work with standard iBeacons already present in over 30.000 buildings and counting.

Having started in Italy, a traditional country, we had to develop a system that is easy to setup for everybody, especially shop owners and non technical people.

Moreover, because Italy is so full of art and ancient artifacts, we developed a very flexible system to be used in museums too. Once the system was flexible enough to be used in two different environments such as shopping malls and museums we discovered that it was ready to be used in other places where localization is important: retail outlets, airports, etc.

Can you tell me something else about the team?

You have to understand that being an international company doesn't erase your origins. So our team uses nicknames. An American might feel like this is something from a remake of the movies The Godfather or Ghost Dog, but this is nothing related to the mob, it's part our tradition.

Our CEO is "Vincenzo Theory" (Vincenzo Dentamaro) because he has studied every conceivable piece of published literature on Indoor Positioning and he always explains his thoughts with citations.

I'm the "The Professor" because of the way I address every issue and apparently I pick an elegant dressing style even when we have to spend the night working in the office.

The third member of the team is "Query Man" (Giangiuseppe Tateo) because he's always ready with his smartphone to send requests to the database.

The fourth member is Marco Bicocchi Pichi, advisor and business angel, the first investor in Nextome.

No nickname here?

Marco is not from our city, so no nickname [laughs].

Tell me more about your city.

We are based in Bari, a shiny city on the sea. We all come from small cities all around Bari and we studied at the same university. It's a lovely place with sun and sea. Unfortunately there aren't any big networks of investors or technology companies.

What have been your best and worst moments so far?

The best moment was when we won the Web Summit 2014 in Dublin as the Most Awesome Alpha Startup voted by popular jury.

The worst was at a pitch investor in Berlin where the jury didn't accept our company.

What's your history of funding?

Funding in Italy is not very easy. All the team have invested their respective savings. Had we failed, we would have had no money at all; not for rent nor for food. We have solved this issue now with further funding, but at the beginning it was a risky decision. It also put us in this state of "sink or swim" that pushes your performance above your normal limits. Ironically, in a startup these kind of irrational decisions are the most rational thing you can do.

Last but not least, what advice would you give to your younger self?

Don't create a technology in search of a problem but a technology that solves a problem.

Second, don't focus just on the technology. Even if your team is made up entirely of technical people, take the time to understand how to make money. Who's willing to pay also provides the best feedback to improve your technology.

Last but not least, be prepared to be defeated, and of course never give up!

Links

Company website
http://www.nextome.net

Robots Won't Just Take Your Jobs

Interlude

I can take better care of your children than you Laura. I don't forget, I don't get angry, or depressed or intoxicated. I'm faster, stronger and more observant. I do not feel fear. However, I can not love them.

— Anita (an android from the TV series Humans)

For three generations, machines have been accused of stealing jobs from blue collar workers. Now, for the first time in history they can threaten white collar employment as well.

Robots can already drive cars (the driverless Google Cars) and answer any question (IBM Watson). Soon, thanks to the rise of Artificial Intelligence, they will be capable of being lawyers and doctors, and performing other intellectual activities.

I am fascinated by science fiction, but this is more than that. This is business and the impact on our society is real and near. Vislab, one of the startups interviewed in this book, was acquired by a multinational company in the weeks between our interview and the publication of this book. Their technology "provides Environmental Perception" - in other words they teach cars to drive by themselves. In a few weeks, the status of their founder, Alberto Broggi, was bumped up from the salary of a university professor to a $30 million exit.

"Displacement of workers from automation is already happening" wrote the Pew Research Center in their 2014 report on robots and the future of jobs. The only point to assess is if automation is going to create more, or less, jobs than it destroys.

In 10 Years

In 2014 the Pew Research Center surveyed 1,896 technology experts about the future of jobs in the following 10 years. People in tech are usually optimistic, but this time they were split almost 50-50 between pessimists and optimists.

Half of the experts (48%) anticipate a future where robots and AI destroy more jobs than are created, with a consequent mass of unemployment, an increase in social inequality, and eventually a breakdown in the social order.

On the opposing side, the optimists stress how technology has always created more jobs than it has destroyed. It's not just a matter of quantity, the optimists say, it's also a matter of quality, since the new jobs are usually better than the old ones. The mechanization of rural areas has moved the farmers to the factories, providing a more stable income and social welfare. One hundred years later, machines have moved these blue collar workers upwards again into better jobs in programming and digital marketing.

In other words, technology has always improved the conditions of workers, moving them from the farm to blue collar jobs and upwards again to white collar jobs. My favourite quote about this scenario comes from Amy Webb, CEO of Webbmedia Group, "The collar of the future is a hoodie."

The pessimistic experts point out exactly the same thing. Technology has transitioned the workers from farmers into blue collars and the blue collars into white collars, but there is nowhere to go after that. Once robots start performing white collar jobs, the only option for humans will be unemployment.

Greed Is Good

Ironically, the optimists' strongest line of defence is that the big corporations are too greedy to allow unemployment. Andrew Rens, chief counsel of the Shuttleworth Foundation points out that "an entrepreneur will only supply goods and services if there is a demand, and those who demand the goods can pay. Therefore any country that wants a competitive economy will ensure that most of its citizens are employed".

"Only greed can save our society" is definitely an intriguing phrase.

Here Is the Proof (Maybe)

Since we are talking about robots, here is a curious aside. The first robot officially recorded in history (at least in Western history) dates back to 4 B.C., when Archytas of Tarentum created a mechanical steam propelled bird called The Pigeon. The modern Tarentum is Taranto in South Italy and at the time was part of ancient Greek culture.

Apparently The Pigeon didn't outlive its inventor for two reasons. Firstly because the technology was so sophisticated that it required a genius to work it, and secondly because employing leisure slaves was much cheaper.

This may prove Andrew Rens' point in a way. Indeed greed seems to be one of the most powerful influencers in human history.

The One and Only Thing Everybody Agrees Upon

There is only one evaluation that almost every expert surveyed by the Pew Research Center agrees upon: the educational system is doing a poor job.

Schools and universities "are still sitting students in rows and columns, teaching them to keep quiet and memorize what is told to them, preparing them for life in a 20th century factory" (Howard Rheingold).

It's not a coincidence that an analysis conducted before the 2012 Olympics found that 9 out of 10 British millionaires never graduated from college.

Sir Ken Robinson in his famous TED Talk—one of the most watched TED videos of all time—stresses how schools prepare our children to sit still and memorize basic information. In other words they are trained for a life of obedience in a factory that doesn't exist anymore.

He adds "Our education system has mined our minds in the way that we strip-mine the earth: for a particular commodity. And for the future, it won't serve us."

Sir Ken Robinson is not the only one. In 1999, the U.S. Department of Labour estimated that 65% of grade school students would be going to work in jobs that didn't yet exist.

This is not the evaluation of some self made entrepreneurs, but the judgment made by the Department of Labour. Seen from another angle, it means that schools teach 65% of students something that is soon going to be useless. Now this something to think about.

In a Few Words

There is an agreement between the almost totality of 1,896 technology experts; robots will take over white collar workers, and almost completely wipe out blue collar jobs. The only questionable fact is if enough new jobs will be created. It sounds alarming but it's also an incredible business opportunity for tech startups.

There is also another possibility. Robots could help to redistribute the labor workload and create more leisure time for everybody. Hal Varian, chief economist at Google, points out how the working week has fallen from 70 hours in a factory to 37 hours in a modern office, and this trend could improve in the future.

Depending on which of the experts you prefer to listen to, the future will either be dark or bright. They all agree on one point though: the near future will be very, very different.

Links

1. Google Self-Driving Car Project
http://www.google.com/selfdrivingcar

2. IBM Watson
http://www.ibm.com/smarterplanet/us/en/ibmwatson

3. Vislab - Environmental Perception in many different fields, including Intelligent Vehicles
http://vislab.it

4. AI, Robotics, and the Future of Jobs
by Pew Research Center
http://www.pewinternet.org/files/2014/08/Future-of-AI-Robotics-and-Jobs.pdf

5. Sir Ken Robinson's TED talk
http://www.ted.com/
talksken_robinson_says_schools_kill_creativity

6. U.S. Department of Labour
Futurework - Trends and Challenges for Work in the 21st Century
http://www.dol.gov/oasam/programs/history/herman/
reports/futurework/execsum.htm

7. Download "Robots Will Steal Your Job, But That's OK"
by Federico Pistono
http://futurecitiesbook.com/115

Nicolas Steiner

Fintech Circle

Following the classic path to success is effective only up to a certain point.

— Nicolas Steiner

I've invited Nicolas for this interview for two opposing reasons. First of all, he has an eclectic background that you can enjoy in the interview. From this point of view, Nicolas is unique and well worth knowing. Second and opposite reason, he's in some way a "normal guy". Nicolas is an angel investor without being on the cover of a magazine. He didn't found a unicorn—a startup valued at more than $1 billion—but he's started a few tech companies, and he mentors many more.

In short, he has some considerable experience in the startup ecosystem, but he's living proof that you don't have to be Steve Jobs or Elon Musk to do something interesting.

You might not be able to emulate Nicolas's unusual career, but you can definitely be part of the ecosystem even if you are not going to found another Facebook. The Startup Game has one defining characteristic: there is no limit to the size of the team. The more we are, the more exciting the match.

The Interview

Welcome Nicolas. Let's start with a summary of your unusual background. If we hadn't known each other for many years I would have confused your life with a movie.

You started your career as a sound engineer in your native country, Switzerland. Then you took a long sabbatical in California practicing surf and paying your bills by playing jazz music. Back in Europe you worked in engineering, open-innovation and marketing strategies for companies such as Bosch, Swisscom, Reliance and Orange, and you have been an entrepreneur and an angel investor.

Last but not least, you are one of the founding members of Fintech Circle, the biggest angel investor syndicate in Europe specializing in financial technologies. Traditionally, the financial industry is run by conservative bankers, but you, Susanne Chishti (the CEO of Fintech Circle) and a small group of founders, created something cool and informal. I don't think I've ever seen anybody wearing a tie in any of your meetings.

I guess the first question is "What's your secret to living such an eclectic life?"

Believe me, I didn't plan any of it. It just happened. Whether growing up in a traditional country like Switzerland, or working in big corporations, I have always been a creative person less interested of following the "classic" career path.

When some of my former colleagues were completely focused on climbing the corporate ladder and some of the music world I was in touch with was completely focused on following their passion, I was doing a bit of everything. I was not really capable of stopping playing music because I loved it I was not capable either of stopping doing business because I really love building new products and experimenting new ideas.

However, when you do so many different things, it can be also harder to get tangible results. You spend 110% of your time to reach 30% of your goal, meanwhile you see so many of your peer having success in what they do or more free time. I have been concerned by this 110-30 rule for years.

What I didn't realize at the time is that following the classic path to success is effective only up to a certain point. Many of my former colleagues initially had exceptional careers in their filed, which then slowed down. Specialized engineers were too specialized to jump into top positions, or artists were too "arty" to scale their business.

It's what they call the "Leapfrog". You don't achieve something immediately because you are powering up your legs for a big jump.

In our post-industrial world, having multiple experiences is a must. Whoever is following a traditional and specialized path will be in front of you for some time, but eventually you'll pass them all in one big leap.

I would have appreciated learning these things at school where I was sometimes bored in learning what people were telling me to learn.

By the way, I think that many young and potentially great entrepreneurs or managers are in the same position. One of the main goals of an organization like Fintech Circle or Startup Home is to share our expertise with the new startups and entrepreneurs.

In Fintech Circle we spend a long time meeting the startups, simulating pitches and investor deals. In Startup Home, we aim to provide affordable accommodation and a remarkable community to startuppers and young professionals moving to big cities. They can spend time with like-minded people as well as more experienced profile. They can see as well that what they learned at school and in a traditional career is a baseline. (A/N I'm not going to ask any further questions on this subject because I have a conflict of interest: Nicolas and I are working together on Startup Home).

Talking about innovation, what's the biggest mistake related to innovation in each of these communities: the corporate world, the startup ecosystem, and the government?

These three communities share the same common mistake: they confuse technology and innovation. Technology is a vehicle for innovation, but the innovation itself comes from social interaction between people. Ideally you need to provide an entrepreneurial environment in order to ensure that people have the freedom to execute an idea.

The startup ecosystem is less guilty of this mistakes than the other two, however it's also the community with less financial and workforce resources.

So it's imperative for a country to be successful that the other two communities — corporations and politics — understand this mistake and try to build a proper environment.

The European corporate world is not very actively offering this environment for now.

The good news is that I can see some typical behavioral changes of mature industries facing disruption. Some corporation are moving from frontal competition attempt with in-house product developed into a more collaborative approach.

So, today I see more open-innovation teams in the big companies, working with external parties in a more collaborative approach, and this is very good news.

Since you are talking about the European market, last year Europe produced 13 unicorns — companies with a $1 billion plus valuation. The United States produced 22 unicorns in the same period, and their average size tends to be larger. What's your take on that?

Europe is catching up with the classic US tech player scene, and this nice to see. However there is still a big difference mainly considering that US still invest more easily and massively in a companies providing a strong customer centric vision.

The interesting consequence is that recently I have been contacted by US and Asian companies looking to spot the next potential unicorns in Europe, by having people based in London to monitor the market.

So my comment is to not worry too much. A more challenging market has its own opportunities, although they may be less obvious and harder to find.

Can you mention some of these companies interested in the European market? Or, if this is confidential information, can you at least provide a general idea of what kind of companies are looking into the European startup market?

Well, some of these companies require confidentiality at this stage, some do not, and some are very open to the idea that we talk about them. Talking of their nature, they tend to be private funds as well as big technology firms managing their own investment portfolio, such as SingTel, Verizon, T-Mobile, KPN, Sales Force or Samsung.

Most of them seem to already be heavily connected to Silicon Valley and Tel Aviv, however I can see a growing perception that

Europe might be able to produce some deals cheaper than those offered by some over-rated traditional Silicon Valley company.

Secondly, they understand that if you are successful in a very fragmented market such as Europe, there is a good chance that you will be able to distribute your innovative ideas successfully in other markets. So again, being in a more challenging market like Europe has its own positive aspects. It just requires a different approach to find them.

If someone wanted to offer the same service that you provide, what does he or she need to do?

At the moment you leverage your network with big companies, funds and startup accelerators on one side, and your contacts with the startups you advise or mentor on the other. Being in the middle means you can find strategic partnership and smart investment leads. Someone else may not have a network that's as good as yours, but they may have enough contacts to get started.

Well, first of all what a company needs and what a company wants may be different (and they usually are).

If a manager has enough contacts to provide smart investment leads, his company would really benefit from giving him a part time job. The manger has a recurrent income to live on during the initial period, then he can spend the rest of his time mentoring startups, improving his network, building a clients portfolio or investing in early stage businesses.

On the other hand, the company has access to highly relevant external innovation insights for a very low cost.

The reality however is that company often doesn't understand how badly they need these external innovations insights. The industries about to be disrupted are usually in a defensive behavioral mode. So they need a certain level of maturity and definitely some strong leaders to understand that they can't do everything by themselves.

Unfortunately, some big companies wait until the very last minute and then either disappear from the market — think about Kodak — or they spend billions to acquire already mature and expensive startups.

Instead, these companies should have employed someone to regularly scout out what was going on, and invested in low cost early stage startups.

So if someone wants to quit his 9 to 5 job to work on providing insights, building distribution channel and finding smart investment leads, he could ask his company for a part time job, but he has to be patient because the company probably doesn't know that they need him. During this waiting period, he could join an acceleration program to mentor startups just for a few hours a month, in order to get his face in the game.

Going back to your experience as an investor and as a consultant for investors, what is your top advice to whoever is building a startup with a focus on future cities tech?

I have four pieces of advice.

The first piece of advice is to avoid the big mistake that we were discussing at the beginning of the interview. Technology is a vehicle for innovation, but it's not innovation in itself. They should not be confused.

Many startups focus on their technology, but they don't solve a problem that customers really want solved. So swallow your pride and make something that may be simple but is useful.

In future cities tech this is even more important than in some other tech segments, because most of ideas will require expensive hardware, and the distribution is very often B2B (business to business) and less sexy.

The second piece of advice is to remember how fast this market moves. You should show the investors that you understand the trends and that you are building a team capable of safely navigating the future challenges that change brings.

My third piece of advice, and probably the most important for your survival, is to remember how slow the selling cycle is. It could sound counterintuitive to the previous point, but it's really like that. The market moves fast, but the sales cycle is very slow. Future cities tech is mostly B2B or B2B2C and your customers are often big companies and government agencies. Even if they love your product, it could take a year for all the departments to accept your order. You have to think now about how to pay your bills during that time, or in twelve months you might potentially be very rich but in reality very broken.

My fourth piece of advice is to carefully choose who you approach to raise funds. Startups in future cities tech tend to develop very niche products. It's not like a videogame or a social media app that anybody can understand. If you pitch to investors that don't understand the industry, or don't believe in you, they will try to force your company down an unhealthy, traditional path. You will regret having this kind of shareholder. So in future cities tech, more so than in other areas, go for the smart money.

The first three points depend on the entrepreneur, but the fourth one —focusing on smart money only— depends also on the presence of a community of investors. One of the other interviewees in this book, Jimmy Garcia, is biased against Europe because in his opinion the communities are not strong enough. What other suggestions would you give a startup about raising investments?

I would suggest looking for a specialized angel syndicate. I don't want to sound like I am over-promoting our own syndicate, but it's the example that I know best. So I hope you can excuse this conflict of interest.

At Fintech Circle we only do Fintech (financial technology) and we only have five sessions per year. So we can meet many times with the startups, they can simulate their pitch and together we improve their presentation and their focus. We also understand what they do and we try to match them with the appropriate investors.

Even in a niche area like Fintech, not all the investors are equal. Some angels may own or consult for a retail franchise and they can introduce customers to a startup offering a payment and loyalty program.

Others work with government bodies and could offer more help to a different kind of startup. And so on.

In other words, even if at Fintech Circle we are sitting on the experienced side of the table, we spend quite a lot of energy doing our homework. A startup should pretend the same from investors.

If an investor has a big name but he doesn't have the time or the inclination to help the startup, of if he doesn't understand the niche industry at all, then it's better to leave. Startups have become very trendy lately, but they can pay a very high price if they focus too much on being glamorous. This is a business, and you can be unsexy, but you still have to make money.

Sounds like more than enough. Is there anything else you would like to share or shall we call it a day?

Yes I would add two points from my personal manifesto. My call to European governments is to carry on developing friendly policies for entrepreneurs. There are many innovative minds out there, but they may find it difficult to become entrepreneurs. Innovation is made by entrepreneurs not by technology itself.

My call to whoever is thinking about becoming an entrepreneur is that startup failure rate is high, but the barrier of entry has become lower. In other words, you will probably fail the first time, but what you will learn will be highly valuable and very useful when you will start again. So you never know if you do not try.

Links

1. Fintech Circle
http://www.fintechcircle.com

2. Fintech Circle Innovate
http://www.fintechcircleinnovate.com

3. StartupHome
http://startuphome.io

Patrick Morselli

WeWork

Don't tell yourself stories. Check what your startup is really doing and where it is really going.

— Patrick Morselli

Just this month, WeWork and its global community of shared workspace has been evaluated at approximately $10 billion. That's two times the amount of Pinterest and more than three times that of Regus, an international player funded in 1989. (WeWork was funded in 2010).

From a technical point of view, these valuations are not comparable. Pinterest is an app, the valuation of WeWork is based on an investment round, while Regus is a public company, thus they are the only company in the group to have received an "official" valuation.

And yet, with a funding round of $355 million in December 2014, and another round of $433.9 million in June 2015, WeWork is a company to follow.

This is not an interview with WeWork, but with Patrick Morselli, their Head of International Expansion. What follows are his own personal views, and not the views of the company. Nonetheless in his role, Patrick has a privileged overview of what's happening in the startup community both globally and from a local point of view.

The Interview

So Patrick, thanks to your position as Head of International

Expansion at WeWork you have a privileged view of what's happening in the startup community all around the world. Moreover, WeWork is itself connected to the subject of Future Cities.

What do you think is the reason behind the recent $10 billion valuation of WeWork, and what could other companies learn from your experience?

You know, as a company we were born in New York City and we disrupted the way that New York City works.

The first reason for our valuation, I think, is that we allow people to do what they love. We allow them to get access to a workspace, to a community and services in a way that nobody else has done before. We don't provide just an office, but a place where entrepreneurs can develop their network and — why not? — have fun.

The second reason is that we have demonstrated to be able to bring the idea and the model of WeWork in other countries in the world that are not necessarily similar to the New York market. So we first showed that it can work domestically within the US, and then we have shown that it works outside the US as well.

We are trying to solve a problem, satisfy a need for not only entrepreneurs, startups and freelancers, but also for small medium and bigger companies to work in a way that makes more sense for them. It is more aligned with their values and gives access to a larger community of entrepreneurs, but we also offer them the possibility to be flexible about it, so to grow inside our space saving time and money, instead of always looking for new offices if this is a company that grows a lot.

How much do you think your community building process is part of this valuation?

I think it's a huge part. What really make WeWork very different from the competitors is that we really care about the community, we care about how the members interact, we care about the events that we do with the community, that people actually have fun and they can connect with each other and they can meet new people.

We care enough to design the space in a way that allows people to move around the space and find opportunities to meet new people and share their ideas with them.

This is a powerful trend in every workspace and accelerator. The office is no longer just the place where you work, but a place where you can find partners, investors, mentors or simply feedback for your ideas. In a way, an office was a mandatory cost in the past, today choosing the right office can be an investment. I see the same trend moving to bigger companies. In the past, it was a point of honour for a corporation to have your own building dedicated to your employees. Now many of these corporations want a presence in a building with multiple companies to access innovation and networking.

Yes, there is definitely a trend for big companies who want their employees to work in an environment that is more social and more fun, in a way that they can actually meet with other companies.

Now if a big company comes to WeWork, they have access to younger companies that are also typically more innovative. So they get access to innovation, to a lot of ideas, and to a very exciting startup environment. Which is what the bigger companies are interested in nowadays.

You are head of global expansion so you have an overview of what's going on in many countries. Do you see one hot trend common among startups? It could be even more than one trend.

I think it's hard to identify one specific trend in startups, in fact there are several trends that involve the startups world.

Startups are definitely more confident, they have a more common identity today rather than few years ago. Just five years ago the idea of a startup was mostly in the Bay area, in Silicon Valley, when as now startups are in many other cities; London, Berlin, Tel Aviv, Paris, Beijing, Tokyo, Singapore, Sidney.

Now startups are everywhere. There were startups before, but nowadays we can define them, we can see them, and they have a stronger identity, a stronger voice in terms of what they need.

Do you see the startups having specific characteristics based on the country where they are located?

Not really. Because there is so much connection nowadays, and barriers to travelling and communities worldwide are smaller and easier regardless where you are based, it is possible to take your value everywhere in the world. It is becoming easier for startups to not necessarily be linked to the country or culture of origin.

On the other hand, the ecosystem is still important at the beginning. I see many startups moving to London, to Berlin and to a few other cities, but I don't see it happening the other way around. Things change when you have traction and revenue, but picking the right city to start in is still very important. At least, this is my opinion. What are your thoughts about that?

Definitely when the startup needs funding, they move where the funding is. It doesn't mean necessarily that the city is richer but that the ecosystem is more into startups, with a landscape of venture capitals and angel investors.

But there are also startups that are relatively indifferent to funding, because they are bootstrapping and they are not interested in founding, or they are of a certain size and generating revenue, and for them whether they are or not in a specific city is not so important.

So I don't see a trend of startups that are going into cities that are richer, on the contrary I definitely see that enabling teams to communicate when they are typically located in different geographical locations around the world, is a startup trend by itself.

So there are different trends in startups, and they are happening at the same time.

Last but not least, what's your one suggestion to a new entrepreneur? I don't want to say young entrepreneur, because more and more people are becoming entrepreneurs at all ages.

Be aware of what's happening around you and don't tell yourself stories. Check what your startup is really doing and where it is really going. If you are telling yourself stories about your company and your success, try to confirm that story through objective data.

Fundamentally the media are very mono-thematic. They can easily focus on a few very successful startups, and they insist on them. Forget these stories, and be aware of what's really happening in your market. Be aware of where you want to go with your company. It's your story, and you can control it only if you can confirm it through real and credible data.

Links

Company website
http://wework.com

Where Can I Buy My Knight Rider? Insights on Driverless Cars

Interlude

Driverless cars are not yet on the market, but four US States have already passed a dedicated legislation to allow their use. Someone non politically correct could point out that it took 30 years for just one State to recognize same sex marriage. From 1970 when the first couple went to a Minnesota Court and lost the case, to 2000 when Governor Howard Dean made Vermont the first state in the U.S. to give full marriage rights to same-sex couples.

Cars and marriage have nothing in common, so I am not going down this path. I will just point out that the driverless car industry is currently valued at 2.4 billion US dollars and a 2015 report by Lux Research estimates that the market will grow 50 times in just 15 years, with a valuation of \$102 billion by 2030. These numbers may have influenced the politicians' decisions more than their love for innovation and technology.

Being Unsexy Is Attractive

The most famous player in the driverless car industry is of course

Google. The idea of jumping into a car, playing with your smartphone for the entire trip, and leaving the car to park itself, is so attractive to the media that news about Google Cars comes out every week.

There is another market less sexy but potentially as big and strategic: trucks. Just this year, the first driverless truck hit the road in Nevada. The first company to get the approval of Governor Brian Sandoval is Daimler, which own Mercedes-Benz, among other companies.

Trucks are not as glamorous as cars, but they are still critical for the economy. After all, you can move around a city without a car thanks to public transport, but you can't move goods without trucks. In fact trains can move from station to station, but not to an the end point.

Martin Ford in his book *Rise of the Robots* writes about driverless trucks, "the staggering destructive potential of these vehicles probably means that someone is going to remain in the driver's seat for the foreseeable future". In other words, humans are going to become backup for robots. Now that's interesting.

Keep Your Enemies Closer

Moving back to cars, Google has unexpected allies in Uber and the other apps providing driver services. Uber keeps 20% of the fee as a lead generation, and gives 80% to the drivers. It's easy to imagine that Uber will benefit greatly from moving their fleet to driverless cars. On the other hand, because of the worldwide presence of Uber, they could be Google's best customer, spreading Google Cars worldwide.

This mutual interest has not being missed by the executives of the two companies. In 2013 Google Venture—the venture capital of Google—invested 258 million into Uber, with the probable return of having Uber purchase Google Cars.

Uber's smartphone apps for drivers and passengers are based on Google Maps, giving Google inside access to the transportation patterns of their ally. So Uber was obviously not happy when at the beginning of this year rumors suggested that Google was developing their own taxi app. A Bloomberg title at the time stated "Google and Uber are going to War". The crisis has cooled down since then, but in the meantime Uber is apparently building a team to develop their own maps. Not only that, but Uber is launching their own research center to develop driverless cars in partnership with Carnegie Mellon University, one of the top campuses in the world for robotics research.

The two companies are not really enemies, nor allies. Silicon Valley has historical examples whereby potential competitors helped each other; the most famous case being the investment of Microsoft in Apple when the latter company was going to risk bankruptcy.

Jonathan Zittrain, law professor and co-founder of the Berkman Center for Internet & Society at Harvard University said "It's a good example of co-petition".

There is another quote that I found even more appropriate, from Lord Palmerston, Foreign Minister of the British Empire in the distant 1840's "We have no eternal allies, and we have no perpetual enemies. Our interests are eternal and perpetual, and those interests it is our duty to follow."

An Unstoppable Force

Part of my job is to try to anticipate innovations to help investors and big companies in their decision. When it comes to driverless cars, there are many elements that make their growth in the market unstoppable.

1. Saving Lives

The first element supporting driverless cars is of course the potential number of lives saved. A typical statistic states that approximately 90 percent of deaths on the road are caused by human error. Remove the human, and you'll remove the error. The phrase has a worrying double meaning, especially visible for whoever follows sci-fiction, but the truth behind it can't be questioned.

2. Humans Don't Want the Job

The new generation is less excited about owing a car and driving than generations before them. But the real point is not connected to cars, but to business trucks. The American Trucking Association estimates a shortage of 240,000 drivers by 2022. Humans don't want to drive a truck for long journeys, especially knowing that new speed limits could force the truck to maintain a low velocity (in the USA it is usually 64 mph) thus reducing the number of trips and therefore the drivers' profits.

3. Companies Want Profit

Sadly this is the stronger element of the three in favour of a future of driverless cars. Companies want profits, and machines are cheaper than humans. No matter if a company owns trucks or, like Uber, runs private driver services, they can save enormously without a driver.

4. The Court System

Ironically the court system that is trying to protect the rights of the drivers is only accelerating the extinction of the entire category. This year the Californian Labor Commission ruled that Uber drivers are employees, while the company sustains that they are independent contractors and the app is a simple marketplace to put customers and drivers in contact. In this specific case, the Labor Commission ordered the company to reimburse the drivers for costs incurred while driving for Uber. These are minor costs, but the ruling may set a precedent for the responsibility of the company in every aspect, including insurance and health assistance.

At the moment, Uber point out that the Commission's decision is an exception, and they can count on favourable rulings in 5 States. But, if you match this risk with the consideration that the driver keeps 80% of the fee and split the remaining 20% with Uber, it's easy to imagine that Uber, Lyft and similar companies are potential investors in, and customers of, driverless technology.

In the short run, this ruling is going to create some extra difficulties for Uber. In the long run, the ruling is simply going to speed up the acquisition from Uber and its competitors of a fleet of driverless cars. The Commission is killing the very same job belonging to drivers that they want to protect. It doesn't mean that they are wrong; it just means that sometimes there are unstoppable forces. Driverless cars are one of them.

When Can I Buy One?

Since the success of the hit TV show Knight Rider, the public has been crying out for a car that can drive itself. This is finally happening. There are slightly conflicting estimates regarding the exact year when driverless cars will be on the market, but all the experts agree on one point: they will be available "soon".

DMVcom reports that "Google is confident that it will be able to launch a self-driving car by 2025, and Nissan is even more optimistic, saying that it will bring an autonomous car to the market by 2020."

Quoting Cisco technology trend watchers, in 5 years it will cost us more to drive our cars than to let them drive us.

No matter the exact time, it's quite probable that the generation attending high school today could be the last generation to apply for a driving licence.

Links

1. Uber Technologies Inc. Vs Barbara Berwick
Labor Commission Appeal
http://futurecitiesbook.com/116

2. Download "Rise of the Robots: Technology and the Threat of a Jobless Future"
by Martin Ford
http://futurecitiesbook.com/117

3. DMVcom
http://www.dmv.com

Goncalo Agra Amorin

BGI / MIT Portugal

For a first time entrepreneur it is extremely easy to become entangled in what we call "startup tourism" events that will just soak up the entrepreneurs' money and will get them nowhere.

—Goncalo Agra Amorin

If you are looking for an expert in smart cities in Europe, Goncalo Agra Amorin is "the Man". Venture capitalist, director of one of the biggest acceleration programs for smart cities, expert in innovation for the European Union, I'm not going to add anything else, since this is already a very, very long interview.

The Interview

Goncalo, you work in venture capital at BGI S.A. and at the same time you are the executive director of MIT Portugal IEI—the biggest startup accelerator in Portugal. This is one of the few programs in Europe that attracts entrepreneurs from all over the world.

Why do you think foreign startups are moving to Portugal and not, for instance, to Silicon Valley?

And what do you think other countries should do to mirror your success?

My responsibility within the MIT Portugal, Innovation & Entrepreneurship initiative (IEI) was to come up with a novel model.

We kicked off this activity in 2010 as a "venture competition" with €1 million aiming at attracting and awarding some of the most promising ventures in the world, in 4 verticals (Medtech & health IT; Smart cities; Enterprise IT & Smart data and Ocean "blue" economy).

We got hundreds of applicants from nearly 40 countries and with this experiment we proved that there was plenty of space for innovation and "connecting the dots" in different entrepreneurial ecosystems.

For instance, you saw companies from Brazil in the medical device space wishing to enter the European market and companies from Europe in the Medtech and ICT sectors applying to enter the US market place.

In both of these instances, the Founders wanted to explore and leverage our global network with over 200 expert mentors from all over the world and our more than 15 thousand business contacts. So, in effect we acted as a glue and connector for these tech-based *globalpreneurs* (as we like to call this new breed of global entrepreneur) and the marketplace.

When did you decide to upgrade this competition into an accelerator and fund?

BGI as an accelerator, the acronym for Building Global Innovators, was launched in early 2013. You can see it as a spillover effect of the MIT Portugal program.

We wanted to leverage the results we had attained in under 3 years and saw the opportunity to create a "hybrid" accelerator with the help of one of Portugal's largest public VC, Caixa Capital. They brought in an annual commitment of €1 million (A/N $1.1M) in non dilutive financing to the top 4 ventures in the batch of 20 accelerated ventures every year.

Caixa also retained a right of first refusal upon series A with an associated discount of 15% in the round caped at €1.5 million. It was a simple model and innovative in its own right, having been praised by top VC's all over the world.

The underlying premise of Building Global Innovators accelerator is that Portugal is capable of world class "deep innovation".

Silicon Valley is, and will be for many years to come, an important reference ecosystem in the creation and support of new ventures. It is a powerful magnet bringing together great ideas, talent and global capital.

One of the quotes I use when I mentor startups, is "The best revenge is to prove them wrong"

Indeed. Many times we were told that it would be impossible to achieve the critical mass (from Portugal) to launch new ventures and support them. At the same time, we realized that the valley value proposition would soon be challenged with unprecedented scalability issues, such as rocketing property prices, which would drive up wages even more and this would create space for disruption at the lower end of the value curve.

In turn this would attract more and more wannabes and false positives. In the Valley you get the best and the worst in the world: top talent but also the opposite. It's not all roses. You have to be able to navigate the ecosystem well and for that you need, more than ever before, the right connections and networks.

For a first time entrepreneur it is extremely easy to become entangled in what we call "startup tourism" events that will just soak up the entrepreneurs' money and will get them nowhere.

The opposite is also true, I believe. Sometimes it's not a competition between keeping a talent in Europe or in Asia or anywhere outside the Valley. The real deal is growing new talent, no matter if they end up moving to another country later.

Sergey Brin of Google was born in Russia, Elon Musk of Paypal and Tesla in South Africa, they moved to the Valley but the entire world uses their innovations.

I believe that there are many Sergeys and Elons around the world who never discover their talents because they didn't grow in the appropriate ecosystem. That's why it is so important to build local ecosystems, in connection, and not in competition, with Silicon Valley, and—why not?—Singapore, or Lagos or San Paolo. Don't you think?

Yes, in fact there is a lot of talent emerging in many European cities— and for that matter in other geographies—that is being wasted due to the lack of "ecosystem connectivity" and networking opportunities.

So, there you go, the international mentors, the funding structure and the undiscovered talents, altogether this was our secret sauce that we used to develop the BGI hybrid acceleration model.

So, all we did was to execute on these asymmetries. In other words we said to ourselves: what if we keep the technology talent (back office) at the origin and move the management, business development, and sales to the US (front office)?

Maybe with this model we could achieve 5x to 10x savings on startup development costs in the initial years. In practice it all boils down to this: When a competitor from the valley raises US$1 million, what this means for one company in the same space — this time based in Portugal — is that they need to raise €100k to €200k to get to a similar stage of company development.

If you consider that 2/3 of the financing provided at this stage (seed) is based on convertibles, then what you effectively have is a model that is much more effective in terms of early stage dilution. Moreover, a lot of these European and non-US based companies do get venture financing from top global VC's series A at pre-money valuations of over $US10 million. Both founders and Venture Capitals love this as they appreciate clean cap tables and straightforward due diligence, which in turn keeps everyone's lawyers fees down.

So, in this context it is easy to see why the BGI model could never have emerged in Silicon Valley, the UK, Germany, or France etc. The answer is simple: because in all these places you have a minimal critical mass in all the components you need to have a full fledged entrepreneurial and innovation ecosystem, from ideation through to company formation to exit.

In other words "(Small) size matters"

In small countries like Portugal, Ireland, and Scandinavian countries like Sweden (and to a certain extent Italy) you have smallish home "markets for these components" which means that you have to build on complementarity from day one.

Israel got this about 20 years and executed. They are now able to attract top VCs to their country as they have a sufficiently mature ecosystem. It takes time.

I really feel we can take the BGI model to another level by

leveraging a highly connected hub strategy. We are at the moment planning our third phase of growth, more to follow soon.

The next question is sensitive and I hope you can answer it. From 2014 you have served as an expert in innovation for the European Union. It means, among other things, that you are asked to evaluate public funds dedicated to startups and other small to medium enterprises.

What do you think the European Union is doing well? And what do you think they can improve on?

Europe is an extremely diverse and rich space, both culturally, historically, and technologically, but also in the way you conduct business, and their traits etc. Europe is far from a homogeneous space when compared to the US. Europe has also a big problem with stalled growth combined with high unemployment, which is something that is threatening its own existence.

Even though the Eurocrats may pray, even after 30 years of the creation of the "single market" and more recently with the single currency, Europe is quite a way from being a united marketplace. It is a collection of small and fragmented marketplaces, which favor large companies and hamper the growth of small, nimble startups.

The regulatory hurdles are high (legal issues, for instance), which means that for an entrepreneur with limited resources getting into every single country in the EU becomes a great challenge, and is also a very expensive and inefficient process time wise.

In BGI we have experienced just this. Being a "Euro-land patriotic" has almost resulted in killing a few of our fragile startups. A combination of lack of urgency, the lack of the right attitude towards collaboration with new ventures, risk aversion and different regulatory environments proves almost fatal for most startups in Europe, when scaling up.

We also have evidence to support that. When you think about it, many of the successful European startups have been acquired (Eg. Skype, Nokia, HockeyApp, Mojang, Vision Factory, Deepmind Technologies, Rangespan, DrawElements, Botobjects, ShareMyPlaylists, etc etc) or acqui-hired — which is more problematic — by US counterparts.

The irony of the situation is that when you look in detail at the sources of the venture funders in the US based VC funds you unleash a surprising finding: a considerable proportion of the dollars invested come from Europe! Isn't that amazing?

So, there you have the market talking: the private investors from Europe that are looking for high returns for their buck prefer to invest in the US when compared to other geographies. I think this is a very clear argument, which deserves some serious attention from our Eurocrats.

If you can give the Eurocrats one piece of actionable advice , what would it be?

My advice to them is to read a book by a gentleman called Clayton Christensen, The Innovators Dilemma and then imagine they are the CEO of a large firm which is called the European Commission.

Are you optimistic?

I am not, sadly, so optimistic. Big companies which are heavily subsidized in the space, aerospace and automotive spaces, for instance, in 10 years will suffer serious competition from newcomers from Asia, particularly China. Companies like Airbus could be seriously threatened in the next decade by the Chinese and other newcomers. All the right ingredients for an innovator's dilemma are in place.

Having said that, Europe has a highly educated population and some advanced science. We just don't know how to commercialize it on a global scale. As I am involved in commercializing activities on both sides of the Atlantic there's no doubt in my mind that Europe has a long way to go.

The VCs tend to be local, smallish fund investors and there's very little cross border activity. There are very few funds in Europe that are run by former entrepreneurs; most have a finance background which does not help. In turn there is a higher mortality than necessary in the startup formation and early stages, as it is easy for startuppers to reinvent the wheel with less smart investors.

Europe is at least 10 years behind the US in the art of

commercialization when compared with the US. Horizon 2020 provides some hope with the SME instrument, FTI and other instruments but I fear it will be not enough to have a huge impact on commercialization of new science, technology and Venture Capital to aid bridging the valley of death.

I believe Europe should look at devising more aggressive measures and very concrete strategies aimed at startups & spinouts that could help lower the risk aversion barriers by creating better conditions for first time founders. For instance an instrument similar to SME but oriented for startups up to 5 years old would be a good starting point. Another area that urgently needs tackling is to provide the right incentives for more cross border VC investment. And the EU has the right instrument to do that via the EIF, for instance.

What's the current status of your startups?

Most of our companies can be expected to fail in a 10 year horizon although the survival rate after 5 editions — thus 5 years — still close to 70%.

We expect to have at least one unicorn in this horizon. We like to think along the lines of achieving long term impact and avoid trends and too much buzz.

The talent available in the Cambridge US ecosystem (A/N BGI runs their program in conjunction with Cambridge University) when compared to other places is extremely sophisticated and it is always possible to find the right person with the right background and skillset within a few square miles.

It is also the only place I know in the world where you can fit in 8 or more half an hour (in person) meetings per day. And this is only possible due to the extreme density and concentration of thousands of startups in a couple of miles radius.

You don't find that in the valley, it spreads for over 50 miles, which means you have to drive around, which means that you need at least 1h in between meetings for travel. In Cambridge and Boston the furthest you can be is typically an under 15 minute trip and it normally means just crossing the street or getting into the elevator.

All this translates into the following: if you are a startupper, you can learn more in the 2 week BGI accelerator in Cambridge than in 1 year lost in and around Europe! And that is all an accelerator is about: acceleration, right connections and networks that can help you build a great product faster than the competition!

This amalgamation of resources results from top universities such as MIT and Harvard, but also from other dozens of universities and top notch research centers.

You tend to walk everywhere which means that you won't be able to avoid bumping into great people that, if you are smart, you will get to know.

In my interviews I usually ask the question "If you had $10 million to invest in startups in Future Cities, what areas would you pick?" Well, you have access to $10 million. In what areas of Future Cities do you think investors will be more active in?

Almost every process I look at in a city, from water distribution and treatment to garbage collection to mobility can and ought to be improved. Governments can become much more efficient machines in the way they spend tax payers' money.

I truly believe that more information based on M2M and IoT will be able to much better educate our politicians about where and how they should spend our money, and also in terms of transparency of procurement processes and accountability. And this is an area where I see a great opportunity.

More informed decisions leveraging on a combination of already existing technologies such as Artificial Intelligence (AI), machine learning, smart data, dashboards, fraud detection etc. The possibilities are immense. BGI alumni startups such as Veniam Works and Movvo are doing just that and grew from an idea to full stack companies and multi million dollar businesses in just 2 or 3 years.

Tech can be expensive. Do you see the gap between cities in rich countries and poor countries growing in the future?

As far as I see it, cities are made of 2 basic pillars: people and physical resources, which come with a specific location in a given point in the globe. If you can get these ingredients right you can even create new cultures.

If I was a governor in a poorer country I think a great experiment could be creating the foundations, for instance, of a startup city where every process is thorough and designed by entrepreneurs.

Such a city could be dedicated to frugal innovation which is a process that is very much underestimated (so far) but that is, potentially, able to generate tons of impact with very little resources and disruptive technologies. So to a certain extent, such cities in emerging countries could and ought to play a very important role in shaping the future of such countries. Hence, they could also help to bridge the gap, sure.

Last but not least, what advice would you give to your younger self??

Do not reinvent the wheel and before you start spending money on building up a product make sure that you have done your homework in terms of mapping out the competition (existing and emerging).

Once you have done that, you will be able to see the opportunities and challenges that lie ahead in a much more realistic and convincible manner towards your prospective customers and future investors as well. Smart cities are a complex beast and you will need all the help you can get.

We have designed BGI as an accelerator which can provide extremely valuable help in all of the above. In fact we dedicate over 1000 hours of our expert mentors' time to each of our companies per year. And that is not an easy thing for anyone to do. But I believe that the results speak for themselves.

Links

1. BGI - Building Global Innovators
http://buildingglobalinnovators.eu

2. MIT Portugal
http://www.mitportugal.org

3. Caixa Capital

http://caixacapital.pt

4. Download "The Innovator's Dilemma: When New Technologies Cause Great Firms to Fail"
by Clayton M. Christensen
http://futurecitiesbook.com/118

5. Veniam Works - An Internet of Moving Things
https://veniam.com

6. Movvo - Tracing the Path to Retail Excellence
https://movvo.com

James Swanston

Voyage Control

Business can be pretty pressurized, and yeah, there are a lot of things that can go wrong, but it's not quite the same as being on the front line in Afghanistan getting shot at. (Serving in a war zone) helps to provide a bit of perspective.

—Captain James Swanston

This is an interview with James Swanston, founder and CEO of Voyage Control. I am not going to write anything in the introduction, because I don't want to spoil the surprises in the interview. There will be quite a few unusual questions and answers. I'm sure you'll enjoy it.

The Interview

James, you have an unusual background for a tech startup. Let's start by introducing yourself.

So my name is James Swanston, founder and CEO of Voyage Control. Originally from Australia. I was involved in my first business at university in the wine industry. That was my first experience of distribution and logistics. After university, I actually joined the Australian Army.

James you are being unusually humble, it may be the presence of a recorder. For the readers, when James says "I joined the Australian Army" he means he served in three different combat zones and he was awarded the US bronze star for his service in Iraq.

Yeah, I've served in East Timor that was my first combat zone. I was in the Australian Peacekeeping Force, when East Timor got their independence. I served in Iraq back in 2004, and then I was in Afghanistan in 2009, 2010. So I've had some really interesting experiences in war zones, which has been fascinating in many respects and also quite tough.

What's the most useful skill you learned in the military that you can use in a startup? If there is one.

That brings up an interesting point about the military. Business can be pretty pressurized and yeah, there are a lot of things that can go wrong and everything like that, but it's not quite the same as being on the front line in Afghanistan getting shot at. It's an existential experience when you're in a war zone. It helps to provide a bit of perspective that even though things go bad in business, it's not life and death.

You could have listed any kind of practical skill—such as leadership or teamwork or even logistics—but the first skill that came to your mind was, in a way, spiritual.

It may sound like a cliché, but I met many successful entrepreneurs when I was a consultant, and the super successful were never just about money. They always have a sort of philosophical view of their business.

Could you list a few practical skills learned in the military as well?

My experience in the military has actually been really valuable in many aspects of the business. I've commanded quite a lot of people in the military, so I think the leadership training you get in the military is invaluable for that.

And it's also invaluable in terms of understanding the things that you need to do to help build a robust team. Teamwork is very important in the military and it's very important in a business context, so that's very valuable.

And another incredibly valuable skill in the military that you learn is about delegation, because ultimately if you're trying to build a scalable successful business, you need to be able to delegate and trust your team to execute things.

A number of our team are ex-military as well and again that's useful, because I have a common background to some of the guys, most of us have all served in war zones.

This is also interesting from another point of view. The social imaginary of a startup founder is a brilliant and weird programmer or an economic genius. As a result, many young men and women may turn down a practical job, because they want to start their career directly at a high level.

Indeed. So my first experience with logistics in the wine industry was a very manual, laborious process, a lot of stuff was done on paper, using faxes, and that's 20 years ago and that still hasn't changed a huge amount since. That's really informed my thinking about the business.

And in the military, again it's about being able to know what's going on and have real time situational awareness and a common operating picture, so you can make far better decisions.

That experience very much shaped how I look at the logistics industry, because I just see it as a highly fragmented industry where people are not making the right decisions, because they don't have the right information and therefore it's really inefficient. And you don't learn this at school, but by doing it.

They say "Weapons win battles, but logistics win wars"

Yeah, absolutely.

What about your team? How big it is and how big a team do you think that a startup needs to build at the beginning?

We're sitting on about 18 people in the business now, and I think that will grow to about 30 before the end of the year.

We are from many different countries and a lot of different backgrounds, and I think having diversity in a team is actually very valuable, for just getting different perspectives on life and business.

We have members of the team in London, in New York and in various other places.

How is the team important in achieving success versus having a disruptive idea?

Many people have good ideas but really it's about how you execute. So it's all about bringing together the people with the right skills at the right time, who can execute a vision and who are flexible enough to adapt to changes.

Because in a startup you can be sure that you will change often. We have completely changed what we do, we have changed our branding, we've changed almost everything.

Many startups have to recognize that whilst you start with one idea, you have to quickly iterate until you get you product-market fit.

Flexibility is a key part of a business. And you achieve flexibility only when you have the right team.

I've seen you in action in the last six months and you clearly inspire people. But who's your own inspiration?

My childhood hero was Captain James Cook, who sailed through unknown seas looking for what ended up becoming Australia, back in 1770. And the idea of guys going out on small wooden ships 250 years ago to explore the world, I think just always fascinated me. So guys like that have always been big heroes of mine.

An interesting example in the entrepreneurial space is a guy called Norm Larsen that most people haven't heard of, but he was an industrial chemist who was trying to come up with a solution for helping rockets getting in to and out of space without getting too much ice on them. So he tried to come up with a solution to do this and he failed 39 times, and his 40th attempt he got it right. And that product is called WD-40 which basically everyone uses around the world.

And the interesting story there is really that sometimes you just have to try repeatedly until you get your successful outcome, and sometimes that successful outcome is very different from what you initially envisioned. So that's just an interesting little example of the importance of determination in doing business. There's a range of people that I draw inspiration from, but they're probably two good examples.

What's your relationship with trying and failing?

I've failed in one of my businesses and it was really tough. It's not nice losing all your money, my stock broker referred to it as my million dollar MBA.

Then you pick up the pieces and start again. It's like when you fall off a horse, the best thing to do to jump back on and start riding again.

The whole thing about failure is still funny though. People who aren't entrepreneurs don't understand that. And even back in Australia, the idea of failing was pretty toxic for a lot of people to consider.

Let's switch to the future. What do you thing is going to happen in 5-10 years?

Well yeah, I think the whole increasing urbanization is a really significant issue. As populations become more about moving to big cities and consumption is going up, there's going to be a lot of requests for big changes about providing services in a smarter way to these masses.

At the same time, there are real issues around climate change.

The next 5 to 10 years is going to be very important in terms of how we — as humans — try and adapt to a very changing environment. And how do we maintain standards of living, given that so many people are moving into these big cities?

Technology will be able to assist with that, if we use it in the correct way.

In greater detail, what do you think is going to be a real disruptive or game changing technology? We can formulate the question in another way. If you have $10 million to invest, and you can't invest in your own startup, what would be your choice?

I think it's all about investing in macro trends. What are the technologies that are going to enable cities to flourish? I think it comes down to smart management of buildings, 3D printing, and other technologies that can create a smarter city. Any technology that does that is part of a big macro trend and in theory should do really well.

Links

Company website
http://voyagecontrol.com

How Millennials Are Going to Reshape Your City

Interlude

The future is not something we enter. The future is something we create.
— Leonard I. Sweet

This year, 75.3 million Millennials (born 1981-1997) are going to hit the market, overtaking the number of Boomers (the generation born after the Second World War, 1946 to 1964). The Millennials, also nicknamed Generation Y by the media, are going to be the largest generation in history, with the highest number of potential customers —at least in the West—and by 2020 they are estimated to be half of the workforce. Their desires can shape entire product lines, and they will definitively shape our cities.

Generation Y have different aspirations, but one in particular is going to disrupt the urban scenario: they are the first generation not particularly interested in buying a car.

Our entire system of cities is built around a society of car owners, with offices and leisure downtown, and houses in the suburbs, connected by a massive network of roads. For a long time, buying a new car has been one of the top ambitions of a typical male worker. Not anymore!

However, there are some differing opinions. The prestigious magazine Bloomberg published an article entitled "Millennials Embrace Cars, Defying Predictions of Sales Implosion". Just one minor problem, the author was wrong.

The analysis that excited car makers and car lovers is based on one assumption: Millennials bought 3.7 million cars in the United States in one year, against 3.3 million cars bought by the previous Generation X, therefore Millennials love cars.

What the author forgot to check was the total number of customers in each generation. Millennials are a group way bigger than Generation X. In reality the number of car owners drops from nearly 74% of Generation X to less than 48% in Generation Y (the Millennials). This reality check shows a different story that could be quite scary for auto manufacturers. Not by coincidence, the smarter car manufactures have already announced research and development in the area of driverless cars and trucks.

John Zimmer, co-founder of Lyft, estimates that most Millennials won't own a car in 5 years. This trend goes on in the following generation. In fact Generation Z, born between the end of the '90s and mid 2000s, are also more interested in buying gadgets and into travelling than buying a car.

73.5 million voters will definitely have a say about the future of their cities. They will push urban scenarios towards more public transport, more driverless cars and more bicycle routes, as they tend to be more environmentally aware than previous generations.

A New Car, a Nice House and a Garden with a Dog

The second characteristic of Millennials that is going to disrupt cities is their lack of passion for owning a home. A new car and a nice house with a garden has been the dream for so many generations of employees. The collapse of the industrial system and the rise of online workers and freelancers has changed that.

The Millennials, and the following Generation Z, are not as interested in buying a house as much as previous generations. They have the technology to work anywhere, and they live in a global interconnected market. Many of them don't want to be stuck in a city with a property and a mortgage, but be free to travel at will.

In reality that many of them will not move to other cities and countries, despite the fact that they have the technology to do so. Technology is just a small part of the equation; ambition and commitment are way more important. Still this idea of freedom is very popular and it's going to impact the real estate market and therefore the structure of any city.

The Forever College

Jean M. Twenge, professor of psychology at San Diego University and author of the book "Generation Me", points to a generation of individualist, narcissist and entitled men and women. Her book is a must read as it's based not on stereotypes but data from surveys.

The combination of these characteristics plus a third point that will reshape cities is that narcissists and individualists—not necessarily in the bad sense of the words— want to live downtown, even if they can't afford it. They want to be extremely independent, thus they prefer to live alone, but they are narcissistic enough to feel lonely.

The sum of the three parts—expensive location, living alone, feeling lonely—is pushing major cities towards a new kind of real estate, "micro-apartments". These are very small and self sufficient apartments, sometimes measuring just 9 to 20 square meters, located downtown, in a building mainly inhabited by other young professionals.

The Millennials can come home after a day at work and spend the evening alone surfing the Internet or watching Netflix. If he feels lonely, he just needs to move to one of the common areas where other lonely young professionals are also looking for occasional companionship.

Friendships are born, business relationships are created, all in an individualistic environment without family ties.

This is what I call in my reports for big companies, the "Forever College". In these sessions of "innovation management" —a popular buzz word used to describe chatting about business chats—I like to make it clear that the personal aspirations above are much more powerful in shaping the market than any new technology. A startup could invent the Star Trek teleport tomorrow, and Millennials would still want to live downtown in a Forever College.

Meet Joe Millennial

Joe Millennial is a character who shows up in many of my innovation keynotes. When Joe leaves the office, he taps his smartphone to inform his smart apartment that he's coming home.

The apartment checks Joe's location (through his smartphone's GPS), checks the bicycle locker in the building (the bicycle is not there, thus Joe is riding his bike today), accesses Google Maps and City Mapper, and the traffic data, in a fraction of a second, and decides the best time to switch on the heaters to save energy yet welcome Joe home to a warm apartment.

Depending on Joe's routine, or by an extra tap on the smartphone, the apartment could switch on only a heater in one room, because Joe is not going to use the other rooms, saving money and the environment at the same time.

The apartment could switch on the microwave or order a healthy organic take away, that will be ready just a few seconds before Joe arrives home.

This scenario would have been science-fiction or a scene from the luxurious life of a millionaire just a few years ago. Today not only can it be done, but it can be done for a very low cost.

Landlords or real estate developers can add smart features and the Internet of Things to their estates with a small sum, attracting Millennials and even more importantly, retaining Millennials in case of economic downturn.

If a bubble explodes, or there is an economic crisis, the previous generation used to move to a cheaper suburb, and use their car only for longer trips. On the contrary, Millennials will probably not leave their fancy neighbourhoods, eventually saving money due to they didn't buy a car and they don't have a mortgage. They will not leave a smart apartment for a "normal" building, even if they have to pay a premium price.

Home Is Where the Laptop Is

Generation Y and Z have the technology to be digital nomads. Not all of them, but many of them. This is another element that may impact heavily on the real estate business. Soon we'll see rent offers like "Pay a fixed amount and live anywhere you want".

Our friend Joe Millennial, from London, could decide to spend two weeks in Singapore for a conference and some tourism without booking a hotel or Airbnb accommodation. He will simply go to a building in Singapore owned by the same company that rents his usual apartment, and use the same smart key to access a local apartment with the same features; Wi-Fi, laundry service, etc. In the meantime, a young manager from Kuala Lumpur just arrived in London is enjoying Joe's apartment.

Joe does not even need to carry luggage. Companies like Dufl can store a luggage with everything you need, and ship it wherever you want as soon as you tap on your smartphone. The luggage arrives when you arrive. And when you leave, you can leave the luggage behind. Dufl will take your clothes, clean them, and store them ready for your next trip.

Today Dufl describe itself as a luxury service, but it's easy to imagine that the service will become more common and cost less sooner rather than later.

Of the four Millennial characteristics shaping the cities, digital nomadism is the most fascinating but the least powerful. Because even if today technology allows almost everybody to work online, not many people and companies will choose that path. People still love to live in cities.

On the other hand, the niche group that choose this path will be very committed. Companies developing services for this vertical market will find a limited but very loyal customers base.

Links

1. Pew Research Center
http://www.pewresearch.org

2. Download "Generation Me"
by Jean M. Twenge
http://futurecitiesbook.com/119

3. Dufl
http://www.dufl.com

Nic Shulman

Block Dox

The Internet of Things is going to go way beyond your fridge telling you when it needs restocking.

—Nic Shulman

Nic Shulman—CEO and founder at Block Dox—is a lawyer turned publisher and event organizer, and now founder of a tech startup. If you think that lawyers can't be cool, you should meet Nic.

He founded the UK's leading publishing and events business about property management: News on the Block. They publish a bi-monthly magazine about residential building management, and organize professional conferences, training and events for property managers.

This could kill any workaholic, but not a lawyer. In fact Nic is the organizer of two award ceremonies for the industry including the Property Management Awards, many other conferences and training events and is now the founder of Block Dox.

The Interview

Hi Nic, I've already introduced you and your company to the readers. Before we move on to the business, I have a personal question for you. How did a lawyer decide to launch a tech startup?

I guess exactly because I was a lawyer. We lawyers are trained to find problems and fix them.

I run a publishing and events business about property

management: News on the Block. So for many years, I've had a front row seat in the problems and issues faced by building users and operators, how this can be improved and what best practice should look like.

You have a degree in law and you're a qualified lawyer. And yet you turned down an offer from a prestigious Wall Street law firm to become a publisher—I know you prefer to keep their name confidential. Can you identify a specific moment when you decided to take a direction in life?

I could come out with an amazing story set in an exotic country, but in reality everything started in my own apartment. During my studies, I was living in an apartment building. The business of real estate hasn't changed much in the last generation and it's ready for disruption. The need for change is in front of our eyes, if you know where to look.

I guess I was just looking at my building with the eyes of a lawyer. The legal profession trains you to find every small issue in a case that needs to be fixed. Lawyers are great in finding problems, but they typically have an extremely risk averse personality which means legal practice can be quite a stifling environment, particularly for innovation.

I decided that in order to fix that problem, I had to look outside the legal profession. I am still a member of the Law Society, and there are many aspects of law which I enjoy. I have friends and family in the legal profession, but my interests extend beyond legal practice alone.

So when I got an offer from Wall Street, I was forced to decide. In or out?

And you chose "Out"!

Correct! Fundamentally, law is about helping people and problem solving. I had a virtual conveyor belt of clients coming through my office with one problem after another which I would diligently help them to resolve.

However, instead of advising clients one by one, I realized in addition to continuing my legal practice I could help more people and solve bigger problems outside the legal profession too.

From lawyer to publisher, organizing awards and events. Now working in a geek environment. Can you describe the best and worst aspects of each of them?

Lawyers have many transferable skills which are also useful in a tech startup environment, for example: attention to detail; prioritization and organization of workload; understanding value of time; and of course, working late and at weekends.

Law is also about rules, and legal practice is well structured with tried and tested methods and processes for doing things within defined boundaries.

Technology is similar, particularly when it comes to coding and development. There are also plenty of unwritten conventions, a concept lawyers are familiar with.

Yet, technology has a creative flexibility you don't find with legal practice. Labels such as 'hacking the system' and 'being disruptive' — probably coined by frustrated lawyers! — describe exciting opportunities for being creative and innovating and show how the perceived norm can change quickly to a new accepted reality.

Let's go back to your business. Or I should say businesses (plural). Could you tell us a bit more about Block Dox?

Block Dox is an award winning platform for enhancing building management with real time and predictive intelligence.

This is delivered via an app, and various IoT sensors to detect and measure KPI's from the way the building is used and operated. These are then analyzed and reports presented to the building operators through a dashboard hub so they can make better, more informed decisions about building performance. In turn, better building performance leads to better business performance for the firms owning and managing property, and a better experience for building users.

The market is huge and ready to be taken. Building management is complex and costly. Building users expect high standards of customer service, with mobile access to information 'on the go'. Building operators want to manage and maintain their portfolio in the most efficient way possible.

This is the "secret sauce question". Why you? Why should an investor bet on your company and not on a competitor?

We understand the business thanks to the experience developed in our publication and event business. When you run something like News on the Block you have a chance to meet, interview and study every successful business out there—and a few unsuccessful businesses as well.

Every company can access its own expertise. We can access the expertise of every company.

We know the issues and have solutions connected to occupancy. And occupancy is the currency of smart buildings. Without occupancy data, smart building systems such as energy and lighting are just blunt instruments.

For instance, our technology can tell building operators the real time occupancy levels in the building so that, for example, during holiday seasons they can make better informed decisions about heating or cooling the building properly.

What about the team?

Our team is a mix of seasoned property and technology professionals. My fellow board members have many years experience working for some of the largest owners, developers or managers of property in the UK. Our development team used to build the UK's leading property app RightMove (A/N RightMove is a very successful real estate startup).

Your company has still two souls: publications and events on one side, and tech startup on the others. Is this an issue with investors?

No, not in my experience. Fortunately, as we have an established business we have been primarily able to self-fund Block Dox. So we haven't been forced to ask for external VC investors yet. Although, those we have socialized with think the association is innovative.

What's your grand vision for the future of your company, and in general for cities?

Our company aims to be the leader and pioneer of new smart building technology.

The future is bright and challenging. The Internet of Things offers vast untapped potential for improving lives across the world and we are just at the very beginning of that process. This is going to go way beyond your fridge telling you when it needs restocking.

In the coming years, we will see a drastic transformation in the way people interact with their environment. I think we will also see existing and new cities reach a new level of prominence as they harness the power of the internet to make our cities and homes more livable, and the use of urban resources more efficient.

Last but not least. What advice would you give to your younger self?

Doing a startup is not a beginning but the end of a phase of careful research and planning. So, make sure you have the groundwork in place before you begin.

And if you are thinking of exploring beyond the legal profession, then you will also need to find a new use for your suit and tie wardrobe.

Links

1. Company website
www.blockdox.co.uk

2. News On The Block
http://www.newsontheblock.com

Michel Willems

BimBimBikes

In every company I've owned, the very best moment is when you receive the first order from somebody you don't know. It's the first real proof there is demand for your product or service.

—Michel Willems

Once upon a time there was a small boy who upon passing a dyke on his way to school noticed a slight leak as the sea trickled in through a small hole. The boy know that he would be in trouble if he were to be late for school, but the running water was going to enlarge the hole collapsing the dyke, and flooding the his town. The boy pocked his finger into the hole and so stemmed the flow of water. He spent the entire day and night until eventually a passerby saw him and went to get help.

Any child in The Netherlands grow up with this story of Hans Brinker, the "Brave Dutch Boy". It's just a legend, but there are two interesting effects.

First, Dutch kids learn that acting fast you can get results even with limited resources. A child could stop a flood.

Second, Dutch kids are unstoppable. Laura Dekker, a teenager from the Netherlands became the youngest person in history to successfully circumnavigate the world by sea alone. Not only that. When the local authorities prevent her from departing alone because the minor age, she sue the Government and won.

There is also a cool short movie about Laura — the *"Maidentrip"* — winner of the SXSW Film Festival. The movie combines real time video she shot during her two year voyage. It's a must watch when I mentor startups, but you will enjoy it even if you are not in business.

Believe me, it's worth it.

What's the link between Hans, Laura and our interviewee Michel Willems? They all come from the Netherlands of course, but in addition to that, they all achieved something remarkable at a very early age.

Due to a love of travelling, Michel wanted to start a company in the travel industry. This is how BimBimBikes was born. After just 1 year they are present in 35 countries and counting. Without further ado, let me introduce you to Michel, the new Brave Dutch Boy.

The Interview

Hey Michel and welcome. Let's start with your elevator pitch. What your company does? What pain are you going to kill?

BimBimBikes is the booking.com of bike rental. Rent a bike, anywhere, anytime.

Travellers and tourist are used to book everything online. Hotel rooms, cars, ski's, museum tickets and even free beds through couchsurfing.com are reserved. It's strange there wasn't a booking platform that makes the bicycle rental market transparent.

Talking to our first customers we found out that they didn't realize the booking platform was new. They just thought it was logical that a service like this existed. We don't have to explain to them why we exist, we just have to reach them.

Bike rental companies like our concept as well. Everyday new companies join our platform.

If I own one bike, may I join your platform too? In other words, do you put in touch only companies with customers, like Booking, or also customers with customers like Airbnb?

We are not the Airbnb of bike rental. We believe in the sharing economy, but most people don't rent a bike by themselves. The typical customer is a group of friends or a family.

Since most private persons don't have a lot of bikes in different sizes, it's hard to find a match between the supply of bicycles of private persons and the demand of travellers and tourists.

Professional bike rental companies provide all kind of bikes and sizes to picked up at the same location!

Since we build up a bike rental company community, we can get stronger together. For instance by sourcing bikes or other goods needed together and using our combined buying power.

Tell me about your secret sauce. What makes you different?

We are the first platform that makes the worldwide bicycle rental sector transparent. This first mover advantage brings us opportunities to set the standard, shaping the market and create a strong network.

Can you briefly introduce the other members of the team?

Sure. We have a multicultural team and this is part of the fun.

Ben Weiland, Dutch, development guru, a technical genius.

Yakup Ilbasmis, Turkish, design guru and creative wonder.

Giulia Girardi, Italian, started as country manager Italia but became marketing manager by taking care of everything that was not taken care of.

Ramadan Qoslaaye, Somalian/Dutch/British, country manager UK & Ireland, who thinks the rest of the world belongs to that region

Polyvios Dimiou, Greek, country manager who shows us that Greek people are ambitious and efficient.

Felix van den Aker, Dutch, eager online marketeer.

Pelayo Yniguez, Spanish, charming country manager for Spain and the latin hemissphere.

Harm Wolterink, Dutch, cofounder and Getting Things Done master.

Let's talk about your city. Why are you based there? What do you love, and what don't you love so much, about this place?

We are based in Rotterdam, the no-nonsense getting things done city in Holland. Not charming, but rough and beautiful. Ambitious people and growing startup scene.

Some people of Rotterdam do have the "second city syndrome".

Amsterdam is more internationally famous. My challenge to them is simple. Why complaining about Amsterdam instead of enjoying your own great city?

What was your best moment and your worse so far in BimBimBikes.

In every company I've owned, the very best moment is when you receive the first order from somebody you don't know. It's the first real proof there is demand for your product or service. So the first booking at BimBimBikes.com made us really, really happy!

Worst moment? The cancelation of the same order! True story in this startup. I'm glad it was just an exception.

Anything you want to add about funding? I know you are working on a specific project.

Yes, we will start a crowdfunding campaign later this year. Holland has an openminded culture and is a pragmatic trading country. So it's a good base for funding. We can't compare the investment culture with regions like Silicon Valley, but it's getting better. In our case, we have an important customer base who love BimBimBikes so we will probably skip the traditional investment and go for a crowdfunding.

I'll keep an eye of your crowdfunding campaign. What's your grand vision for the future of your company and in general about your market?

We believe cycling is great way to make your vacation or trip even better. Good for tourists and travellers, but also for the environment.

By setting up a worldwide network, we believe we are not only able to make the booking process easier and more transparent, we believe we can help to innovate the sector. Think of smart bikes, tracking and tracing, unlocking by the customer's smartphone etc.

I could talk hours about it. My message to anyone listening or reading this interview, if you need more info, please don't hesitate to contact me! There are solution that are not so publicized by the media, but can improve your travel, or boost your business if you are in tourism and travel industry.

Do you think there's going to be a bubble in the tech sector?

Yes, like there will be future bubbles pumped up and exploded in every growing sector. No problem though. Sustainable companies will survive and growth. A great company is not about hype, it's about adding value to customer lives.

Can you name a person—dead or alive—who inspire you or your company?

Willem Elsschot, a Belgian writer. At the age of 16 I read his classic comedy 'Kaas', a book written in 1933. It tells the story of a failed startup in the time new companies were not called startups. Elsschot really makes clear what kind of personality makes an entrepreneur successful or not! I couldn't stop laughing about this book from the thirties.

Last but not least. What advice would you give to your younger self?

First read the book "Kaas" by Willem Elsschot above or it's English translation "Cheese". If you recognize yourself in the habits of the main character, just go for it! Be an entrepreneur.

Links

1. Company website
http://www.bimbimbikes.com

2. Download "Cheese"
by Willem Elsschot
http://futurecitiesbook.com/120

The Present and Future of the Internet of Things

Interlude

We tend to overestimate the effect of a technology in the short run and underestimate the effect in the long run.

— Roy Amara

The Fourth Industrial Revolution

Ah *"Revolution"* — this word doesn't have much of a place in politics anymore, but in technology, it seems that we have a revolution almost every day.

The Internet of Things itself has been defined as the fourth industrial revolution. Really? We can see plenty of fancy gadgets but not many of them really matters. And I mean "Really Matters" with capital letters, as in "Life Changing" and "Revolution(ary)".

When you spend a few years working with startups, you notice a common rule. New technologies tend to be promoted to the consumer market first.

There is usually a lot of public excitement — *Hey, I can ask my fridge if the milk has expired!* — but the real impact is limited. After all, my grandmother has the technology to check the milk too. She opens the fridge and has a look inside.

At some point, someone realizes that the same technology can generate more money in a business environment. The innovation moves upwards from consumers to businesses, then downwards again from business customers to their own users — this time in a different format. That's when the new technology has a real impact on society. That's when everything changes forever.

If you love formulas, have a look at this one:

B2C -> B2B -> B2B2C

Think about email. At the beginning, email was used by a small number of professors, then moved upwards to companies. Millions of employees got used to sending emails at work, and brought this technology home.

This is exactly what's happening with the Internet of Things. The technology is hot and creates excitement among the general public; however it is at the initial stage. Don't get me wrong, the technology is already advanced. It's the commercial use that is at the initial stage.

Over the next few years, the IoT will become pervasive in every city, building and transport system; that's when everything will change forever.

Fancy Some Data?

There will be 14 billion connected devices by 2022, ranging from cars to heating systems and — of course — the omnipresent security cameras. Smartphones and tablets alone will count for 3 billion of them (Bosh White Paper).

The financial opportunities around the IoT are estimated to be in the area of €596 billion (US $675 billion) by the same year. Smart cities and connected buildings will count for €233 billion, almost 40% of the entire IoT budget.

As a comparison, the manufacturing industry, even with all its robots and technology, is estimated at "just" €17 billion — less than 3% of the IoT budget.

The impact is political as well. General Electrics expect that the "Industrial Internet" will add $15 trillion to the global GDP. That could mean recovery or recession for many countries, based on whether their policies attract or repel talented entrepreneurs and innovations.

Top 5 Financial Opportunities in IOT

The top five areas are estimated to access €471 billion of the total €596 billion— about 80% of the total market—with all the other areas sharing a mere 20%. Future cities tech alone accounts for 40% of the entire budget and half of the top five opportunities.

Connected Buildings: €213 billion
Automotive: €176 billion
Utilities: €44 billion
Smart Cities: €21 billion
Manufacturing: €17 billion

Future Cities (Connected Buildings + Smart Cities) = €234 billion

Investors and Acceleration Programs

The rise of the B2B (Business To Business) IoT has not been missed by big corporations and investors. Just two examples:

Intel, Cisco and Deutsche Telecom have set up a startup accelerator exclusively dedicated to the IoT.

The MIT has a partnership in Portugal that specializes in smart cities.

Investment in IoT is growing faster than in any other area except Fintech (financial technology). Consider one market—the nascent drone industry—in 2014 it topped $108M across 29 deals, with an increase of 104% year-on-year.

The most active investors in the IoT in 2014 according to CB Insights were Intel Capital, Qualcomm Ventures, Sand Hill Road, Sequoia Capital and Kleiner Perkins. If you run a startup in this area you definitely want to contact them.

Links

1. Download "Capitalizing on the Internet of Things – How to succeed in a connected world"
by Bosh
http://futurecitiesbook.com/121

2. Worldwide and Regional Internet of Things (IoT) 2014–2020 Forecast
by IDC
http://futurecitiesbook.com/122

3. The Industrial Internet by the Numbers & Outcomes
Free analysis by GE
http://futurecitiesbook.com/123

Laurence Kemball-Cook

Pavegen

Social media is a free marketing tool, so exploit it.

— Laurence Kemball-Cook

If you have an investment fund or an accelerator, Pavegen is the startup you want to see in your portfolio. They are not another social media platform or a lifestyle app. They have a real product: flooring tiles that generate electricity from footsteps, and they are also extremely good at marketing.

Pavegen has a strong European presence, with their pavements being used in Heathrow Airport and at the Paris marathon, but they also have an international presence spanning from the U.S. to Asia. Their business model is attractive to the media since it allows every single citizen to produce green energy, but they also have an eye for making profit.

This year alone, the charismatic CEO Laurence Kemball-Cook has met prime ministers from multiple countries, and his company has raised more than $3 million in seed investments.

As always, it takes many sleepless nights to make an overnight success. Laurence spent 5 years building a team without a budget and producing enough revenue to attract investors for the $3 million seed round. If you read about Pavegen in typical media outlets everything seems glamorous and easy. You know how this works as well as I do. Stories about overnight success attract more readers, but not me. I am always more intrigued by stories of relentless persistence instead.

I was thinking about whether to include Pavegen in the

interviews or not, as I am one of their investors and I want to avoid any conflict of interest when I am writing. They solved this dilemma themselves by closing the funding. They are not in the book because I chose them, but because they are already in the spotlight. Besides I am confident that they will keep on catching the public's attention for a long, long time.

The Interview

Hi Laurence, let's start with your elevator pitch. What is Pavegen?

Pavegen manufacture and develop flooring tiles that generate electricity from footfall. Every time someone steps on our tiles, the weight of their footstep is converted into electricity that can be used to power lighting and applications.

We provide a unique patented technology which combines digital and physical worlds to engage people in their environment.

You just closed a crowdfunding for equity campaign; one of the fastest in Europe. Now everybody can see that crowdfunding was the right decision, but it was not so obvious at the beginning. Why did you decide to raise money through crowdfunding? And what advice would you give to another startup about launching a successful campaign?

You are right. Pavegen is the fastest clean technology campaign on Crowdcube (A/N one of the biggest crowdfunding for equity platforms.) We managed to reach our £750k ($1.17M) target in just two days!

At the end of the campaign, we have raised more than £2M ($3.11M) from 1,555 investors, equal to 275% of our target. We see this as the right opportunity to enable our next stage of growth for Pavegen.

Our technology empowers the crowd to take part in the energy saving process and we thought why not let the crowd empower Pavegen to reach our immediate investment goals too? This way the whole community can be part of our journey.

About giving advice on crowdfunding to other startups, I'd tell them to fully prepare. Investment on such a public forum takes months of planning and you have to be sure you can face the world's attention for the entire campaign. Additionally, it's important to focus on emphasizing qualities the investors will want to see: market potential, the idea, the team.

What is the main obstacle in this kind of venture?

Since the recession, investors want to see some revenue in the company. Our problem was achieving such revenue without staff. A typical executive in an energy company has a salary that we were simply not able to afford.

And yet you did. Any practical suggestions that you can share with other startups?

In situations like this, you need to find people who believe in you and the potential of your technology. We were gradually able to form an experienced team of engineers and marketing people, prepared to work for us on favorable terms based on their faith in our company. It's more difficult to find these kinds of people; on the bright side they are highly motivated.

We know about you, the company and your funding. Can you briefly introduce the other members of the team?

Sure. Our board of directors:

Charlotte Mason from NED (A/N Non Executive Directors), an INSEAD Executive MBA. Charlotte has a Masters in Manufacturing Engineering & Management and holds various board seats including a NED of INSEAD National Alumni Association UK. She is also a professor at HULT International Business School, a mentor to London Business School's Entrepreneurship Summer School and has delivered lectures at Cambridge Judge.

Chris Smith, CFO. Chris is an experienced SME Finance Director with 20 years' experience of working with rapid-growth early stage technology companies. A commercially minded chartered accountant who thrives on change, Chris helps his businesses to ensure that they are investor-ready, that funding plans are complete, understandable and realistic, and that companies have appropriate systems and controls in place.

Richard Kemball-Cook, also NED Chairman. As a Chartered Accountant Richard was Chief Accountant to the Royal Ordnance Factories (A/N the collective of UK government's munitions factories in World War II, in operation until privatization in 1987). Hired by British Telecom, he maximized profitability on the company's engineering processes as its network changed from fixed line to mobile. He became an expert witness on inter-utility network disputes before co-founding Pavegen in 2009.

Don Eungblut, Investor NED. Don is an experienced board-level mentor, advisor and investor in early stage technology-based companies. He brings a wealth of knowledge from a wide ranging career encompassing telecoms, IT digital media, international marketing and management consultancy.

Craig Webster, CTO. Craig was co-founder and director of the successful clean-tech start-up Aveillant Ltd and Head of Clean Technology at Cambridge Consultants. Craig is an experienced technical leader and now works to aid the development of the Pavegen product.

Let's talk about your city, London.

I dislike the pollution in London, and the conservativeness of policy-makers towards the adoption of new technologies.

I like the fact that London is an international hub for business, commerce and technology. As 90% of our market is overseas, it's easy to work to different time zones and keep our partners happy.

What have been your best and worst moments so far?

Our best moment was creating the world's first people-powered football pitch, in partnership with Shell. We installed 200 tiles in a football pitch in Morro da Mineira, Rio de Janeiro; powering floodlights in the favela and empowering action through sport, as part of Shell's #makethefuture campaign.

I don't believe in regrets, as I see every 'bad moment' as an opportunity to learn and develop. Growing an innovative company in a competitive energy market is always a challenge and I firmly believe and encourage the notion of 'knowing no boundaries' and 'going till you get the job done'.

What's your grand vision for the future of your company?

We aim to become part of the fabric of urban infrastructure; powering smart cities of the future, equating the cost of our tiles to standard flooring and uniting communities in a positive renewable energy generation.

There are almost 4 billion people living in our cities; imagine the power we could produce together by harnessing energy from every footstep.

Last but not least, I usually ask what advice would you give to your younger self. You are not even 30, so I will ask a slightly different question: what advice would you give to a new entrepreneur?

Persistence is key. Social media is a free marketing tool, so exploit it. Take part in startup programs. Network as often as you can. Don't be afraid to take a risk; being an entrepreneur is about quick wins, and even faster fails.

Links

1. Company website
http://pavegen.com

2. Crowdcube - Crowdfunding for equity
http://crowdcube.com

Fabien Girerd

Jooxter

Launching a new startup is very exciting but it is a hard time with moments of doubt. Your family can support you or break you.

—Fabien Girerd

You can't write a book about startups without featuring a French entrepreneur or two. If you are following the news about Uber, France looks like a dark fortress against innovation, or an enlightened stronghold against the US Invasion of Europe. They are good or bad depending on your point of view, but never entrepreneurial.

This could not be further from the truth. I had the honour of working with France Telecom at the beginning of my career, and spent some time in the country. The bureaucracy is massive, but the entrepreneurial spirit is alive and kicking.

Sure, in France the idea that the entrepreneur is a hero has never been as widespread like it is in the USA and other countries. But is this not truly heroic in itself?

French entrepreneurs fight and prosper in a market where the state can tax you up to 60% of your revenue and wide sections of society prefer to work in a public office. And still, many of the biggest companies in the world are French, as Jeremy Rifkin points out in his book "The End of Work".

Both the French entrepreneurs interviewed in this book have their headquarters in France, and they don't plan to leave their country. But it may not be a coincidence that I met one of them in London and the other in Palo Alto, Silicon Valley.

If one day I have a coffee with the French President, I would probably suggest to give a public speech about "entrepreneurs as an example to follow". They don't need to hear that, they are doing their job anyway. They just deserve it.

This is an interview with Fabien Girerd, founder and CEO of Jooxter.

The Interview

Hi Fabien, let's start with you. Can you introduce yourself to our readers?

With pleasure. My name is Fabien Girerd, CEO of Jooxter. I grew up in the South of France, in a place that produces one of the best, if not the best, wines in the world, the "Hermitage".

I am a life science engineer who started his career 20 years ago in Paris as a management consultant. I then joined the corporate world running big IT projects and teams in major companies such as Warner Lambert, GSK, Holcim, and Johnson Controls.

I really enjoyed these initial years working on challenging projects, travelling across Europe.

What happened to change your mind?

Not what but who. My 10 year old son asked me a straight question: "Dad, what is your job?" You can answer an adult by telling them your salary, your benefits and your status. Adults focus on the details and in doing so they lose the big picture. You can't do the same with a child.

If you can't reply to the simple question of a kid with a simple answer, it means that you have no answer. Then it's time to reflect.

While I was struggling to answer my 10 year old son, I realized that I could not explain what was really involved in my senior position at Johnson Controls. I also realized that I had lost the passion to wake up every day for a long time.

It was time to make a drastic change in my career, time to innovate and create a truly smart solution for the building managers I was working with to really improve their workplace.

Let's talk about your company. What "pain killer" do you provide?

We solve a specific issue in the market: bad occupancy.

Everybody talks about smart technology, but it's not really useful having a smart building if it's not occupied. Today, most commercial buildings have an average occupancy rate lower than 50%.

In addition, occupants are complaining about their workforce wasting time every day, trying to find a place to meet or work, or even find colleagues.

At Jooxter, we optimize the use of workspace and the quality of life inside such workspaces. Our technology already improves the occupancy by up to 25% and it's growing smarter every month.

What makes you different?

Our secret sauce is a combination of ingenuity and years of experience working alongside property management organization and strong expertise in automation, and artificial intelligence.

Through plug & play sensors positioned across the building, we use advanced micro-localization technology to truly understand what's going on inside the building and provide the appropriate solution for every space. Just a few examples:

We provide real time and predictive analytics to drive building performance. For instance, the scheduled optimization of meetings rooms, the predictive occupancy analytics to monitor energy management.

We push real time services to improve life at work: For instance, finding the nearest available collaborative places, locating colleagues, and path finding are a few examples from many.

I'm very proud to see large corporations selecting our company as part of their new workplace technology standard. Very proud also of being recognized as one of the technology innovators shaking up the property industry after we were one of the few startups selected for the Cognicity acceleration program in Canary Wharf.

Who are the other members of the team?

Thomas Thelliez is a co-founder of Jooxter. I met Thomas when I was looking for a contractor to develop my first MVP — Minimum Viable Product.

It took only a few weeks of collaboration, to realize that we could create something special together. Thomas began his career 8 years ago as a software engineer then software architect in Lille, Paris and Brussels for major international groups before creating his first innovative startup, Eenox in 2011. He also taught artificial intelligence courses in several French universities. He brings to Jooxter his expertise in computer sciences and his passion for future technologies.

Henri Wallart is a graduate in computer science and passionate about mobile development. Henri started last year on an internship, went to Canada to finish his masters degree, and decide to continue with us.

Philippe Boddaert brings 10 years of software development experience and left a large technology firm to join us as Service Delivery Lead.

Nicolas Steiner, one of our Mentors from the Cognicity programme, is now our partner who accelerates our international business growth from the UK.

Let's talk about your city (Lille). What do you love and what do you not love so much about your home?

Lille is a lovely city of the North of France. It is also a very strategic location because it is an hour from Paris, an hour and twenty minutes from London and thirty minutes from Brussels by train.

Basically I can get to the office in London faster than many of my colleagues who live in London.

In Lille, we are based at Euratechnologies, one of the largest innovation campuses in France, who help startups grow in business incubators.

I love Euratechnologies for the passion the whole management team shows every day to make Lille the leading place for the French Tech ecosystem. It's a great place for entrepreneurs to start a new business away from the frenzy of big cities. A great place to find young talent thanks to the many universities.

The only thing that I can't love in the city is the weather. Considering that I was born in South France where the weather is practically perfect.

I am also not completely happy that only a few large companies are taking the risk of supporting startups at the early stage.

Anyway, we have growth now and even if the main R&D stays in France, we have a presence in other cities.

Moving on to a personal question. What have been your best and worst moments so far?

Since I have been an entrepreneur, I have experienced the best and the worst moment alternated on a regular basis.

The worst moment is not one moment but this rollercoaster. It's a feeling shared by many entrepreneurs. Kyrill of eCozy describes this feeling as seasickness. Could you point out one specific moment anyway?

One of the worst moments was probably the first time I had to pitch in two minutes about my project and no one understood what I was talking about.

The best moment was recently when we won our first contract for a large project, and were chosen instead of a big and well established company.

What's your grand vision for the future of your company? And for the future in general of your area?

We are making Jooxter a global brand for smart buildings, with our technology being installed over millions of square feet in megacities across the world.

The future in general is to use technology to focus on the wellness of people and to improve the efficiency of daily life.

The way companies own and occupy commercial buildings will also dramatically change. Large organizations occupying an entire building belongs to the past. We are entering a new paradigm for workplaces with more collaboration, more sharing of spaces.

At the same time, new generations of workers will expect wellness, flexibility but also freedom.

Can you name a person—dead or alive—who inspires you or your company?

My father.

He became head of his family when he was 9. As a self made man, my father harnessed his strength and courage to never give up and found the energy to move mountains. Launching a new startup is very exciting but it is a hard time with moments of doubt. Your family can support you or break you. My father was the first kind.

We tend to close our interviews with the following question. What advice would you give to your younger self?

Go ahead and become an entrepreneur.

Times have changed since the last century when big names were great places to work and gain valuable experience. Nowadays, entrepreneurship is the best way to start a career.

There are many bestsellers which provide good advices such as Running Lean or Business Model Generation. Have a look at them, then jump in.

If you believe in your idea, go for it and search for feedback rapidly to check if it is worth pursuing. If not, find another one.

Links

1. Company website
http://www.jooxter.com/

2. Euratechnologies
http://www.euratechnologies.com/en

A Tale of Two Cities: From the Car Economy to the Internet of Everything

Interlude

Someday soon, you will look into a computer screen and see reality.
— David Gelernter (Mirror Worlds)

The 1939 World Fair in New York and the 2010 Expo in Shanghai are considered by many to be the two most important international exhibitions in the last 100 years. Indeed they represent not only two different moments in history, they seem to showcase almost two different planets.

New York 1939 was the domain of General Motors. The popular car maker introduced their vision of a future world organized around the 'car economy'. Offices concentrated in the city center, factories built in one specific area, and vast suburbs connected to them by the omnipresent car. The belief "One car in every family" sounds very similar to the Bill Gates dream of "One computer in every home".

Personally, I like a good laptop more than a car. Having lived for a few years as a digital nomad, I can see its value. Anyway, both of these aspirations were brushed aside by their peers as promotional overstatements, only to be proved as understatements in the long term. Families ended up having more than one car and far in excess of one computer.

If cars were the true disruptive technology at the 1939 World Fair, and General Motors was the hottest company, the 2010 Expo in

Shanghai told a different story. A short movie by Cisco had almost no trace of cars in it, yet attracted over half a million Chinese viewers. In the video family members speak to each other through video walls, smart watches control the health of a pregnant mother, doctors are informed of the status of their patients and consult with their colleagues through portable gadgets, and a baby is born in a storm thanks to smart technology.

Cisco was the hottest company at the 2010 Expo, just as General Motors was in 1939. In their short movie, in the Shanghai of the (not so distant) future everything is connected. The *Internet of Things* becomes the *Internet of Everything*. The future is not just the sum of many smart objects, but many smart objects that together create a smart grid.

Smart Grid and Smart Business

The term 'Smart Grid' is first and foremost used for the power grid. Many countries have already moved households to smart meters, but this is only a small part of the business. The Smart Grid means power plants or power nodes that can adapt in real time to the exact needs of the city's smart buildings. This information is communicated to the grid not just by multiple sensors in the buildings, but by the smart gadgets in our hands. Billions of smartwatches, appliances, cars, wrist bands, and every other object connected to the grid, become part of the grid.

The Smart Grid is one of the areas that startups tend to forget. In our regular lives as consumers we see the smart meters and the smart gadgets, but not the entire grid. As a consequence a large percentage of new companies tend to build small hardware for consumers and forget the opportunities in business to business.

From Boring Energy Saving to Gamification

Creating a Smart (Power) Grid in your city means first and foremost saving energy. Smart buildings can decide when to shut down the air conditioning in an area without customers, they can switch on the heaters in a room only if a family member is present, and so on in a series of automatic activities that don't require any human decisions.

Yet smart buildings have a limit. They can't force human beings to be more sensible with regards to energy consumption. But a *Smart Grid* can.

To understand how we need to go back to 2009 when the Sacramento Municipal Utility District was in the middle of a campaign aimed to reduce energy waste. They didn't use any sophisticated technology, they just provided their customers with one extra piece of information: the energy consumption of their neighbors.

Each new utility bill included the amount to pay (as usual), plus the consumption of neighbors with a similar property. On top of these numbers, each customer received a big smiley face on his bill if his consumption was less than his neighbors.

It's a silly example of *gamification*. Each bill became a reason to compete with the neighbors. The funny thing is that the system works. This is not a solitary case. Other companies such as OPower, Xcel Energy and Commonwealth Edison experimented with the same smiley face and got the same positive results.

The only limit of this system is not in the system itself, but in the technology. The customers only received one bill a month and comparisons could only be drawn between customers with the same electricity provider and a similar fee.

Moreover the customers can't interact with each other. It's a one way relationship with the energy provider, and that kills much of the fun.

All these limits are going to disappear in maximum of 5 years. Sensors and smart gadgets everywhere will create a Smart Grid and connect it to every daily activity. So for instance the customer could engage with his neighbors in an energy saving game on Facebook, and receive the results in real time.

Facebook is already in every home, and on almost every smartphone. It will probably be on almost every smart gadget too. Android is an operative system that will soon be present in many household appliances. Like Facebook and Android, there are many others apps and systems already used by virtually every customer.

The consequence is that a new startup doesn't need to reinvent the wheel to be successful. Instead of developing another trivial app or another to-do list and then convincing the customer to use it, they can find a way to bring advanced *gamification* to an existing system. An app for Facebook that talks with the Smart Grid and engages the customer in a game to save energy is just a silly example. Go out and find your own silly idea, because Sacramento proves that being silly often works.

From the Smart Grid to the Rhythmic Whole

If the term 'Smart Grid' is used in connection with the power grid, the Internet of Things is giving birth to many other grids out there. Scientist and visionary Nicola Tesla wrote in 1926 in Collier's magazine "When wireless is perfectly applied, the whole earth will be converted into a huge brain, which in fact it is, all things being particles of a real and rhythmic whole". It sounds like sci-fi but as a person who works with startups in the areas of the Internet of Things and Smart Cities, I can guarantee that Tesla's vision is not only very accurate, it's also already happening.

The Difference Between the Internet of Things (IOT) and the Internet of Everything (IOE)

The Internet of Things (IoT) is expected to be a 7 trillion market by 2020. This value sounds impressive, and yet it's limited to the 'Things'; the smart hardware and software. What Cisco likes to call the *Internet of Everything*, and Nicola Tesla the *Rhythmic Whole*, is much more than that. It's the sum of the 'Things', the 'People', the 'Data' and the 'Processes' that connects them all.

If you work in these areas, the concept sounds easy. If not, you could probably use this example. If the price of a smart watch is $300, two smart watches have a value two times that, i.e. $600. This $600 is the value of the Internet of Things.

However if a doctor and a patient each have a smart watch, and the first one checks the health of the second, the value is much more than $600. The doctor can bill a fee, which has a value, and the patient extends his life and his health, which has a very high value.

The watch, plus the people, plus the data concerning the health status of the patient, plus the process that the doctor uses to serve his patient, all come together to form the Internet of Everything.

This Internet of Everything will be one of the richest and most important markets for the next 10 years, not only in the area of future cities, but in tech in general. Not by coincidence are Cisco making great efforts to promote and explain the term 'Internet of Everything'.

As for me, I use the same wording as Cisco because it has become common language in tech, although I would rather call the phenomena like Tesla did. The *Rhythmic Whole* would be such a better name, don't you think?

Links

1. Cisco Short Movie at the 2010 Shanghai's Expo
https://vimeo.com/12841328

2. Download "Mirror Worlds: or the Day Software Puts the Universe in a Shoebox"
by David Gelernter
http://futurecitiesbook.com/124

Calum Chace

Author

No-one should be under any illusion: life in a startup is hard, generally poorly paid, and most of them fail. But when they work, the rewards can be enormous.

— Calum Chace

This is short interview with Calum Chace, a journalist turned entrepreneur, turned consultant, turned author. Calum has a specific knowledge and passion for AI—Artificial Intelligence—and his background in business make his books unique. As a former journalist he knows how to tell stories, but the reason why I enjoy to read his books is his experience in the field. Calum is not an academic futurologist; when he writes about something, it is probably going to happen sooner than you think.

The Interview

Hi Calum and welcome. Let's start by introducing yourself to the readers.

Hi everybody, my name is Calum Chace. I write both fiction and non-fiction books, mainly about the likely future impacts of Artificial Intelligence and related technologies. This has been my main occupation for three years, before which I had a thirty year career in business and journalism. I started as a trainee journalist with the BBC, then moved into marketing with BP for five years. After taking an MBA I spent fifteen years in strategy consulting, including five years as a director at KPMG. Finally I spent ten years running entrepreneurial businesses, and I still chair and coach some of these.

Would you like to speak briefly about your books?

My novel "Pandora's Brain" was published in March. If you like science fiction it is science fiction; if not, it's a techno-thriller, in the tradition of Michael Crichton.

My non-fiction book "Surviving AI" will be published later this summer. It traces the history of AI and the enormous benefits it can bring us, and also the serious challenges it raises — in particular the current wave of business disruption, the possibility of widespread technological unemployment, and the possible development of superintelligence (A/N This is not a mistake. Superintelligence as one word is a newly created word in our vocabulary due to the rise of artificial intelligence).

What's going to happen to our cities in five to ten years? What's the one thing that is going to impact more upon our lives?

Cities will be at the forefront of the revolutionary waves generated by the rapid improvements in AI — Artificial Intelligence. More than half the world's populations now live in cities, including many of our most innovative and entrepreneurial people.

The linking up of semi-intelligent sensors and devices (aka the Internet of Things) will be most apparent in cities, and self-driving cars will have a huge impact there, greatly reducing road injuries and congestion.

If automation produces technological unemployment on the scale that many of us expect, the effects will be felt most keenly in cities, whether for good or ill.

Artificial Intelligence, driverless cars, intelligent devices; to many people they sound like a first world problem which will heighten the gap between rich and poor countries, and between rich and poor cities in the same country.

Some of my other interviewees think the opposite; that, developing countries finally have the tool to create low cost technology to reduce the gap. Do you support one side over the other?

I take a broadly positive view of the likely impact of the profound technology-driven changes we are living through. I think these are exciting times, although certainly not without their challenges. Accordingly, I think technology will create more opportunities for all of us, and inequality, while unlikely to disappear, will decline as a source of injustice and anger. If we don't succeed in meeting the challenges, however, it could go the other way!

You have sat on all sides of the table: journalist, entrepreneur, consultant and now author. What would be your advice to your younger self?

No-one should be under any illusion: life in a startup is hard, generally poorly paid, and most of them fail. But when they work, the rewards can be enormous, both in terms of money and in terms of intellectual stimulation and personal growth.

There are two types of people who should definitely be in startups. First, the born entrepreneurs, who will stop at nothing to succeed, have enormous energy and determination, and are usually very bright. They have the ability to envision a future which has no right to exist and then walk through walls to make it happen. These people are very rare indeed.

The second type is the person who has genuinely found a way to offer a product or service that people will pay for, and do it significantly better than is being done today. They may be working for an incompetent boss, or they may have invented a new way of doing things. People in this situation are more common, but not ubiquitous.

Everyone else should think twice or three times before taking the leap. My advice would be "Do your due diligence!"

Links

1. Calum's Blog
https://calumchace.wordpress.com

2. Book's Website
http://www.pandoras-brain.com

3. Download "Pandora's Brain"
by Calum Chace
http://futurecitiesbook.com/125

Jarkko Hämäläinen

Intelle Innovations

Iterate your idea at least 10 times.

—Jarkko Hämäläinen

"Amazon is just selling books online, nothing sexy." This is not true anymore, Amazon is much more than e-commerce today, with cloud services and logistics, but go back to the '90s and they were skyrocketing on the stock market as a pure online bookshop. That was not enough to impress Jarkko Hämäläinen and his team.

The quote "nothing sexy" is attributed to one of his colleagues, but it was probably the general feeling in the team in Finland. In fact Jarkko was a manager in one of the sexiest companies of that period, Nokia, the mobile phone manufacturer.

It's hard to understand if you were not in telecom in the '90s. Impossible, if you are a millennial and your first smartphone was an iPhone. In the '90s I joined a telecom company as employee number 8. By the time I left, the company employed 6,500 people. I had the opportunity of following the growth of telecom in Europe and believe me, Nokia was not just a mobile phone manufacturer, but "The Mobile Phone Manufacturer". The best company for some, one of the best for many others.

They were recognized for having way longer battery endurance than any of their competitors, an easy to use interface (for the time), and Symbian, the operative system that was so good that it eventually became one of the reasons for Nokia's downfall. Like Blackberry in more recent times, their system was so advanced that they didn't feel the need to change it.

This quest for building something sexy and over performing has stuck in many Finnish minds. Finland is a very small country, with less than 6 million inhabitants, but they have one of the highest concentrations of startups and new technologies in the world.

So when I ask Jarkko about their elevator pitch, the answer is very much in line with his quest 'We are doing something sexy for the construction business'. His company transforms notes into 3D designs. You can see your building one year before it's built. And this is not just a sales platform. With Intelle Innovations you can check everything, from hidden cables, to interior design, to materials and change the project accordingly.

This gamification for business has demonstrated its popularity in the last few years in every sector. And Jarkko's startup is already generating profit. When you are a business to business company producing net revenues, it's always easier to access investors. So on top of the revenue, they also raised €2 million funding ($2.2M).

Ask Jarkko what he loves about Finland, and he replies without hesitation; '"We have highly educated and experienced software development professionals, a secure environment to grow and very diverse weather. Of course we have also sauna". I'm not sure if the reference to sauna is Finnish humour, or if he's talking about Startup Sauna, the famous startup accelerator, but I avoid asking. I like the answer as it is.

Jarkko's inspiration is not Bill Gates or Steve Jobs — who in a way killed his beloved Nokia with the iPhone — but Jack Welch, the former chairman and CEO of General Electric. During his management, GE's value rose 4,000%. Jack Welch entered General Electric as a junior employee, and when he left, he got the highest severance payment in history, $417 million. Jack Welch's story is not about overnight success but persistence, like Nokia at the beginning, and like Jarkko's vision for his company. Not by coincidence, one of Jarkko's main pieces of advice to a young entrepreneur is to "iterate your idea at least 10 times". In a way his motto is that to build something sexy, you have to work in a very unsexy way.

Links

1. Company website
http://www.tridify.com

2. Startup Sauna - Accelerator
http://startupsauna.com

A New Kind of Money Is Reshaping the Cities

Interlude

When the winds of change blow, some people build walls and others build windmills.
— Chinese Proverb

According to McKinsey & Company there are 2.5 billion *"Unbanked"* — adults who don't use banks or microfinance institutions to save or borrow money. The largest part of these potential customers is based in Asia and Africa, with an outstanding 800 million adults living on less than $5 a day.

This huge mass of humanity is not served by traditional banking because they are too expensive to reach. This is going to change, and it is changing already, thanks to the mobile payment technology.

Smartphones are cheaper and more popular than ever: 1.9 billion users estimated in 2015. In this scenario, Android is the game changer. Xiaomi, a Chinese brand, came out with its first Android phone just in 2011, but they are on track to sell 100 million smartphones this year.

Giving access to non-cash payment and banking service to 2.5 billion people is going to impact the future cities just as much as driverless cars, smart grids and other smart cities innovations.

The first and most obvious change is in the daily life of the users. This evening an old lady in Kuala Lumpur can run a street food stall without cash in hand, reducing the risk of being mugged. From her point of view it's just a tap on her phone, a tool that she already uses every day. That means more people in business, especially women, and more money to pay for the education of their children and grandchildren.

But there is more. From a financial perspective, the old lady from Kuala Lumpur is pumping money in the banking system. The sum is small for each merchant, but multiplied by hundred of millions of merchants every day this cash flow could energize entire economies. Moreover, the profit for the companies behind these payment systems is going to inspire more investors and more startups, thus generating more research and development, thus creating more profit, and so on in an unstoppable virtuous circle.

This area of tech is traditionally called Fintech – financial technology – but mobile payments, loyalty programs and smart retail tech have such a big impact on the life and growth of the cities, that Fintech and Future Cities tech overlap.

This tech attract top investments in London, Silicon Valley and New York, and in general in the Western world, but it's going to have a the biggest impact in the so called 'Developing Countries' where 35 of the 40 estimated megacities will be based. Not by coincidence, in the last year Venture Capitals have invested massive amount of money in the local startups. It's the 'Rise of the Rest', and it's here to stay.

The Magic Cake

Alice H. Amsden borrowed the same phrase for the title of her book, *"The Rise of the Rest: Challenges to the West"*. In the emerging countries, Amsden sees a direct challenge to the supremacy of the West. China, Taiwan, Korea, Turkey, Mexico and all the other new members of the international playground want a piece of a limited global cake. In this vision, more guests at the party means less cake for everybody.

Her book is brilliant, but I don't share this view about a limited amount of resources. The global cake has magic powers and its size can grow in tandem with the number of players. The West could share the cake with more guests and have a bigger piece for itself at the same time.

Think about M-Changa, a startup from Kenya. Their app allows lending and micro-crowdfunding for school fees, emergencies and even wedding and funeral expenses. The concept is nothing new. This practice of mutual support— *Kuchanga*—has been around for centuries but this startup has made it accessible to hundreds of millions of people in real time. Their escrow account also reduces the risk of travelling with cash.

M-Changa was also a member of Startup Bootcamp Fintech, an acceleration program based in London where I was one of the mentors. During the year, I've seen a mutual exchange of expertise between the startup, the mentors, and the community.

At the end of the program, M-Changa has raised part of their funds from European angel investors. This is not a charity operation, where the West gives and Africa takes—or sometimes is forced to take against their interest. This is a business investment, and everybody wins. M-Changa gets funds, the investors get profits.

M-Changa is living proof that the Rise of the Rest doesn't necessarily mean a downsizing of the West. Micro-crowdfunding in Africa is a new market and it could serve hundreds of millions of customers. We—Western investors—may enjoy a piece of this new and freshly baked cake exactly because the Rise of the Rest.

What Goes Around Comes Around

There is another benefit that is too often forgotten: thanks to the Rise of the Rest new cakes are baked in our own countries too.

Try to Google "prepaid meter"—the prepaid system for electricity. If you are based in the UK, you'll see a list of the most advanced companies in the country, with almost a half a million results. However the first massive use and development of prepaid meters didn't happen in the USA nor in Europe but in South Africa.

Back to the '80s, a large number of South Africans without a proven address or a credit history found homes in the newly built districts around the country. These customers tend to be served on a prepaid basis, because a subscription contract is too risky.

The most popular prepaid system at the time was inserting

coins in your electricity counter. You can still see some of these old counters in London. Apparently a counter full of coins in your basement in the middle of a new South African development was considered too risky. That's when they developed the new modern prepaid meter. Today South Africa is seen as a world leader in prepayment technology and many other countries have adopted their standards.

There Is Something New Under the Sun

The *Developing Countries* have large masses of new customers and low resources to manage them. This combination has produced negative results, until now. These masses with a smartphone are no longer unreachable. The combination of new customers and low resources inspires companies and startups to develop low cost but effective solutions, ready to be tested in the local market. Then these technologies may be exported to the richer West.

Besides, this is not a dual market anymore, with rich Westerns and poor customers anywhere else. After recurring economic crisis and job losses, many in the Western population are struggling to survive until the end of the month. Western customers are more similar to the "other" customers than anytime in the recent past.

Young unemployed and retired individuals — the first victims of this series of crises — benefit greatly from low cost technologies. Technologies that have developed in Africa or Asia could be more beneficial to these groups of people than the new fancy apps developed by a startup in Silicon Valley, London, or New York for wealthy Millennials.

What Is Really Happening

I started being interested in Asia in the '90s. It was Japan first, then teaching Italian to the Koreans. Then backpacking in China and studying their history. Step by step I've gone deep into the entire continent. During my years as a consultant I had a chance to work with India, Pakistan, China, Thailand, Indonesia, and

Malaysia. I still follow what's happening over there and in the last few years the growth of a startup community is amazing.

If you want to know more about the top startups and innovations in this area, have a look to the Fintech Book, it can be downloaded online (I'll add the link at the end of this article). I wrote one of the chapters in the book "The Rise of the Rest in Fintech" that includes an overview of what's really happening. This article is an excerpt from that chapter.

No matter if you believe that the 'Developing Countries' are going to compete for our piece of the cake, or are going to increase the size of the cake (it will probably be both), the 'Rise of the Rest' is here to stay. The only possible choice is to embrace the new order and make the best of it.

Links

1. Download "The Rise of The Rest"
by Alice H. Amsden
http://futurecitiesbook.com/126

2. The Fintech Book
http://thefintechbook.com/

Bill Clee & Peter Jaco

Asset Mapping

Don't get distracted by little pots of gold. Keep your eyes on your primary goal.

— Bill Clee

This is an interview with Bill Clee and Peter Jaco, co-founders of Asset Mapping. We had a good, long chat about the unique characteristics of each of them. I don't want to spoil anything in the introduction, I'll take you directly to their story.

The Interview

Bill, let's start with you. Can you introduce yourself to our readers?

Hi everybody, I'm Bill Clee the founder of Asset Mapping. My career started as a designer within the Oil, Gas and shipbuilding industries. As you would expect, the systems we used were extremely accurate and you really had to know how all the different systems connected together, and accurate build data was critical.

It was only when I started to work on the London 2012 Olympics that I realised that the construction industry had a huge opportunity to improve its accuracy of the data they used to manage large complex projects. As soon as a building or site drawing was printed onto paper it was out of date, and the designs were constantly changing.

At the time, there was no central system that managed the information flow so that everyone working on the project was aware of what was going on and when during the installation phase of the project.

To remedy this problem I started to look at why the problem exists, and focus on the core information that the engineers and technicians needed and the information they capture during the construction and on-going maintenance. It is this experience and research that led me to launch Asset Mapping to help solve the problem of managing complex buildings and estates.

Peter here is our Angel investor and Commercial Director, He has been involved in over a dozen fast track start-ups in the Internet of Things and cyber security space.

Peter what about you? You are a Canadian serial entrepreneur with kids who lives in Edinburg, Scotland and run two startups in London. How did you end up here?

And what suggestion do you have for other entrepreneurs who are expatriates and with a family?

I have been involved with start-ups in the UK since dotcom 1.0. Way back in 1999, I left my stable city finance job and joined a start-up where we raised €250 million and also spent most of it. All a great experience on a very fast roller coaster ride and nothing like my previous business experience had prepared me for so we all learnt, and made most of it up, as we went along.

Since that start-up I have been involved with over a dozen start-ups as co-founder CEO, Non Executive Director, Chair and over the last few years have become an active angel investor with a focus on IoT, cyber security and encryption.

What's the best way for a startup to approach you? Do you have a specific investing strategy?

My model is fairly simple. I like to invest very early in truly outstanding teams of people with great innovative ideas and the strength of character to commit to what will be a journey of several years to build a successful start-up company.

I also like to join the team on an interim basis to help as the first commercially focussed team member.

Both to begin to help build the go to market strategy and focus on first revenues but also to ensure that we begin to profile the technology with investors and the world leading technology firms who may one day distribute the technology or indeed acquire the company.

Tell me more about your life between Edinburgh and London.

It has been a balancing act living in Edinburgh and working in London, but it is also nice to have a little break sometimes in Edinburgh which is a beautiful city. You can never get away from start-ups for too long as I have now been involved in a number of start-up projects in Scotland as well.

My family are used to the start-up life with my children both growing up with an entrepreneur for a father they both are interested in business and languages and have both interned at friend's companies during their university holidays.

In some ways, I feel fortunate that when they were younger a lot of my early start-up work was totally virtual (still is!) so I go to be very involved with their early lives, possibly more so than a father who was catching an early train off to work. Saying that I also was travelling a lot with trips to over 50 countries pursuing startup interests.

Looks like a good life-work balance. Do you have any specific suggestion for us?

My only advice to family people who want to work in start-ups is to take some quality time out when you can. We can all spend all day on our laptops if we choose, but sometimes the time you turn off your tech and spend time with your family is worth more than sending a few more emails. Also smell the flowers along the way.

Things hardly every proceed to plan with a startup so you need to be able to handle disruption and sometimes disappointment. You will also have very positive experiences too. Good luck and enjoy the ride.

Bill, it's your turn. You are the original founder. What's your elevator pitch? What pain are you going to kill?

Asset Mapping is an open, non-proprietary platform that helps building managers and engineers to visualise the location and health of building assets in real time across a whole building, estate or city.

Asset Mapping makes sure that engineers have the latest and most accurate information, and that this will help to save a lot of wasted time, reduce the cost associated with building management and energy across complex estates by providing a single source of all buildings and their equipment used to operate them.

Where do you find all the data?

We gather data from the historic information stored in silos such as CAD drawings, BIM, Building Management Systems and Security Systems and show all the buildings assets on a single intuitive digital map where users can see the asset's location, along with important contextual information, in real-time.

When we first install Asset Mapping on a customer site, we create a "single source of truth" about the building and more importantly an entire estate from legacy and live system data. This information is continually updated by technicians in the field, or from the real time systems that automatically populate other management systems and energy efficiency specialist systems.

As we are compiling data from all these different systems we capture valuable asset performance data that can help customers analyse the performance of all assets on their estate. This meta data on asset performance is not currently available as most building systems delete the data after a certain short periods.

Can you explain these features from a customer point of view?

We can help our customer use this data for further analytics to improve the performance and even predict when equipment needs to be serviced or when they might fail. This data can also help building owners and facilities management companies improve their procurement and insurance as they have data sets that demonstrates the performance of a certain asset or asset class by manufacturer.

For the first time Asset Mapping offers an accurate real time asset management to really help the people tasked with installing and maintaining our buildings and cities equipment.

Tell me about your secret sauce. What makes you different?

We take a different approach to other systems, we don't offer a "walled garden solution" so we "talk" to all systems used already to manage the building or estate, acting as an 'interlayer' between the different systems.

A lot of large companies have been trying to sell a one system fits all Smart Cities solution but this will not work if you already have existing buildings running on a variety of different proprietary vendors management systems.

We take the view that we need to first help the technicians that operate with legacy buildings systems and understand their challenges.

We are building great relationships with a number of leading technology firms who are working with us to help us build and integrate our technology including Intel, Cisco and SAP.

For all the geeks reading your interview, can you mention one specific partner or technology particularly important for the project?

We are using Intel's secure "chip to cloud" Moon Island IoT gateways to connect to different buildings systems and publish live data from these systems onto Asset Mapping.

If there an asset failure such as a light, camera or air conditioning unit our system automatically alerts the maintenance staff with accurate information about the asset and its location. We are focused on helping to create and gather fast actionable data that enable rapid and accurate management of a building.

Besides you and Peter, would you like to introduce other members of the team?

Our CTO is Greg Klimaszewski who is an integration, security and cloud expert and is leading our tech team to deliver our platform.

Lastly, our Chairman is well known IoT expert Andy Mulholland who has held a number of senior CTO jobs in industry including at Cap Gemini where he was Global CTO.

Let's speak about your city (London). Why are you based here? What do you love and what do you hate this place?

There is huge start up buzz in London right now and we are certainly surfing that wave. The Internet of Things has captured a lot of interest from Venture Capitalists as well as companies looking to find disruptive technologies and deploy them into their customers so we are very busy fielding interest and getting projects started.

We love London and think in Europe it is the best place to run a start-up and find the best talent, although expensive, it's also a great place to live and bring up a family.

We have been based in two of the many innovation hubs in London, at Canary Wharf Group's Level 39 where we were asked to support their Cognicity Smart Cities innovation program and picked up our first order from them. Not a bad first customer!

We are now located at Cisco's Shoreditch innovation centre IDEALondon which is a curated innovation space focused on IoE. The sponsorship from Cisco has been fantastic for us and has really opened up some commercial opportunities with Cisco customers and partners and we are building good relationships with other resident cutting edge innovation companies.

I guess our concern is not London centric, but there is also way too much hype about happy, smart or futures cities. For us it's pretty simple. Can we add value by connecting disparate systems and help customers save money on engineering time and energy costs? We don't like hype, we like building systems that work and add value to the real world.

That was all about your company and your business. What about you personally? What was your best moment and your worse moment so far?

There have been loads of best moments so far. First revenues, great partners, media coverage, being recognised as a true innovator, people 'getting' our tech, global tech firms taking us seriously and actively supporting us, interest from VCs, making stuff work, solving tech challenges and one of the best of all is building a great team doing things we believe in.

I guess a slight frustration is how long some things can take sometimes, and the aforementioned industry hype, but hey, that's just the way start-ups and the industry work.

Another personal question. Can you name a person — dead or alive — who inspire you or your company?

George Nakashima, the Japanese American furniture maker. He took something as simple as wood, keeping the rough edges, the totally unique character of the tree, and spent months planing the surface to create staggeringly beautiful furniture. What looks very simple to make, can only be done by masters of their craft.

Time to speak about money. What's your history of funding? What do you think about rising funds in your country?

We have closed an angel round, and also received grant funding from innovation awards won from the UK Government innovation funding group Innovate UK. We have also won another project where we are the Smart Cities lead company of HyperCAT, Innovate UK's new IoT Open Standard. We are planning our next A round for Q1/2 2016.

With respect to the many VCs we know there is still a bit of a lack of sectoral focus in the Internet of Things. Often we know an awful lot more about our space than potential investors we meet so we are sometimes left wondering about their value add above and beyond any cash.

The UK market typically is very development capital orientated rather than more risk orientated like the US market so there is a real UK funding gap. There seems to be lots of Angel cash with tax efficient schemes like SEIS / EIS but not a lot of intermediate pre-A round capital.

What's your grand vision for the future of your company. And for the future in general in this area (future cities, smart home, connectivity, sharing economy, etc.)

We are excited about the future, however we are not hanging around waiting for it to happen. Using available technologies we are currently trying to build practical solutions to solve the fundamental challenges faced by cities around the world.

We are also keeping an eye on the amazing technology coming out of innovation companies both large and small, and how it can be applied to help us deliver a market-leading platform. New chipsets from Intel paired with forthcoming nano-sensors such as mass spectrometry is a technology tipping point in IoT and in the way that we perceive our environment and it's going to cause huge disruption for the companies that can't adapt quickly enough.

Last but not least. What advice would you give to your younger self?

Focus Focus Focus - don't get distracted by little pots of gold. Keep an eye on your primary goal but also be prepared to pivot if things aren't going your way. You will learn a lot on the journey. Make sure you keep an open mind and also network network network. Its important to surround yourself people you trust and that inspire you that your will work hard for.

Links

1. Company website
http://www.assetmapping.city/

2. Download "The Soul of a Tree: A Master Woodworkers Reflections"
by George Nakashima
http://futurecitiesbook.com/127

João Marques Fernandes

CityKeys

If you don't follow the common knowledge and you survive, there should be something good in what you do.

—João Marques Fernandes

If you like startups, you should definitely read this story. João Marques Fernandes—CEO and founder of CityKeys—is a modern Yanez De Gomera, the Portuguese adventurer created by the writer Emilio Salgari. Like the fictional character, João is capable of entertaining the modern notables (the investors) with some of the funniest stories.

When they joined Cognicity, the acceleration program in London, their startup was a platform showing real time data to road users. Just one minor problem. In our neighborhood there are no road users at all. Canary Wharf, the smart district where the startups test their models, boasts a myriad of underground and over-ground trains, buses, taxis and Uber cars.

And yet CityKeys survived and made a name for themselves. They did what all tough startups do: pivot. And it was not just a minor twitch, but a complete u-turn: From a platform providing real-time data to road users, to an indoor and outdoor navigation system with augmented reality for tourists and shoppers.

Next time your project doesn't match the needs of your potential customer, think about João, read one or two stories by Emilio Salgari, than twist your business for the better.

The Interview

Hi João. Can you tell us a bit about you and your background?

Hi Stefano, good to be here. My name is João Marques Fernandes from Portugal. I come from the advertising world. I started out doing indoor advertising for retailers and moved on to digital advertising.

Although I am not a programmer, CityKeys is my fourth startup. I have always had this sort of (good) obsession to connect developers with the public.

How did you come up with the idea of CityKeys?

I wanted to solve a worldwide nuisance: traffic. After years of study I found out that the biggest traffic problems are caused by disruptions: construction, accidents, engineering works, sporting events. So we created BuzzStreets, a platform that shows real-time data to road users so they can better plan their route (A/N BuzzStreets was the initial company name, then changed to CityKeys).

Once we had the app, we applied to the Cognicity challenge but we soon realized that Canary Wharf doesn't have traffic jams so we tried to find a solution in integrated transportation. That is, how to get there by car or public transport and once there, how to get around the area. We gathered the technology from BuzzStreets and put it in this new app called CityKeys that does indoor navigation too.

Do people really not know their whereabouts when indoors?

We're not talking about indoor navigation at home! In places like Canary Wharf there are more than 100,000 workers who know very little about the area. People either get lost or don't go shopping because they don't know where the shops, the cafes or the restaurants are. This is a real shame for them and a real loss for the businesses in the area so we decided to address this challenge by creating CityKeys.

What differentiates CityKeys from its competitors?

We're the only company mixing indoor and outdoor GPS with augmented reality. Augmented reality means we can add information to what you're seeing. For example, you can receive push notifications from the stores that inform you of promotions without even going inside the store. The technology has existed for years but nobody has put inside and outside maps together with augmented reality. That's our secret sauce.

Do you already have a grand vision for your company?

I try to make my ideas useful for society. Everyone hates traffic or getting lost in the shopping mall, so the first goal is always to solve one real problem for one single person. This real live feedback is what makes me happy.

At the same time, my ideas need to be profitable and in that sense the plan for CityKeys is very ambitious. We're talking with infrastructure and service operators as well as with major companies who own shopping malls. Big retailers are interested because it makes the experience of spending time in their real estate not only efficient but extremely pleasant.

An app that prevents people from getting lost and gives them the pleasure of discovering new places means they'll spend more time and money in the area. Tenants will be happier too and willing to pay more in rent for their spot so it's all connected. I'm convinced that CityKeys is a great idea which can be useful for people, retailers and boroughs alike.

Your country has a long tradition of trading and travelling. Would you consider moving to Silicon Valley?

Most of the young people setting up startups think they should get to Silicon Valley as fast as they can. I don't have that opinion. I think we can do pretty good things in Europe, especially with programs like Horizon 2020 in place, which are giving great grants to tech companies.

Let's close with a question about you. Can you name a person—dead or alive—who inspires you?

I'm not that inspired by public figures and millionaires. My inspiration has always been my wife. She's been my companion during my entire journey, from my early job in advertising to four companies.

This is a very European thing, and I mean the old traditional South Europe. We may look less competitive, because we consider success in business slightly less important than other cultures, but we have a reserve of energy and inspiration in our families unknown to other nations.

That's why I am optimistic about the future of Europe. It seems that we are always on the verge of collapse, and yet we always survive. It's not a coincidence.

In a startup, if you don't follow the common knowledge and you survive, there should be something good in what you do. Nations are no different. Taste the quality of our lives and our families, and you will enjoy a different way of living.

Links

1. Company website
http://www.buzzstreets.com/

2. Horizon 2020
The biggest EU Research and Innovation programme ever with nearly €80 billion of funding available over 7 years.
https://ec.europa.eu/programmes/horizon2020/en

Crowdfunding in Future Cities

Interlude

Running a startup it's like a man riding a lion. People look at him and think, This guy's really got it together! He's brave! And the man riding the lion is thinking, How the hell did I get on a lion, and how do I keep from getting eaten?

—Toby Thomas

One Thousand and One Nights to Overnight Success

Sandra Sassow—interviewed in this book—had the expertise, the team and the prototype—an innovative waste bin that transforms leftover food to electricity. That's when she decided to launch her startup, SeAB.

Just one "minor" problem. Sandra needed more than a million dollars to go to market. This issue of funding is true for any startup, but it's particularly important in future cities. In our industry, companies are rarely founded by two kids in a garage.

In the consumer apps market, small but brilliant teams can build great products with practically no initial cost. Facebook, Instagram, Snapchat were all built like this. On the contrary, smart cities and smart buildings require costly hardware, expensive research and patents.

Experienced investors understand the difference. Goncalo Agra Amorim—also interviewed in this book—runs an acceleration program that specializes in smart cities and other business to business startups. They support companies for up to 5 years. As a comparison, a typical acceleration program for consumer apps runs for about 4 months.

Unfortunately experienced investors are still uncommon in the future cities market.

A Look into the Mind of an Investor

A typical investor looks for a quick minimum viable product and a fast return. This attitude is usually a complete disaster in smart city technology.

It's not always the media's fault, but media plays a part. They are all about consumer apps and overnight success stories. Smart City tech simply doesn't work like that.

Because apps are cheap to build, there is a long queue of startups lining up in front of any angel investor. We investors have learned to filter this queue by asking for a product and a list of customers.

This is a great strategy in the app industry, but it doesn't work for smart cities and smart buildings. Research and hardware require an investment of millions. Jimmy Garcia—a serial entrepreneur interviewed in the book—talks about a goal of one hundred million dollars.

Crowdfunding Is the Unexpected Child

The result of this attitude is a high infant mortality rate of startups in the business of smart cities. They fail before they can test their product. Sandra Sassow recalls that many investors were interested in her company, but they didn't commit because they were waiting for a final version of the product.

In the end, Sandra and her cofounders decided to invest a few million euros themselves. The startup today is successful and they are growing a customer base of hotels, hospitals and prisons. The investors know that they lost an opportunity, but they will probably behave in the same way with the next startup they see.

Of course, not many founders can afford to invest millions in their startup, so the problem remains.

The unexpected effect of this attitude among investors is the growth of crowdfunding among many startups in smart cities.

Two Proven Case Studies

eCozy—interviewed in this book—chose Indiegogo, the popular crowdfunding platform. Kickstarter and Indiegogo are the two biggest reward based crowdfunding platforms. The companies pre-sell their products before they are built.

Pavegen—also in this book— chose Crowdcube, an equity based platform. On these platforms you don't sell products but equity—shares in your company. The backers become shareholders. The two biggest platforms in our market are Crowdcube and Seedrs.

These two startups were both successful. Pavegen reached their target in approximately 48 hours, and they raised an extra million before the closing of the campaign. I should add the disclaimer that I'm an investor in Pavegen, but they have been already mentioned in many major media outlets long before this book was published.

Links

1. Indiegogo - Crowdfunding platform
http://indiegogo.com

2. Kickstarter - Crowdfunding platform
http://kickstarter.com

3. Seedrs - Crowdfunding for equity
http://seedrs.com

4. Crowdcube - Crowdfunding for equity
http://crowdcube.com

Alex Siljanovski

BaseStone

Being an entrepreneur is like living on a roller coaster where there's always an up and a down and an up near success and a down near disaster. When you have too many cycles like that too quickly, it can wear you down. You definitely need very thick skin.

— Alex Siljanovski

An interview with Alex Siljanovski, founder and CEO of BaseStone. We talk about how to win Techstars, pitch investors, and being remembered in the history books.

The Interview

Hello Alex and welcome. Let's start with a question about you, not the company. Do you have a person—dead or alive—that inspires you in your work?

It's the legendary engineer Isambard Kingdom Brunel. It may be fancier to reply Steve Jobs or Bill Gates—they are both great—but at heart we are in construction and engineering. Isambard is considered "one of the most ingenious and prolific figures in engineering history". I would love to achieve even a part of what he did in my career.

Fair enough. It seems a very good goal. What about your business? Can you describe your company in just one sentence?

In a nutshell, BaseStone reduces costs and screw-ups on construction projects.

"Reducing screw-ups" is one of the best elevator pitches I've ever heard. I love it. And what do you do exactly to reduce "screw-ups"?

We empower the people involved in a construction project with a real time collaboration tool. For instance, an engineer on site can access all kinds of data with his tablet. The use is easy and intuitive. Then he can flag a problem also on his table with a couple of taps, and this information is shared to whoever needs to know.

BaseStone can be applied across the entire lifecycle of a project, from concept creation to detailed design to construction and then handed over.

Translated into non technical language, it means that we speed up the construction and we reduce the risk of mistakes through a collaboration platform. In construction, speed and fewer mistakes are the two real variables that make you better than your competitors. Materials and man power cost are more or less the same for everybody.

So what BaseStone really does is to make your company more competitive than anybody else. All our energy focus is dedicated to improving this goal, and this goal only.

Let's imagine that you are in front of an investor panel and you have five seconds to provide a Description by Association. Something like "We are Uber for X" or Tinder for Y". No matter how silly they sound, these descriptions are very popular among some investors. What would you say? "We are Slack for construction" maybe?

Yes, you could say that. If the investors have a specific knowledge of our market, I would probably go for "We are InVision meets Pivotal Tracker for construction"

What about your team (briefly)?

The team is very, very smart. We have an outstanding CTO in Simon McCabe, who is a computational physicist and a PhD. He's backed up by Manuel Zapata, a hugely experienced software developer, a serial startup engineer. We've got Laura Davies on marketing and growth. She has both outstanding field experience and a Masters in technology. She's backed up by Priya, who takes care of all of our events. We are expanding and now there are a total of eight of us.

What's your situation with funding?

We raised a successful seed investment round from angels. We have traction, so I believe we are going to look for venture capital soon. We are close to having both revenue and enough traction for a Series A, so I guess the time for new funding will come soon.

How important is the revenue to raise funds in a Business-to-Business startup? You know where I am going. In the consumer market companies like Twitter and Instagram got exceptional valuations and raised an impressive amount of funding even if they didn't produce enough revenue to cover their costs. In my experience, B2B is different.

B2B is quite hard. The sales cycle is very long and even if you are successful you can still fail. You can have ten CEOs agreeing to purchase your product, but their approval should be formalized through a long process of legal departments, accounting, and so on. So you have these months where you can be rich in theory but your bank account is poor. If you run out of cash before you get the payment, you die rich but you'll still die.

What do you suggest to B2B startups to overcome this issue?

I would suggest to dedicate one or two slides of your pitch to measuring traction against engagement. Basically you would show how the clients don't just pay for your product but how they use it and talk about it.

I would show this to the investors who we have in the pipeline, and compare past growth with current negotiations. For instance, if you negotiated 20 contracts last quarter, and closed 10 of them this quarter, if you are negotiating 40 contracts you will probably close 20 of them in 3-6 months.

If you were negotiating medium sized contracts last quarter, and today you have a couple of big contracts in the pipeline this also means that you are growing.

In short, you don't have to try to oversell the present situation, because the investors are not stupid. They will challenge your analysis and you'll end up in a defensive position. Worse, you will spend the entire pitch discussing the present situation that is not so profitable.

On the contrary, you have to anticipate their objections. Quickly describe the present situation, admitting the reality of it, and focusing on the pipeline to show that you are building a solid and scalable business. It will take some time, but you are going to get there.

I love these kinds of practical answers, and the readers like to hear actionable advice as well. Let's try another one. What are the worst and best moments you've had during this startup?

I need to think of something that you can actually publish [laughs]. There's a term called the Entrepreneur's Despair Cycle. You have ups and downs, highs and lows. I think sometimes the worst moment is staying on that roller coaster where there's always an up and a down and an up near success and a down near disaster. When you have too many cycles like that too quickly, it can wear you down. You definitely need very thick skin.

So the worst moment is not a moment but the rollercoaster?

Yeah. On the other hand, you have some pick good moments. For us, I think it was being adopted by Crossrail.

Crossrail is well known in our sector but probably not as much outside of it. Can you introduce them to the readers?

Crossrail is one of the largest, if not the largest, infrastructure projects in Europe. It's a 118 kilometers (73 miles) railway with a 42km (26 mile) tunnel network underneath London that allows large commuter trains to access the center of the city.

It's valued at about £15 billion in terms of spending. It's one of the most innovative construction projects on the planet. They're doing things that have never been done before so it's, yeah, it's the project to watch at the moment in Europe, and they are using our technology.

Revenue from these types of customers makes our investors very happy. But for us, there is something more. We can work side to side with one of the most advanced projects on the planet; that's pure adrenaline.

It helps with the rollercoaster.

Definitely.

What would be your advice to your younger self? The more practical the better.

To a younger me or to any other person wanting to start a startup, I would actively encourage them to go for it. The risks for a young person of it going wrong are massively outweighed by the positive benefits of the experience.

It looks fantastic on a CV so the risk is very low. If it works well then there's a huge upside. You learn a lot so I'd say definitely do it.

I'd encourage any youngster just out of university who has an idea to test it out for a year. There's no risk to them in my opinion.

Older individuals, if you have a family, I believe you have to find a way to mitigate the risk. As long as you've been smart about it and you give yourself a deadline I think you can do it.

If you do it properly, the risk is relatively low. You can always go back to your career. It will still be there. It's definitely worse to have remorse for never trying for your entire life.

I have left the best questions for last. Congratulations on being accepted in Techstars!

Thank you! Indeed we're in Techstars.

Did you have any secret weapon that you used to get into Techstars?

I think what they look for is the ability to execute on an idea rather than necessarily the idea itself. So a good idea is a good idea but if you've got the team behind you to be able to act, to take that further. You know, a great idea ends up not being executed when it's just something on a piece of paper.

Any actionable tips for a founder who wants to join the next batch of Techstars?

There's not just one pitch but a very long application process. So they vet as you go along, and you only really pitch at the very end, so you've already been short listed by then.

Because I think they are genuinely interested in the team, you may tend to oversell the individual team members. Don't do it. Techstars is one of the best accelerators in the world, they will find out if you are not completely truthful.

Instead you should stress the value of the combination of the members.

If you have a founder who is better in tech and one who is better at sales, stress this point.

If the founders have known each other for a long time and, even better, they have worked together for a long time, stress this point.

A common story of the founders can be powerful. You want to inspire a simple reaction "Well these guys could actually do something good". Even if your initial idea is not super, you want to share that as a team you'll do everything that it takes to build something good. No matter what.

Links

1. Company website
https://basestone.io/

2. Crossrail
http://www.crossrail.co.uk/

3. Techstars - Startup Accelerator
http://www.techstars.com/

Freddie Talberg

Pie Mapping

Get out there and present openly to people your idea, because as you openly present to an audience you start to realize if this idea is nonsense or is something that might work.
— Freddie Talberg

Freddie Talberg — the CEO and founder of PIE Mapping — is an unusual engineer. He created the first motorcycle parking map in London by riding his bike for 3 months from 2 am to 7 am every night. Eventually his very first map was the basis of one of the businesses that he later sold.

He quit one of the most prestigious companies in Europe when "startup" was not yet a cool word, and he was used to build business from scratch when *lean startup* was not yet popular.

Meet Freddie, the "technology based serial entrepreneur".

The Interview

Hi Freddie, let's start with you. How would you describe yourself?

My name is Freddie Talberg. I am CEO and founder of PIE Mapping and I guess I am a technology based serial entrepreneur.

I was born in the Middle East but now reside with my family in London. I served part time in the British Army Territorial Division for more than 8 years.

How did you become a serial entrepreneur?

I typically always build from scratch a business on my own initially, then I grow and employee a team. I have been doing this for now over 20 years since leaving full time employment.

I have a Bachelor of Electrical Engineering and more than 15 years technical experience within the telecoms sector. I worked in BT and then in a high-tech telco software business in the USA and Israel.

I have spent the last ten years working in the mapping and navigation industry which is an amazing and really interesting sector and industry.

If you had to explain the idea of being an entrepreneur with one personal example, what would it be?

I created my first motorcycle parking map of London by riding my bike out for 3 months from 2am to about 7am.

Ok that's definitely an event to remember. As a serial entrepreneur, how many years do you spend on each company? Or—if you prefer— how many years did you spend on the first company?

I set up and sold my first global telecoms business within 4 years. I moved to mapping and geo spatial industry pioneered interactive mapping and geo spatial data collection.

PIE Mapping began as a traditional printed map publisher (The PIE Guide) which is still ongoing. We evolved into the location based (GPS) mapping industry and are an innovator in terms of both data capture and distribution processes for online and in-vehicle navigation and routing products.

Moving to the business, let's introduce your company.

Sure. PIE Mapping is an enterprise SAAS routing and freight management platform with a driver app that helps lorry drivers navigate the city making it safer for all vulnerable road users whilst ensuring they maintain compliant journeys.

We are the creators and operators of the current Transport for London (TFL) Freight Journey Planner (FJP) as well as creators of the VIP and Freight Logistics Journey Planning Platform for the 2012

Olympic Games which was a great success.

We provide journey planning services for hundreds of freight operators saving them on fines for routing compliance, parking fines and save driver hours and time driving optimally in our complex and ever-changing cities.

Tell me about your secret sauce. What makes you different?

PIE Mapping specializes in turning disparate road data from local authorities into services for road users. We are geo geeks and manage a lot of data. We have an awesome routing engine and capability that is different from Google and other players that gives us an amazing capability to create live road networks on the fly.

Basic amazingly complex routing and complex data management (big data) from Local Authorities and all new things mapping and routing that are complex.

Let's say you own a sports car that should not really go over any speed bumps. But your navigation aid gives you the best route. Does it? No it won't be able to customize on the fly. Well our platform and capability will. We will be able to give you a route that suits you and where you want and don't want to drive. Customized routes into your navigation aid.

Can you briefly introduce other members of the team?

I have a very technical team who are experts in GIS (data) and routing. These are Omer Quershi and Mustafa Khokhar.

Also I have the most awesome UK/UI person Max Glaisher that has managed to make our tech come alive and pull it all together.

What was your best moment so far? And your worst?

Creating my first map of London was a fun and liberating experience as well as having my company on 24/7 cover during the Olympics in case of any Journey Planning issues we had to sort out. It was great being part of the whole 2012 Games thing.

The worst moment, I don't have many, but I guess it is when the really bad news becomes a mega reality. I can remember one time in

2001 when the markets and banks were crashing and we had to shut down the company. I guess the worst moment is when the optimism just cannot find any way to surface.

What's your experience with fundraising?

I have raised VC money and lots of angel money before and it is easier when things are going really well and you have good people looking the part and being part of the team.

On the other hand, I had investor angels on my Board and that has been a nightmare.

I have had investors pledge money after I have presented at conferences but they all want a good deal no matter what.

Raising money is hard work and takes longer than it should. Plus there is so much competition. I think the challenge is understanding the amount you want and where the business is in its life cycle and who would be the ideal investors types. It is certainly possible but needs to accelerate and get a lot better.

What's your grand vision for the future?

I have a string vision that our technology will be a major part of the construction and freight logistics movements.

I think there are major opportunities to create a safer navigation capability that caters for all road users and is able to share road space effectively.

I think we need to have a different approach to ensure harmony and calm while driving in cities. I think assurance of journey time will be key in that and I am sure PIE will be a big part of that.

Last but not least. What advice would you give your younger self?

Become a better sales person and start selling your service/product to someone immediately. Get your first customer to part with money and grow from there.

Get out there and present openly to people your idea and project, because as you openly present to an audience you start to realize if this idea is nonsense or is something that might work.

Believe in yourself and your self esteem.

Get good advisors/supporters that have achieved the big time themselves. They will be more candid and have the scars to prove it.

Links

Company website
http://www.piemapping.com

Star Trek Was Wrong. And It's Not a Matter of Technology

Interlude

Success is often achieved by those who don't know that failure is inevitable.

— Coco Chanel

When I was a kid, I was surrounded by a world of amazing technology. It was the world of Star Trek. And if you think that it was just fiction, you should go back and watch the entire series.

The crew would approach a room and the doors slid open, they would tap a small device to talk with a friend, and search for information on a bigger one that was more like a tablet and connected to a limitless source of data. An appliance could create any kind of object from food to a guitar, at the push of a button.

It was amazing to me, but nothing special for a teenager today. Everything is already here or we are getting there.

Appliances are not so advanced as to be printing food (yet), but Electroloom, a 3D printer that prints fabric, has just been funded on Kickstarter and will be released to the mass market at an affordable price.

Only the teleport is really missing—and it will probably be missing for some time. But even Star Trek could not anticipate some of today's innovations. Take Facebook, or the progression of artificial intelligence. You can dislike the first and be afraid of the second, but they are here to stay.

Data, an android with artificial intelligence, wasn't present in the original series; he had to wait until the year 2364 AD. I can't predict the future, but I work and invest in startups and I am confident that we will have something like Data quite some time before 2364 AD.

We Have Their Technology but We Have Lost Something Else

My childhood was all about the exploration of space. It was not just Star Trek. Sci-fi books, movies, and TV shows were all about " Boldly going where no man has gone before."

The Americans, the Russians, the entire human race was pointing outwards to space.

This is not true anymore. Our future is not aimed outwards at space, but inwards, towards our cities.

In a way it's sad. It almost feels like we have given up. However, the new tests may be even more challenging than the old ones.

Scout the space frontier without discovering an alien race, and you'll still have your own home planet to enjoy. But if we fail to improve our cities, we are destined to a miserable life.

What's Really Missing

We have much of Star Trek's technology almost 250 years in advance, but we don't have anything even close to their utopian society.

Don't get me wrong. Technology is fantastic. I've been able to spend five years traveling through over 20 countries while I was working. I lived the life of a digital nomad, all thanks to technology. This would have been unthinkable just five years before.

And yet, this lifestyle will remain limited to a small portion of the population. It's not a matter of technology, but of personal choice.

In 1995, technology writer George Gilder proclaimed that, "Cities are leftover baggage from the industrial era." He was right about technology — progress made cities somewhat obsolete — but he was wrong about everything else. Technology is not enough. You might run a business in front of your computer, but you often start a new one in front of a glass of wine.

After the first market place was established six thousands years ago somewhere in the Middle East, human nature hasn't changed much. We still commute and aggregate for business more than for any other reason.

The least convincing invention in Star Trek isn't the teleport, but the extinction of money and universal welfare.

I would love to see these innovations, but I am not so optimistic about human nature. George Gilder thought that because we have the tools to make cities obsolete, we will use them. It only took ten years to prove him wrong.

It's never just a matter of technology.

Jane Jacobs — in her influential book The Death and Life of Great American Cities — argues that "cities have the capability of providing something for everybody, only because, and only when, they are created by everybody."

It's not the technology that is going to have the biggest impact on our lives but how we decide to use it. This happens with apps and smartphones as well, but with one main difference. An app with a bug can be upgraded to a better version with a couple of taps; cities, once built can't be rebuilt so easily.

That's why I prefer to use the term "Future Cities" rather than "Smart Cities". Because the cities of our future could be smart or dull depending on our choices. They could be stuffed with smart technology, yet the quality of our lives could be terrible.

Guo Bai — author of China's Development and an interviewee in this book — argues that simple smart neighborhood apps could have a better, more immediate impact on our lives than complex smart infrastructures or smart buildings.

The near future isn't going to take us to outer space. Yet it's full of challenges.

To boldly do what no man has done before.

Hamish Watson

Polysolar

Keen to learn however bright you are.

— Hamish Watson

Hamish Watson is the founder and CEO of Polysolar. Of all the startups I've met this year, they have one of the easier to sell business models — they make transparent glass that produces solar energy.

Modern cities are place of skyscrapers, with limited amount of roofs but an extensive area of windows. If Hamish can turn all these windows into solar panels, the city can become self sustainable.

Combine these new buildings with electric cars and you'll have modern cities that don't need combustible fuels at all.

During the year, I've seen Hamish's glass improve from dark and un-stylish to colored and fancy. It will take some time to create a completely transparent window that produces energy even in small houses, but the technology is headed in the right direction.

The Interview

Hi Hamish. Can you tell us a bit about yourself? What did you do before setting up Polysolar?

I was born in London a couple of years ago [laughs] and studied Business in Scotland. I worked at a management consultancy after I finished my degree and ended up moving to Hong Kong in the 90s.

I set up my own consultancy there, advising multinationals moving to China and after eight years I established myself back in

Cambridge with my family. Just before Polysolar, I started a mobile telecom business of data transmission. Now I'm fully dedicated to this project.

Where is Polysolar now and what is your grand vision?

What we were anticipating was selling glass. In reality we are developing the entire supply chain, from creating the components to fitting them into buildings. In the immediate future, we're very excited about a new product which is a completely colorless glass, better suited to the architectural aesthetics of the commercial office building in the West. We estimate it will be in the market in two or three years time.

As regards our vision, we think we can solve the world's carbon crisis. You'd only need to cover a fraction of the buildings that exist today to produce the entire world's electric power. There's no need to cover any land, we can just build with a material that not only generates power, but can generate all the electrical power required worldwide.

Tell us about your secret sauce. What makes you different?

There are not many companies building integrated photovoltaic solar glass and we supply solutions rather than just products. That gives us the advantage of being uniquely skilled in this field. We're also meeting a need which is unavoidable from our customers' point of view.

European regulations dictating what are known as zero carbon buildings mean these have to produce a proportion of their own power. That's fine if you have a warehouse or a factory out in the countryside but as soon as you talk about office buildings you have very little opportunities to generate your own power.

They have little roof space to install solar panels as the plant equipment is usually placed there, so we're now looking at the facades of buildings, which is what we do. On top of all that, our product is cost comparable with conventional glazing.

Your company is based in Cambridge. Does it still benefit from its proximity to London? If so, in what way?

London is the centre for architectural construction worldwide. The big projects may be happening in China or the Middle East, but the big architectural players have their headquarters here. It's great for making connections.

Also a lot of international building regulations are mirrored in the UK. For example BREEAM, an international standard for environmental buildings which has been adopted worldwide, had its origins here.

What do you think of the startup craze? Do you think there will be bubble anytime soon?

There's always been a lot of startups, they are just better publicized now. Entrepreneurship in itself is a good thing, particularly in the UK where we don't have many of our big companies left.

In countries like France or Germany, there are a number of big enterprises where graduates can go when they finish university.

In the UK, there's less of that standard rear progression than in other European countries so you have more natural enterprise by the fact that you can't look elsewhere. I wouldn't worry too much of a bubble.

What advice would you give to your younger self?

Things always take longer than you expect and hard work is the only road to success. The classic dotcom business where you suddenly get millions of pounds out of Google is the rare case. I'd also say try not to close yourself away from advice. It's always a learning curve, even for those who have done it before. Always be open minded and keen to learn however bright you are.

Can you name a person—dead or alive—who inspires you or your company?

This is an easy question for a Londoner with a non-traditional background like me. Richard Branson. Today he's a respected entrepreneur all around the world. But he started his career from a small company here in England. For us he has been an inspiration quite some time before his international fame.

Links

1. Company Website
http://www.polysolar.co.uk/

2. BREEAM
Design and assessment method for sustainable buildings
http://www.breeam.org/

Miguel Rodrigues

Cities2020 Brazil

The world has changed and it's not just Silicon Valley anymore. So to the two points —
be real and be fast — I would add a third point for success: be low-cost.

—Miguel Rodrigues

Miguel Rodrigues is the CEO of Cities2020, the biggest virtual expo in the world for smart cities. But don't get fooled by his bureaucratic title; Miguel is first and foremost an entrepreneur and maker. His interesting background includes building a race car, launching a tech museum in his native Portugal, and much more.

Miguel is bringing innovation to the cities precisely because he has not always worked with smart cities. Sometimes, the fresh eyes of an entrepreneur can be more effective than an expert.

If you have a chance, meet Miguel in person. We had a great talk about what the so called 'Developing Countries' could bring to the society (more than they usually think), the role of a huge country like Brazil in the global economy, and his advice on how to develop businesses in the new economies. Until then, enjoy this interview!

The Interview

Welcome Miguel, please introduce yourself and your organization.

I´m Miguel Rodrigues CEO and Co-Founder of Expo Cities2020, a large, innovative Smart Cities initiative that impacts 200 cities in Sao Paulo State in Brazil, a hybrid event that combines virtual exhibitions over 11 months a year, 24 hours a day and accessible from anywhere in the world.

With the support of Sao Paulo's State Government this initiative aims to accelerate the development of Smart Cities initiatives in 200 cities including Sao Paulo City, the 6th largest city in the world. It is a privileged communication tool between the State and Municipal Governments and all the other players in the smart cities field, such as universities, research centers, startups, and other public or private institutions.

When did you started?

Expo Cities2020 was officially launched on April 29th 2015, and will have attracted more than 500 virtual stands. In the Expo you can find extensive information about tech companies, smart cities solutions and innovative startups.

In addition, a large number of smart cities from all continents showcase their successful initiatives plus much more specific information that will become important, inspirational elements for the mayors of the 200 cities from the region of Sao Paulo.

What did you do before Cities2020?

I've been involved in different smart cities projects from 2007, when I setup the first project for Oporto, my city in Portugal, based on electric and connected vehicles.

In 2012, I moved this expertise to Brazil, where I consulted with many companies and startups around smart cities, smart buildings, and smart retail environments.

In the meantime, with my company MtoM, I developed an app that integrates with Intel hardware, Bluetooth, and RFID technologies to map and interact with people in buildings, streets, parks, and malls. This kind of projects are fun everywhere, but in San Paolo is even better. When you have the opportunities to test an app in one of the top ten biggest cities in the world, it's simply amazing.

If you had $10 million to invest in startups in Smart Cities, and you can't invest in your own organization, what areas would you pick?

Right now if I had $10 million to invest in startups, I would invest in the design of a platform that could coordinate and accelerate the process of making cities smarter.

So WordPress for smart cities?

Yes. More than 65 percent of the population in Brazil already own a smartphone. Cities need urgent solutions to become smarter, more efficient, and more humanized for their citizens. But it's still too difficult to add value to this area. Think about controlling the heat or the water in your building, or aggregate people in a smart neighborhood. There is a lot of hardware on the market and an incredible number of apps, but they don't talk to each other, and you need a very advanced team of programmers to develop a new app. A plug and play platform will solve many of these issues, plus it would give access to local people with revolutionary ideas and a sense of community, but not enough tech skills to develop an entire startup.

Tech can be expensive. Do you see the gap between cities in rich countries and poor countries growing in the future?

Quite the opposite; I see the gap between rich countries and poor countries is going to be reduced. Technology is an important tool to help people to do more with less money. Smart infrastructures are already taking place in the cities of Latin America. The next step is to develop the right applications and platforms to be used directly by citizens in those cities.

The large corporations can be efficient on large scale projects at a Federal Government level, where having huge resources is very important. Think about macro sectors at the level of public transportation, education, health care, and e-government.

But at the municipal level, there's another large universe of potential solutions that can be more quickly developed and implemented by small companies, with less technologic resources. An innovative idea can be rapidly developed and adopted by the city, especially in the apps universe.

So, the smarter cities in poor countries will be the ones that will have more intelligent and inventive public managers to inspire and motivate this collective creative flow of small local companies, micro entrepreneurs, or SME´s.

Soon we will see a new wave of urban creativeness, with entrepreneurs and public managers working closely to produce smart cities solutions. This new way of working will become a natural action.

In this new reality, centers like our Expo Cities2020 will flourish. We can connect all the smart cities players on a global scale, including municipalities, companies, research centers, and public institutions. This is a global game, so organizing the community of your city is not enough anymore. We need centers of global aggregation, and a virtual center is both global and less expensive than having multiple city, state, and country centers. That's why we have decided to invest so much energy in our own project Cities2020.

What advice would you give to your younger self?

Be creative and observe the city environment. Don't focus just on the business but understand the environment as a citizen and from a public manager perspective.

Every startup from Silicon Valley knows that you should find a real solution to a real problem, and execute it quickly. But the world has changed and it's not just Silicon Valley anymore. So to the two points — be real and be fast — I would add a third point for success: be low-cost.

If you produce expensive technology, it would be adopted in North America and maybe Europe. You are going to miss the access to 5 billion customers from Latin America, Asia, and Africa.

Is there anything else you would like to share?

Just one thing: join us at Expo Cities 2020.

If you are not in Brazil: join us too. You will be able to showcase your technology to some of the most dynamic cities in the world, especially the ones based in developing countries. They are starving for new technologies, to help manage a large mass of humanity.

Expo Cities2020 is a tool that Brazilian cities already have available and that is already growing with the cities' needs and demands. We have an ecosystem where they can get a large amount of information regarding the experiences of the last ten years of smart cities, especially in Europe. Our platform will help them to understand what type of solutions have been implemented, what kind of business models have been successful, and what tech companies have been involved. There is a vast amount of available information that European cities didn't have a few years ago when many smart cities projects started.

For a startup or a major company, being on our platform is an immense opportunity.

Vice versa, if you are in the government of a city that is running smart projects, you also have an opportunity to showcase to the major companies.

Whoever you are, if you are involved in smart cities, Expo2020 is great community to join.

Links

Company website
http://www.cities2020.com.br

Songdo, the Story of an Artificial Creature

Interlude

What is the city but the people?
— William Shakespeare (The Tragedy of Coriolanus)

During my university years I spent an entire summer teaching Italian to Koreans. I was fascinated by their culture that combines ancient roots with modern dynamism. I still watch Korean dramas from time to time: Lawyers of Korea, Cruel City, City Hunter, My Girl; an endless stream of urban stories.

It's a *"Pali Pali"* culture, literally "Hurry Up" or "Faster", an expression repeated many times a day by mothers to their sons as well as by corporate executives to their employees.

South Korea is a natural place to rethink the future city. It is not a coincidence that this country hosts the largest real estate project in the world—a $40 billion investment—and the biggest Feng Shui creation in history—a 600 hectare arrow made of streets and buildings pointing to the heart of China.

In fact, the largest real estate project in the world and the biggest Feng Shui creation in history are both in the same place: Songdo, a smart city built from scratch on reclaimed land in the Yellow River.

While London and New York are modernized cities where city planners fight every day to adapt old buildings to modern concepts, Songdo is totally new and artificial. A baby child of the South Korean passion for innovation, born with the size of a muscular teenager.

For John Chambers, CEO of Cisco Systems, it is a city that will "run on information". Cisco has invested about $50 million in the project to build "the city's nervous system".

Every area in Songdo is covered in sensors. Using state of the art RFID—radio frequency identification—you can enter your flat without a key, while artificial intelligence controls heating, water and waste based on the human presence in each area. This system is supposed to cut greenhouse gas emissions by two-thirds.

The city's artificial intelligence knows the location of every vehicle, of every product and—somewhat disturbingly—of every citizen. Not only the City knows where you are, "She" is alleged to predict the flow of people and material before it happens.

The book *Aerotropolis* by John Kasarda and Greg Lindsay describes Songdo as "a weapon for fighting trade wars", mostly by air power. The nearby Incheon International Airport plays a strategic role in the original concept of the city.

Infrastructure is only part of the plan. Songdo was supposed to be a special economic zone, with low taxes and light regulation, inspired by Shenzhen and Shanghai, the two cities which ignited China's economic miracle.

Songdo is planned to perfection, and yet—like in Mary Shelley's novel *Frankenstein*—artificial creations are never exactly how we expect them to be.

The city is not an ugly monster; on the contrary, it's beautiful (for the most part). It hosts the tallest building in Korea, the Northeast Asia Trade Tower, green areas and an amazing waterfront. But many offices are empty and the 10 year plan—supposed to be completed in 2015—is a missed deadline.

In these 10 years two things happened.

The city was planned around the concept of "ubiquitous computing", according to the 2004 vision of the future. An expensive centralized system of RFID sensors is at the very core of the city.

In 10 years smartphones and apps have completely disrupted this vision. The reality doesn't look like a nervous system with a tyrannical central brain. The new world is a railroad grid with a central controller. He coordinates and facilitates the flow of information coming from the people to the center—*crowd sourcing*—or moving between people—*peer to peer*.

There's a joke here somewhere. A $40 billion centralized plan has been disrupted by apps created by a group of teenagers in a garage, and by smartphones in large part produced by two South Korean companies—Samsung and LG.

The second element that disrupted Songdo's plan is not technological but geopolitical. The city was supposed to be a new gateway to China, but the modernization of China pushed the investors to overlook South Korea and invest directly in the mainland.

In just 10 years both technology and politics have changed so much that they've made a $40 billion plan partially obsolete. It's the *Singularity* baby! The growth in tech and culture is not linear but exponential. In the past the difference between the two was barely noticeable, not any more.

I would like to add a third factor to the two above (tech and politic). Songdo was started in 2004 and was supposed to be completed in 2015. But can we really aim to "complete" a city?

Ancient Rome, Paris, London, New York, every city that is strategic, or was strategic at one point, are all live entities. They grow and adapt constantly. When they stop adapting, they don't simply stop growing; they stagnate and implode—think of Detroit.

In the next 10 years many projects will aim to develop new cities or reshape old ones. The CEO of Cisco was right—we have the technology to plan cities that "run on information". This technology may be perfect but the plan can still fail. What about this? Maybe we should simply plan cities that "run on people".

Paul Sheedy

Reward Technology

Too frequently I hear people say that they'll raise the money through advertisement and that's not a solid business model. My advice is: work out how you're going to get physical cash out of somebody's pocket.

— Paul Sheedy

Paul Sheedy, founder of Reward Technology, is a rare bred in Europe: he has made an exit. This would be good in the USA, where the startup ecosystem is almost three generations old. In Europe, where startups are a relatively new phenomenon, it's simply excellent.

We often meet at Level39, the accelerator in London. He's always friendly, never pushy about investments, and makes occasional jokes about the Irish. Paul is Irish and I had a youthful passion for Irish history. Together we can ramble for hours.

The Interview

Hi Paul and welcome. Let's start introducing yourself.

Hi everybody, my name is Paul Sheedy. I trained as a product engineer and got into delivering and manufacturing all sorts of brand new products in China, from speakers to DAB radio (digital radio) and promotional products for Disney and Coca-Cola.

I also set up a data analysis company called Engage Your Customer which analysed loyalty card transactional data in order to work out growth market strategies tailored to each one of the customers.

After the company got acquired by a larger one based in Palo Alto, I started looking at how retailers could move from paper coupons to digital. My view was that we had to move to digital but we have to do it in a simplistic, inclusive way without barriers to entry.

What do you mean by "barriers to entry"?

The fact that your customer may need a smartphone is what we consider as a barriers to entry.

Let me give a practical example. At Engage Your Customer we analysed the loyalty cards of 18 million customers every single day of every week.

We soon realised that the very best shoppers tend to be middle aged females. However, when you look at smartphone penetration rates for that middle-aged female group, it tends to be lower than other groups. So if you're trying to get these customers to download an app to deliver them offers, it's not going to work.

Another issue is that even when your customers have smartphones, they only want to have a certain number of apps. In the USA, out of all the million of apps out there, only five of them take up 80 percent of a person's time. It's kind of futile trying to compete with those five large corporations for your customer's time.

Finally, another thing we looked at is Beacon technology but the issue again is that you're relying on a person having their settings enabled, WiFi on, data running, Bluetooth switched on, and we all know that we either forget to do that or once you're inside a big supermarket it's like a faraday cage, there's little or no reception.

How has Reward Technology removed those barriers?

We embedded a chip and antenna inside loyalty cards that act as a triggering mechanism for us to know who's walking through the door. As soon as that happens, we know the person's email address, mobile phone and other data they've agreed to provide when they signed up for their loyalty card.

We can then communicate with every single mobile phone immediately and show customers the relevant offers for them on that day. For example, if we know that you buy bread every day, toothpaste every month and window cleaning products every six months, we can also figure out what's the right week to send you a specific offer and tell you how much it is going to save you.

What's the future like for Reward Technology?

Our focus when we started this project was completely on retail but we've moved to hospitality, security solutions and smart cities. For example, we're working with a number of companies in terms of how to deliver integrated solutions using security passes.

In the event of a fire, we know that there might be 80 people at a certain floor by detecting the card inside their wallets. Fire marshals can check on a tablet how many people are still at each level and we can also directly call those people to confirm whether they're still inside of the building or they have walked outside.

Let's talk about you city (London). Why are you based here?

If I wanted to be a top watchmaker, I would be based in Switzerland. If I wanted to design racing cars, I probably would place myself in Italy. By this I mean that you have to be in the right ecosystem and the ecosystem for technology right now is being brilliantly run in London. The government is doing a phenomenal job laying down a foundation which is making London the place to be for technology.

Do you think there will be a bubble in the sector?

Companies in London have to figure out how to get by with the little funds they raise. In Silicon Valley, startups raise enormous amounts of money and I would often question the business model behind it.

So in terms of bubble bursting, the scale here is not the same than in Silicon Valley so I wouldn't worry too much about it.

If you could give some advice to your younger self, what would it be?

There are a lot of people with great ideas but no commercial model behind them. Too frequently I hear people say that they'll raise the money through advertisement and that's not a solid business model. My advice is: work out how you're going to get physical cash out of somebody's pocket.

Is there someone who inspires you or your company?

Yes but it's not a person. It's the country of China that inspires me most. They are not thinking about the next election but about where do we need to be in 40 or 50 years time.

They're looking at the bigger picture all the time and they're also very quick at seeing what their weak points are and improving them.

For example, a few years ago you would say that the Chinese are amazing at manufacturing but don't know how to design products. Well, China realised that too and they now have more designers than the rest of the world combined. I personally love that visionary thinking and it has been an inspiration for me for decades.

Links

Company website
http://rewardtechnology.com

Justin Lyon

Simudyne

The sooner you get to the A team, the sooner you get to the big leagues and if you don't have the courage to let go of the B team, you'll never make it to the varsity level.

—Justin Lyon

Justin Lyon—CEO and founder of Simudyne—sold his first company when he was 26. Then he became an MIT graduate.

His company Simudyne is "Sim City for Real Cities" and believe me this is not just a slogan. I've seen the company in action. Governments and businesses can pick a specific city and a specific event—a terrorist attack or a fire—and see what's going to happen before it really happens.

The event is not necessarily dramatic. In fact the company makes most of their revenue simulating new infrastructures and changes that could improve the quality of life in the city.

But when there is a public presentation, you can bet that Justin pulls out one of these Hollywood scenarios from his hat and he wins the attention of a room full of investors and public officers.

Who said that city planning isn't fun?

The Interview

So Justin, your company slogan is "Sim City for Real Cities". What's all that about?

Simudyne is about helping cities and governments and corporations create a safe environment where they can generate, test, and refine their ideas before they take action in the real world. It's effectively Sim City for real cities.

And what about you? How does a guy from Texas end up in London? (A/N Justin is originally from Texas, and he now lives in London)

That's a great question. So in the 21st century, we have the opportunity to operate globally and there are huge numbers of people in Western Europe, Northern Europe, the Middle East and North Africa, and most importantly in Asia.

London sits in a wonderful time zone that allows us to effectively manage West Coast operations but also still be able to work very effectively with our colleagues in Singapore and that's critically important, so it's time zone.

The second issue is that London is a beautiful, wonderful city. It's cosmopolitan, culturally diverse and rich, beautiful. We're based in and we operate in the city of London. We also operate in the Canary Wharf area and both of those locations are phenomenally beautiful, with deep history, and it's just absolutely a joy to work there.

I think sort of the third reason why we chose London is that it's got incredible technical resources, world-class developers who are able to build beautiful, elegant code that we're able to use to solve some of the world's most pressing problems.

And those three things together: the time zone, the beauty of a cosmopolitan environment, and really kick-ass developers, is why I am in London.

Would you like to briefly introduce the team?

Our team is comprised of primarily software developers who use programming languages to develop our software platform.

We tend to focus on technology such as Scala and Lift. Scala is a programming language and Lift is the framework for managing web applications.

We use a tremendous amount of Java and we have APIs and other ways for independent software vendors and developers to use our platform on the Cloud to drive their computer simulations to improve the operations of global corporations, countries, and cities.

And you have been able to raise very smart money. A series of investors who also support the company on a regular basis. Correct?

Indeed, we have a small team of investors who are also working with us.

Ramona Liberoff is one of our key investors. She comes with a deep understanding of our mathematics and modeling techniques, and is helping lead our strategy development.

Miriam Lahage is a former executive with eBay and she's helping us drive our business forward.

The Chief Technology Officer of Shell, outsourced with T-Systems, Dr. Mazin Yousif is on our Board of Directors helping lead our technology strategy and our technology vision.

And our Chief Operating Officer is Mike Morgan, who manages our commercials and runs our team.

What's your best moment and worst moment so far?

I'll start with the worst moment as bad news always travels faster. I think the worst moment is just the sheer relentless effort that's required to deliver great work and great code.

Building a company and building a great platform is not easy and it takes time. The amount of code that we've thrown away is mind blowing. If you don't do that, you fail and your investors just have to get that.

I think the best moment has been winning clients. There's nothing better than deploying your software and seeing it used to make really important decisions better.

Our entire species needs that. We need to be able to engage in this really robust and beautiful dialogue between the things that we've created and the things that have evolved. And it's together that we can actually transform our lives for the better and to make a beautiful, safe, resilient environment for ourselves in the 21st century and for our children's children.

What's your grand vision for Simudyne?

We are going to transform how humans make decisions. The same way that Google has transformed how we search for information.

No more will we rely on pure intuition. Instead, we'll be able to combine our gut feeling, our intuition, the things that we've evolved over millions of years, pattern recognition that comes from trying to escape tigers 10,000 years ago in the jungle, we're going to combine all that with the beauty and elegance of our mathematical knowledge.

We have the ability to solve really difficult non-linear equations using the things that we've created, these digital computers that we've invented and that we've nurtured and that we've built.

Together, the humans and the computers can make a beautiful world for ourselves.

Last but not least, what advice would you give to your younger self? The more practical, the better.

My first piece of advice, think very hard about how long you think it's going to take to make money and then triple it.

So let's say you think it's going to take you two years, it will take you six years. If you think it's going to take six months, you're wrong. It's going to take a lot longer.

Double or triple whatever estimates you have in terms of when you're going to be cashflow positive.

The second suggestion is you sometimes just have to hire the people that are just right for right now. They may not be the A team, they may not even be the B team, they're the team that you can afford.

But never hesitate to make the hard decisions to let them go when you have the money and the resources to hire the A team.

The sooner you get to the A team, the sooner you get to the big leagues and if you don't have the courage to let go of the B team, you'll never make it to the varsity level.

The third thing is that VCs don't care about your vision or about your dreams or about really anything other than how fast can you scale and how fast can you make me a lot of money.

And as soon as you get that through your thick head, the sooner you're going to be able to make a pitch that they're going to understand.

And they have the attention span of gnats. It needs to be two minutes or less and it needs to be credible.

If you bullshit they'll see through it. They see hundreds of people bullshitting them and they know instantly if it's going to make money.

And if you get rejected by a bunch of VCs, quit and come up with a better idea.

Do you have a person, dead or alive, who inspires you?

So a person alive is Dr. Kim Warren. He used to be a professor at London Business School. And what he did was he figured out a way to take really complex mathematics, I mean truly complex mathematics, and dumb it down so that even executives could understand it. And I don't mean that in a denigrating sort of way.

What I'm saying is that executives are under incredible time pressure to deliver value for their clients, for their investors, and for their team. What Dr. Warren did is figure out a way to distill that into a manner that the computer can understand, that the computer can simulate, and so that the computer can then deliver foresight to the executives to make better decisions.

In terms of dead, my inspiration is the Taoist philosopher Sun Tzu. I like the art of winning without fighting. It's truly beautiful and if you can understand that then you're on the path to riches.

Links

1. Company website
http://www.simudyne.com

2. Download "The Art of War"
by Sun Tzu
http://futurecitiesbook.com/128

Future Cities Events and Conferences

Interlude

Once you have experienced the thrill of flight, when you're back down to earth, you will continue to look at the sky.

—Leonardo Da Vinci

Events come and go, and what is dumb today may be cool tomorrow (and sadly vice versa). I keep an updated list here:

http://futurecitiesbook.com/129

If you know of an event that is not on the list, please add it to the comments on the page above. Every link counts. Thanks!

List

(In alphabetical order)

Asia Africa Smart City Summit
Bandung (Indonesia)
http//asiaafricasmartcity.com/

Cleantech Forum Europe
Lyon (France)
http://events.cleantech.com/cleantech-forum-europe/

Cleantech Forum San Francisco
San Francisco, California (USA)
http://events.cleantech.com/cleantech-forum-sf/

Distribution Tech
Orlando, Florida (USA
http://www.distributech.com/

Ecocity World Summit
Abu Dabi (UAE)
http://www.ecocityworldsummit.com/

Ecosummit
London (UK)
http://ecosummit.net/

EmTech MIT
Cambridge, Massachusetts (USA)
http://www.technologyreview.com/emtech

Expo Milano
Milan (Italy)
Only in 2015
www.expo2015.org

Gigabit Europe

Munich (Germany)
http://bit.ly/gigabit-europe

Global Forum
Oulu (Finland)
http://globalforum.items-int.com/

Global Tech Summit
Helsinki, Finland
http://www.globalcleantechsummit.fi/

Globalcon
Boston, Massachusetts (USA)
http://www.globalconevent.com/

Green Build Expo
Manchester (UK)
http://greenbuildexpo.co.uk/

IEEE International Smart Cities Conference
Guadalajara (Mexico)
http://sites.ieee.org/isc2/

Industry of Things World
Berlin (Germany)
http://www.industryofthingsworld.com/en/

Internet of Thinks World Forum
London (UK)
http://iotinternetofthingsconference.com/

IoT Summit
Santa Clara, California (USA)
http://www.iot-summit.org/

IoT Tech Expo Europe
London (UK)
http://www.iottechexpo.com/europe/

iSmart
Jerusalem (Israel)
http://www.ismartisrael.co.il/

Kyoto Smart City Expo
Kyoto (Japan)
http://www.kyoto-smartcity.com/e/index.html

Liveable Cities Conference
Melbourne (Australia)
http://www.healthycities.com.au/

Living Future Unconference
Seattle, Washington (USA)
http://living-future.org/unconference

New Mobility World
Frankfurt (Germany)
http://newmobilityworld.com/

Nordic Edge Expo
Stavanger (Norway)
http://nordicedgeexpo.com/

One Globe Conference
New Delhi, India
http://www.oneglobeconference.com/

PowerUp
Miami, Florida (USA)
http://powerup.opower.com/

Renewable Energy World Conference & Expo
Las Vegas, Nevada (USA)
http://www.renewableenergyworld-events.com/

Smart Building Conference

Amsterdam (The Netherlands)
http://www.smartbuildingconference.com/

Smart Cities Asia 2015
Kuala Lumpur (Malaysia)
http//www.smartcitiesasia.com/

Smart Cities Investment Summit
Mumbai (India)
http://smart-cities-india.com/

Smart Cities Middle East
Dubai (UAE)
https://www.smartcitiesme.com/

Smart Cities Summit & Expo
Taipei (Taiwan)
http://smartcity.org.tw/index_en.php

Smart City 360°
Toronto (Canada)
Bratislava (Slovakia)
http://smartcity360.org/

Smart City Conference
Herzliya (Israel)
http://logtel-conferences.com/smart_city/

Smart City Expo
Barcelona (Spain)
http://www.smartcityexpo.com/

Smart City Event
Amsterdam (The Netherlands)
http://www.smart-circle.org/smartcity/

Smart City InFocus
Yinchuan (China)

https://www.tmforum.org/events/smart-city-infocus-2015-yinchuan-china/

Smart City Startups Festival
Miami, Florida (USA)
http://www.smartcitystartups.com/

Smart City Week
Washington D.C. (USA)
http://www.smartcitiesweek.com/

Smart Energy Summit
Austin, Texas (USA)
http://bit.ly/smart-energy-summit

Smart Home Summit
London (UK)
http//www.smarthomesummit.net/

SSIC - Security of Smart cities, Industrial Control System and Communication
Shanghai (China)
http://www.ssic-conf.org/

Sustainable Smart Cities
Bengaluru (India)
http://nispana.com/ssci/

The Future of Energy Summit
London (UK)
New York (USA)
Shanghai (China)
http://about.bnef.com/summit/

The Technology Expo
London (UK)
http://www.the-tech-expo.com/

ThingsCon
Berlin (Germany)
http://thingscon.com/

Water Innovation Summit
Berkeley, California (USA)
http://events.cleantech.com/waterinnovationsummit/

Alberto Broggi

VisLab

Take one minute every morning to feel the real value of what you are pursuing. You could work less hours and make more money in a 9 to 5 job. Remember what your goal is and enjoy it for an entire minute every morning, and you will never quit.

— Alberto Broggi

Last Minute Update

Between the interview and the publication of this book, VisLab had its exit to Ambarella, a U.S. public company listed on NASDAQ. Ambarella is the company empowering GoPro cameras with HD video and Google wearables. Congrats Alberto!

Back to the Introduction

If you think of driverless cars, you think of Google, right? Google is the biggest player in this field, but not the only one, and not the first one. VisLab, an Italian startup, sent four driverless vans from Italy to China back in 2010, tracing the journey of Marco Polo.

VisLab focuses on Environmental Perception. In sci-fi talk "they teach machines to see". A car, or even a building, with a VisLab system can "see" what's happening around it, recognize vehicles and people, and take consequent decisions.

At the moment VisLab is not interested in manufacturing cars, and they probably won't be in the future either. But any car manufacturer or real estate developer could use their technology to make their cars or buildings sentient. Add to this mix the technological advancement in the field of Artificial Intelligence, and the result is disruptive. We could reduce road mortality and energy waste to next to nothing. Or we could have Skynet, the entity from the Terminator waging battle against humanity. There has never been a time in history where optimists and pessimists both have the opportunity to fulfil their visions.

The Interview

Hi Alberto and welcome. Can you introduce yourself?

My name is Alberto Broggi. I was born in Parma and studied Electronic Engineering at Parma University, followed by a PhD in Information Technology. In 1998 I became an Associate Professor of Artificial Intelligence at the University of Pavia. Since 2001 I've been Associate Professor, then Full Professor, at the University of Parma, where I lead the artificial vision research group, known worldwide as VisLab.

How did you come up with the idea of VisLab?

We were doing research when nobody was working on driverless vehicles, so we had all this experience with exceptional results, but the use was limited mostly to the academic environment. We wanted to share these benefits with the rest of the world, so in 2009 we created a company as a spinoff of the university research program.

Where is VisLab now and what's your grand vision?

We aim to be the provider for the market in autonomous driving solutions. Driverless cars are an inescapable evolution of the auto industry. Car manufacturers have the factories for producing traditional cars and with our technology they can start producing smart cars at a fraction of the cost. There is no need to invest billions in research and development; they can simply use our existing solution. And because we have focused only on Environmental Perception for the last 20 years (A/N the technology behind driverless cars and sentient buildings) our solution is not only cheaper, it's better.

Tell us about your secret sauce. What makes you different?

Our length of experience. We have been in the field for more than 20 years, well before Google and the others. Now many car manufacturers are reaching out to us since we have been involved in this for so long. We have driven thousands of kilometers in autonomous mode and have also recorded data to use in statistics and to improve our algorithms.

Why are you in Parma? Are there any other cities you would consider moving your startup to?

We are in Parma because the university is here and because we started here. It's a great city to live in, but if the Italian government would like to create special legislation for startups as in other countries, it would be easier for us.

What has been the greatest achievement for VisLab so far?

We have set some worldwide milestones: In 1998 driving in Italy in open traffic, and in 2010 driving from Parma to Shanghai in autonomous mode. It's still the longest ever test in autonomous mode so far.

What advice would you give to young startup entrepreneurs?

Take one minute every morning to feel the real value of what you are pursuing.

It's very difficult to feel value in your daily activities. Most tasks don't have any glamour, and you could work less hours and probably make more money in a 9 to 5 job.

Take a moment every morning to remember that your work is bigger than the sum of the single tasks. One day you are going to have an impact on the entire society. Remember what this goal is — in our case it is providing driverless cars and trucks, reducing road accidents and changing the way people move.

Feel and enjoy that goal for an entire minute, and you will never quit.

Links

1. Company website
http://vislab.it

2. Ambarella
http://www.ambarella.com

Karim Fahssis

ZephyTools

Today entrepreneurship is the best way to start a career.

—Karim Fahssis

Karim Fahssis is a globally known wind energy expert and the winner of the 2014 Massachusetts Institute of Technology (MIT) award for innovators under 35. If this sounds interesting, you should check out what he does when he's not working on his startup.

In March 2009, Karim took a gap year out of his work to achieve one of his childhood dreams, along with his dear friend Hubert Beaumont: riding a bicycle from Beijing (where they worked) to Paris (their hometown) through the Himalayas and along the Silk Road.

This adventure took them through 18 countries from China to Europe through South Asia, Central Asia, Iran and Turkey. And since an entrepreneur at heart never stops doing business, after Karim and Hubert returned to Beijing they produced a 12 episode documentary of their adventures, in Chinese for "The Travel Channel".

Let me introduce you to Karim, a very special entrepreneur.

The Interview

Welcome Karim, would you like to introduce yourself and your company?

Sure. My name is Karim Fahssis, I'm a 31-year old French engineer who lived in Asia for the past decade (8 years in China and 2 years in India).

We have developed a digital platform called ZephyTOOLS which lets industry stakeholders generate bankable assessment reports for any given wind project. Using ZephyTOOLS they get reports within a fraction of the time and the cost of any other platform they were used to using. Customers love our business model because it is cloud-based and pay-as-you-go with a super-intuitive interface. As a consequence we didn't need any funding to survive till now; on the contrary, we are generating revenue.

Can you briefly introduce your co-founder?

Tristan Clarenc is the CoFounder and CTO of the company. He has a proven track record of successfully developed wind modeling software products which helped the global wind industry in raising assessment quality standards over the past decade. Throughout his career, he has developed a unique ability to absorb open source technologies and make them become industrial-grade solutions that create user satisfaction.

I first met Tristan in June 2007 when I joined Meteodyn, a small French wind modeling software company. He was the core expert of the company and my first assignment was to go to China for a period of 2 years to establish the Asian branch. Tristan spent the first 6 months with me in Beijing for my training. Since then, we've become great friends, started sharing the same long-term vision for the global wind industry and understood we could start a successful venture together.

Let's speak about your city. Why are you based there? What do you love and what do you hate about this place?

We decided to headquarter our company in Marseille because it is our favorite city in France with a pleasant quality of life (nature, culture, sport).

We decided to settle our China Branch Office in Nanjing because the Jiangsu Province government gave us significant incentives. Even more appealing was the grant and the free office that we received; their offer proved that "they care". They truly want us in their province, and this is sometimes more important than the money alone. I lived in Beijing but I enjoy Nanjing as it is less polluted and more easy-going.

We decided to settle our India Branch Office in Hyderabad because our biggest Indian client is located in that area. Besides I love the local food and the weather is great. Unfortunately it can be noisy and they still lack some infrastructure.

If it's not confidential, can you share an example of what you are working on now, or one of your main goals?

With pleasure. Our main goal is to empower engines with Artificial Intelligence so that there can be innovators and not just operators. It's an ambitious project, but we will get there eventually. You see, a long time ago me and my co-founder decided to follow a famous quote by Ghandi. This has eventually become the motto of our company: "Be the change you want to see in the world."

Links

Company website
http://www.zephy-science.com

Future Cities Investors and Accelerators

Interlude

If you don't think about the future, you cannot have one.

— John Galsworthy

Investors and accelerators come and go too, so I keep an updated list here:

http://futurecitiesbook.com/130

If you know of any organization that is not on the list, please add it to the comments on the page above. I truly appreciate your help (and the readers too).

P.S. This list includes organizations providing grants. Technically they are not 'investors' but if you reading this list, you are looking for money for your projects, not for technicalities. Right?

List

ABC Accelerator
Milan (Italy)
https://abc-accelerator.com/

Alchemist Accelerator
Strong IoT focus
San Francisco Bay Area, California (USA)
http://alchemistaccelerator.com/

Alpha Lab Gear
Strong IoT focus
Pittsburgh, Pennsylvania (USA)
http://alphalabgear.org/

Angel.co Real Estate Angel Investors
You can use Angel.co to find investors who have already invested
in real estate tech (and repeat the search for IoT and other areas)
https://angel.co/real-estate-1/investors

BGI / MIT Portugal
Lisbon (Portugal)
http://buildingglobalinnovators.eu/

Bolt Accelerator
Smart Cities is one of their areas of specialization
Malaga (Spain)
http://bolt.eu.com/en/

Build It
Strong IoT focus
Tartu, Estonia
http://buildit.ee/

Catapult - Future Cities

Not a traditional accelerator but an organization focused on supporting tech and startups in future cities
London (UK)
https://futurecities.catapult.org.uk/

Catapult - Transport Systems
A sister organization of Future Cities Catapult
Milton Keynes (UK)
https://ts.catapult.org.uk/

Challenge Up
IoT accelerator by Intel, Cisco and Deutsche Telecom
http://challengeup.eu/

Cognicity Challenge
London (UK)
http://cognicity.london/

Digital Accelerator by Allianz
IoT, Connected Home, Fintech and other areas
Munich (Germany)
http://digital-accelerator.com/

Digital Greenwich
Focussed to a specific area of London, the Royal Borough of Greenwich
http://www.digitalgreenwich.com/

Ecci Smart Accelerator
Edinburgh (Scotland)
http://smartaccelerator.edinburghcentre.org/

European Pioneers
One of their areas is Smart City Services
Berlin (Germany)
http://www.europeanpioneers.eu/en/

F6s

A directory of acceleration programs and funds. If you are into startups, you probably already know this website
https://www.f6s.com/

Fiware Accelerator
€80 million funding equity free
http://www.fiware.org/fiware-accelerator-programme/

Global Cities Initiative by JP Morgan
http://www.jpmorganchase.com/corporate/Corporate-Responsibility/globalcities.htm

Industrio
Strong IoT focus
Trento (Italy)
http://www.industrio.co/

Infinity by NEST
Hong Kong
http://www.infiniti-accelerator.com/

InnoCité MTL
Montreal (Canada)
http://innocitemtl.ca/

Kraftwerk
Bremen (Germany)
http://kraftwerk-accelerator.com/

Level39
Biggest accelerator in Fintech and Future Cities tech in Europe
London (UK)
http://level39.co

Microsoft Ventures
Microsoft Ventures is a startup accelerator for any area of business; however Microsoft is investing big resources into smart cities projects. Microsoft CityNext provides grants and support in

this area.
Worldwide.
https://www.microsoftventures.com/locations/accelerators
And
https://www.microsoft.com/en-us/citynext

Pi Labs
Europe's first property focussed accelerator
London (UK)
www.pilabs.co.uk

R/GA Accelerator
Strong IoT focus
New York (USA)
http://rgaaccelerator.com/connecteddevices/

Smart City Accelerator
Malmo, Sweden
http://www.smartcityaccelerator.com/

Soul-Fi
Europe, different locations
http://soul-fi.ipn.pt/

Speed Up Europe
Europe, different locations
http://speedupeurope.eu/

Startup Bootcamp Berlin
Specializing into Smart Transportation and Energy
Berlin (Germany)
http://www.startupbootcamp.org/accelerator/berlin.html

Startup Bootcamp Smart City & Living
Amsterdam (The Netherlands)
http://www.startupbootcamp.org/accelerator/smart-city-living.html

Techstars Mobility
This uber famous accelerator has an entire branch dedicated to mobility and smart cities
Detroit, Michigan (USA)
http://www.techstars.com/program/locations/mobility/

Urban Opus
A non-profit accelerator specializing 'in people data and the future of city' (plus they are based in one of my preferred cities, Vancouver)
Vancouver (Canada)
http://urbanopus.net/

Urban Us
Virtual accelerator
http://urban.us/

Valluri Technology Accelerators
Bangalore (India)
http://www.vallurita.com/smart-cities.html

An Extra Note

Smart Cities, IoT, Big Data and other areas connected to future cities are very hot right now. If you have a startup in this area, you can apply to (almost) every venture capital and angel syndicate in your region.

The interview with Simon Menashy of MMC Ventures includes great tips to win these investors. Godspeed!

Pietro Martani

Copernico

You need to take the risk and build big. The downsize is that if you fail, you fail big. But if you go small, you will fail anyway.

— Pietro Martani

Pietro Martani provides the missing link for understanding what's going on with future cities technology and startups. The typical person involved in smart cities is either in tech — a startup or an investor — or in government. Pietro is a traditional real estate entrepreneur who took the risk of moving into the startup ecosystem. His views from both side of the table are a compass in a world made up of hype.

Pietro's main business is in real estate for high end customers and corporate clients. He partners with Ferragamo, the same family behind the famous Italian fashion brand. This is a business that rarely has a downturn. During a market crisis, high incomes and low incomes don't change their behaviour much. It's the middle classes that feel the impact.

And yet Pietro moved a considerable part of his investment from this secure market to build *Copernico*, one of the biggest shared offices for startups in Europe. He didn't piggy back the startup hype with a small accelerator like many others. On the contrary he took the risk of investing in a business channelling an amount of money into a market of not-so-wealthy customers: the startuppers.

Pietro is too much of a good entrepreneur to build *Copernico* just for the sake of helping young entrepreneurs. There is a real potential for business and it's not always the one that the media tells us about.

The Interview

Welcome Pietro. The first question is about this gigantic investment called Copernico, in Milan. It's one of the biggest shared offices in Europe, in the top ten. On one side you moved your investment from a highly profitable market—the high end and corporate rental—to a riskier market.

On the other hand you didn't open an accelerator like many office owners do, but invited startup veterans to move their own accelerator in. You took all these risks when everybody was talking about a startup bubble.

You have a reputation of being accessible to young entrepreneurs with bold ideas, but I don't think that you started Copernico just because you love them. What's the catch? What can you tell us about the market that many others ignore?

I don't think I have any secret information, I just connect the dots. All the entrepreneurs in real estate know that the world of business is changing. Yet it's very hard for a successful company to change a business model that works and jump into the unknown.

If you don't take the risk, in the long run, you die. But the CEO of a company is usually more concerned about today than tomorrow. He has to survive quarterly meetings with the shareholders and he has to deal with a turnover of the top management, including the CEOs, that didn't exist just one generation ago.

Luckily I don't have these issues. I've a limited number of partners who trust me, so I can take the risk today in order to survive tomorrow.

Real estate is not a market that provides accommodation anymore, we provide network and communities. When we connect these dots, what to do to be successful in the new real estate market is easy to see.

In fact, if real estate is not just a matter of accommodation, but a matter of networking, then success comes from different rules. In accommodation the rule is "location, location, location" and reducing the costs. In networking there is a different rule. It's a mathematical lesson: the more people you have, the more collisions you have. The more collisions you have, the more innovation spreads and spreads faster.

So you need to take the risk and build a big ecosystem.

The downsize is that if you fail, you fail big. But if you go small, you are failing anyway. There is no more space for small or secondary investment in startups. You can't be in this business part time just to brag that you are working with startups. You are in or you are out. I've chosen to be in. That's it.

Well, you make it sound simple. Are you adopting the same philosophy in other areas?

Success is a matter of focus. So I am not trying to operate in too many areas. What I do however is to work in connected areas. For instance, to develop a successful shared office, we had to learn how to develop and manage catering and restaurants inside the office. Now that we have this vast experience, we can start a series of catering projects inside other offices managed by other companies. This is one of the next projects that we are already working on.

Where do you think real estate entrepreneurs have to change to adapt to this new market and be successful?

I think that the future of office space is to support business. Companies see an office as a mandatory cost today. But if they leave their office and move to a center based on a different mentality like *Copernico*, they can and they should improve their business. In other words, being in *Copernico* or another modern space, the company should make more money than they spend. Either because they meet potential customers in the common space or during our events. They meet the right providers. They find new ideas for their business.

As an office owner, if you can offer a company more value than they spend in rent, then our offer sells by itself.

Clearly real estate is your main area of expertise. But if you had $10 million to invest in a startup, that you couldn't invest in a real estate business, what area would you choose?

For me the keyword is sustainability. Some key trends, such as the growing number of people living on earth, are unavoidable. All these new people access the internet and know what they are missing. So they move to the cities to get more knowledge and grow their personal network.

This trend is going to overcrowd the cities. So any startup that fixes this problem is almost guaranteed that they will grow in value.

It could be technology providing a more natural quality of life, energy saving, better transport, or access to knowledge. There can be many technologies, but with a common core value. I would invest this $10 million in technologies that improve the lives of human beings living in cities.

Do you think this improvement could be afforded only by rich countries and rich cities, and they would increase the gap between rich and poor? Or, vice versa, do you think that technology is going to reduce this gap?

I believe technology will reduce this gap. Because on one side technology has become very sophisticated, but on the other side, it's becoming cheaper and more accessible to everybody.

For example, if you want to buy a smartphone now, you can do it even if you are on a low salary. In the past, a smartphone was a luxury for the wealthy. So I am optimistic.

Do you think that there will be a gap for other reasons?

Yes and it's not going to be a matter of access to technology, that is becoming cheaper every day, but a matter of access to talent. Bad policies and the mathematical rule of networking that we were discussing before will strongly influence cities.

Some cities will become almost completely deserted and some cities will amass everyone, especially people with talent.

It's not going to be concentrated in one country, like it was Silicon Valley in the past. There will be dispersed centers of excellence among many countries. The difference will be less between rich countries and poor countries, and more between rich cities and poor cities, and I mean cities rich in talented citizens, and cities poor in talented citizens.

Money is a commodity and it moves easily. People will be more valuable than money.

Finally, last but not least. What advice would you give to your younger self?

Don't think of the business as a local business, but understand local nuances.

In other words. Don't think of the business as a local business. The previous generation was used to growing in one country and maybe expanding abroad later. Sometimes they just stuck to being in a strong position in one country and ignored the rest. You can't afford to do that anymore. Think of your business as global from day one.

On the other hand, recognize that each country is different, sometimes differing even by region or city. Technology is the same everywhere, people are not (yet). Like the old saying, "When in Rome, act like the Romans". Do this everywhere, not just in the most important cities.

So develop a global vision of your business, but pay attention to understand the specific characteristic of the next place where you are going to expand your business. "If you understand that, you can beat any competition that thinks just globally, no matter how overfunded or bigger than you they are.

Links

Copernico
http://www.copernicomilano.it

Sandra Sassow

SEaB Energy

If you have an idea, go off and try it out. So what? So you fail? It doesn't really matter. You just do the next thing. That's not a reason not to do it.

— *Sandra Sassow*

There is a moment in the story of Sandra Sassow— founder and CEO of SeAB —when you can't stop thinking about one of the most famous founders of our time: Elon Musk.

He raised a fortune in the exit of PayPal and he could have easily gone without working for the rest of his life. And yet when his last startup Tesla didn't find enough investors, he gambled his entire fortune on his own company.

Sandra and her co-founders didn't have the same amount of capital as Elon Musk, and yet when investors didn't react quickly enough, they invested quite a few million euros of their own money in the company.

"Go big or go home" sounds like an appropriate slogan for this interview.

The Interview

Hello Sandra and welcome. Let's start with a brief introduction about you and your product.

Yes, I'm Sandra Sassow, I'm the CEO of SEaB Energy. And we have a waste-to-energy device that converts food waste and organic waste on a site back into energy and water for the site's use.

What's your typical customer?

Our typical customer is catering waste producers, so hotels, hospitals, prisons, any of those types of businesses that have a food waste and have a need to get rid of it. And we would convert it back into energy and water for their site.

Can they use the energy produced by the device in their own building?

Yes, the energy can be used in the same building.

I like the concept. It saves costs of waste management. It saves costs of energy. At the same time, it helps the environment. A win-win-win. However it looks like a project that requires an important research and development and of course sales. What's the situation with your team?

So there are 14 of us in the team, mainly focused on engineering and product development. And now, as we're scaling into delivering product to market, we have service and installation engineers coming on board.

We have a background in scaling businesses, from startup all the way through to successful exit.

We have technical background in the sector that we're coming into, so the waste sector, from both the sales angle as well as the product development angle.

So you have already growth and sold a startup in the past?

Yeah. Some of us have worked directly all the way form start to exit. Some have invested in startups that successfully exited. So definitely yes.

You are a serial entrepreneur so you are the best person to reply the next question. What was the worst moment and the best moment of your startup?

I think best moment was the very first alpha or beta test site that we secured, being able to start the discussion on a Monday and have the site agree to pay to try the equipment on the Friday. That was quite key. I think that was probably our biggest success in terms of a move forward for the business.

It should have been quite a release. Because you were self funded for quite a few million dollars at the time. Correct?

Yes, we self-funded because there was a lack of appetite in the market for a B2B to business. If I look at the business plans that we did, when we went out to market to raise capital, we've met every target, which is great except that we've had to do it with our own money.

So, you know, if we had not had the financial capability to do that, we would have gone under a long time ago.

I guess another great moment was proving those who refused to invest in the company wrong, right?

Yeah, you could say that [laughs].

It's surprising for me that investor didn't see green energy as a good area of investment.

They thought that we were a late entrant to the party for green energy. Renewable energy and wind projects were not all showing great returns. So there was a negative appetite there.

They based their analysis on the existing technology, but our technology was new and different.

We came to market with two technologies—the device that you see today and a wind energy tech—which was viewed as a negative as well.

When we didn't see funding, we focused our effort on one product because we knew we had financial resource to be able to bring that all the way to market.

What suggestion will you give to your younger self?

Oh definitely, do it. If you have an idea, go off and try it out. So what? So you fail? It doesn't really matter. You just do the next thing. So that's not a reason not to do it.

But you need to really, really believe in what you're going to do as a startup because you will encounter 99 people out of a 100 that will tell you it's the wrong idea, and it won't work, and it won't happen, or it's not possible.

So you will hear the negative more often. And, if you yourself don't believe strongly enough, you'll lose confidence.

On the other hand, the most common reason of failure on B2B startups is that the founder are not open to change their idea. How do you reconcile this issue with the fact that you should keep going no matter what the other say?

Yeah, there's feedback, and then there's openness to change. So you've got to be very astute to differentiating between the two.

First of all, you should pick good advisors. This is one of the first actions to do for a startup founder.

But advisers have only the advice of what they know. And if you're coming with something that is disrupting the current marketplace, they may not understand how big the business can be or where the business is going to fit.

If you look at companies such as Kodak, they would have had any number of excellent advisers who would have been telling them that they were on the right track. And yet, they missed the market completely.

They were at the top and the forefront of the photo industry. And now, they're not really anywhere. So advisers' advice has to be always put on a platform and questioned.

And then as an entrepreneur you have to make a decision. And it's you who are taking the risk. In my view, you listen, you digest, and then you make a decision, right or wrong. And it's your decision.

Links

Company website
http://seabenergy.com

Horseshoe Nails

Goodbye

For the want of a nail the shoe was lost,
For the want of a shoe the horse was lost,
For the want of a horse the rider was lost,
For the want of a rider the battle was lost,
For the want of a battle the kingdom was lost,
And all for the want of a horseshoe-nail.

– Benjamin Franklin

In *Foundation*, a novel by Isaac Asimov, Seldon leads the *psychohistorians*, a group of renegades who have developed a "branch of mathematics that deals with the reactions of human conglomerates to fixed social and economic stimuli."

In *Dune* by Frank Herbert, the *Bene Gesserit* direct humanity along a path of insight and stability through a series of small social interventions.

The novel *In the Country of the Blind* by Michael Flynn points out how history can be influenced through minimal but well calculated actions.

These are 'just' three sci-fi novels, however their stories are based on a powerful concept: you can influence history without having huge resources if you look for the horseshoe nails; small events capable of generating a snowball effect. This is the message of Benjamin Franklin, one of the finest inventors and diplomats of all time.

The opposite is also true; we can waste huge resources without having any effective result. In *Foundation* and *Dune* the respective empires are powerless to change their future precisely because they focus only on their superior resources and power. They play hard, not smart.

So I'm skeptical when a politician or a corporation says that we can't change the world around us because we don't have huge resources to invest.

In the next 10 years we'll see big corporations disappear for the very same reasons as those empires, and new small startups emerge to take up leadership. The life expectancy of a company in the Fortune 500 was around 75 years in the XX century. Today, it's less than 15 years and that's declining all the time.

Accommodating nearly 70% of the world's population, the cities will be the main battleground between companies. It will not be a battle between evil corporations and good startups, but between innovation and stagnation. Some big corporations will be good, some small startups will be bad, and vice versa.

Add Artificial Intelligence, the Internet of Everything, robots, drones, smart grids, driverless cars and 3D printers to the mix and you can tell that in the near future the world will be a very interesting place.

STEFANO L. TRESCA
San Francisco, USA

One More Thing

If you want to go quickly, go alone. If you want to go far, go together.
– African Proverb

In the age of the e-book, each and every review counts. Plus you can help drive the book you just read to Amazon's home page. Please take a moment to leave a review (and thanks, I owe you one).

This is the easy link to Amazon:
http://futurecitiesbook.com/100

More Books

Call it a clan, call it a network, call it a tribe, call it a family. Whatever you call it, whoever you are, you need one.

– Jane Howard

Check Stefano's Amazon author page for more books:
http://www.amazon.com/author/stefanotresca

Or search "Stefano L Tresca" on Apple iBooks, Kobo, Nook, etc.

Printed in Great Britain
by Amazon